GW00648289

CLIMBER AND FELLWALKER
IN LAKELAND

Uniform in this series

A CLIMBER IN THE WEST COUNTRY
CLIMBING AND WALKING IN SOUTH-EAST ENGLAND
COASTAL PATHS OF THE SOUTH-WEST

all by

EDWARD C. PYATT

CLIMBER
AND FELLWALKER
IN LAKELAND

by

FRANK MONKHOUSE and
JOE WILLIAMS

DAVID & CHARLES
NEWTON ABBOT

ISBN 0 7153 5459 0

To our long-suffering wives

COPYRIGHT NOTICE

© FRANK MONKHOUSE AND JOE WILLIAMS 1972

All rights reserved. No part of this publication may be reproduced, stored in a retrieval system, or transmitted, in any form or by any means, electronic, mechanical, photocopying, recording or otherwise, without the prior permission of David & Charles (Publishers) Limited.

Set in 10 on 12pt Times Roman
and printed in Great Britain
by Clarke Doble & Brendon Limited
for David & Charles (Publishers) Limited
South Devon House   Newton Abbot   Devon

CONTENTS

LIST OF ILLUSTRATIONS

7

FIGURES

PREFACE

WHILE this book represents our forty years' experience of the Lakeland hills, specifically it is the result of a four years' planned programme, during which we have been fortunate enough to have been on the fells two or three days a week, winter and summer. It does not set out to be a detailed guidebook either to fell walking or to rock climbing (there are plenty of these, as indicated in the bibliography); rather it is a topographical analysis of the Lakeland mountains and crags from the point of view of the climber of average competence. The criterion for inclusion of a particular fell walk or rock climb is that we have found it enjoyable and satisfying; every one discussed in any detail has been climbed by one or other of us, usually both and frequently together, during these last few years. Admittedly this is a largely subjective basis for choice, though the climbs are not described in a personal or reminiscent way except where this might illustrate a specific point; mainly we want to convey the 'mood' of a mountain, the 'feel' of a climb, the joy of a free-striding ridge walk and the attainment of a summit. Severity of grade is by no means the only criterion for the inclusion of a climb. The élite class of Extremely Severe (XS) climbs, the province of a relatively small though increasing number of leaders, is not described except in passing; those who can lead such climbs need no information, since they after all are the pace makers. A selection is given in an appendix of our 'hundred best climbs', chosen from an extensive range of crags over the categories of severity from 'Difficult' to 'Hard Very Severe'. In the text, rock climbs are given in italics, the select hundred being indicated by a prefatory asterisk, thus *New West. The individual crags, 110 in number, are listed in a table on p 200, together with their National Grid references, and located on figure 13. In the text the consecutive number of each is given after its initial mention, thus Gillercombe Buttress (35). A table is also appended of peaks over 2,000ft (610m), with their National Grid references.

The first two chapters are concerned with the physical anatomy of Lakeland and with the evolution of climbing from both the psychological and technological points of view. Then follows an analysis on a regional basis of the seven main sectors into which

Lakeland may be conveniently divided, starting with Ennerdale and working in a clockwise direction round to Wasdale.

The photographs were specially taken by Joe Williams, and the maps and line-drawings prepared by Alan Hodgkiss, senior technical officer, University of Liverpool. The colour photograph was taken by Mrs Doris Williams. The manuscript was typed by Mrs Josie Hill and checked by Mrs Tess Monkhouse.

We are more grateful than we can say to many who have helped, directly or indirectly, in the production of this book, especially Ian Angell, Colin Greenhow and Jo Palmer, who climbed with us, acted as models in the photographs and patiently checked typescript and proofs.

It is hoped that this book will be read by those contemplating a climbing holiday in the Lake District, perhaps for the first time, and by those who enjoy their climbing either in retrospect or vicariously in an armchair; in short, by all who are interested in our Lakeland mountain heritage.

F.J.M.
J.S.W.

Ennerdale
English Lake District
April 1971

1

THE CLIMBER'S LANDSCAPE

THE English Lake District is a compact piece of country, little more than thirty miles across and nine hundred sq miles in extent. As long ago as 1810, William Wordsworth in his *Description of the Scenery of the Lakes* recognised something of a radial pattern in the arrangement of the ridges, valleys and lakes; he visualised '. . . a number of valleys . . . diverging from the point on which we stand, like spokes from the nave of a wheel . . .' Each valley, each lake, each mountain has its own individuality, yet it is the sum of these features, a unity in diversity, which gives what John Ruskin called '. . . this large piece of precious chasing and embossed work . . .' its unrivalled charm.

The Lakeland massif consists of a dome of ancient rocks, elongated in a general west—east direction, which because of their differing resistance to the forces of earth sculpture—running water, glaciers during the past Ice Age, and weather—are basically responsible for the details of the scenery, whether soft, rounded and subdued or rough, bold and craggy. From the more gentle slopes stand out prominent masses of rock, the crags which are the climber's playgrounds. He is in effect a practical geologist, concerned with the character of the rock, its lines of weakness, its roughness or smoothness, its soundness or unreliable quality. Some kinds have a rough abrasive nature or reveal incut notches and sharp-edged cracks; climbs on such rocks may go successfully even when it is wet because of the positive holds. By contrast other types are smooth and slabby, providing splendid routes when dry, and the climber in tight-fitting, rubber-soled footwear can balance up confidently on sloping exiguous holds, though they may present a very different proposition when damp or slimy.

The rocks occupying the heart of the Lake District can be divided into three main groups (figure 1). The oldest, known as the Skiddaw Slates, outcrop mainly in the north; the Borrowdale Volcanic Series occupy most of the central area; and in the south various limestones, shales and grits form the lower country around Coniston and

Windermere, where few hills exceed 1,000ft. These ancient rocks are surrounded by a discontinuous frame of others appreciably younger: limestone, coal measures and sandstone underlying the foothills and undulating lowlands along the Solway coast, Morecambe Bay and the Vale of Eden. The sandstone projects boldly into the Irish Sea as St Bees Head, on which the 'hard men' of West Cumberland have worked out a number of severe climbs.

The Skiddaw Slates consist of dark grey slates and shales, with occasional beds of coarser grit and sandstone. They form most of the northern uplands, including Skiddaw itself and its neighbour Blencathra, the Grasmoor group and some of the hill country west of Loweswater and Ennerdale, while an outlying mass in the southwest projects towards the coast as the prominent hump of Black Combe. These uplands for the most part are rounded in profile, for the slates tend to weather and break down uniformly, masking their slopes with sheets of shaly debris; the northern slopes of Skiddaw and Blencathra are smooth enough for skiing. Yet some of these mountains reveal remarkably deep valleys and sharply defined ridges, and beds of massive flags or coarse grits may form impressive crags. This is shown in the Grasmoor group, with Dove Crag high up on its north-eastern flanks, Eel Crag on the east, and Hobcarton Crag on the northern side of Hopegill Head. But these cliffs, though lending a sombre grandeur to the view, are as far as the climber is concerned splendid deceivers, best left to the ravens, for almost all are characterised by a crumbling instability. In just a few places the slates have been hardened (metamorphosed) by the effects of great pressure and heat associated with later earth movements, as at Angler's Crag and Bowness Knott on the shores of Ennerdale Water and at Buckstone How on the northern slopes of Honister Pass, where some good climbs have been made. The Skiddaw Slate uplands, therefore, are on the whole of little value for rock climbing, though their prominent ridges and broad summit plateaus offer good fell walking.

The heart of the Lakeland dome consists of a great thickness of material poured out from volcanoes which erupted some 500 to 450 million years ago; since the resultant rocks were first studied in Borrowdale they are known collectively as the Borrowdale Volcanic Series. Beds of hard, almost flinty lava alternate with deposits of fine-grained ash (tuff) and of larger angular fragments (breccia)

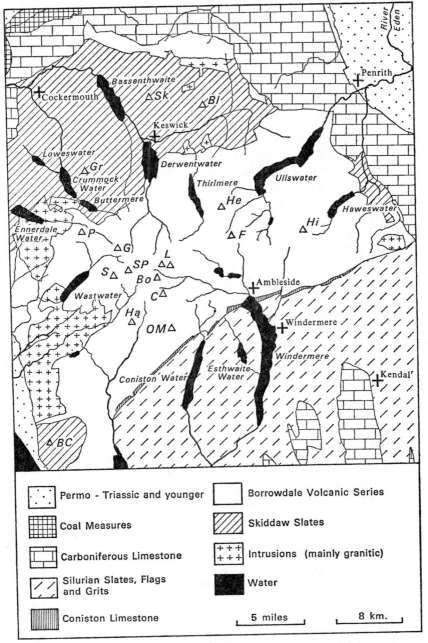

·.·. Permo - Triassic and younger	Borrowdale Volcanic Series
Coal Measures	Skiddaw Slates
Carboniferous Limestone	+++ Intrusions (mainly granitic)
Silurian Slates, Flags and Grits	Water
Coniston Limestone	5 miles 8 km.

FIG 1. Geological map of the Lake District

(Based on the official Quarter-inch maps, by permission of the Geological Survey of Great Britain) which were compacted by subsequent pressure and heat. In places the tuffs have a distinctive banded appearance, as on the Shamrock Traverse leading to the east face of the Pillar Rock, and very strikingly in the 'Tiger-banded Rocks' of the crags under the eastern summit ridge of St Sunday Crag overlooking Grisedale. These igneous rocks include bluish-grey, fine crystalled andesite, of which most of the major climbing buttresses are composed, the yellowish rhyolite, and types of porphyry, a coarse large-crystalled rock found, for example, in the crags around the head of Buttermere. The texture of these rocks varies widely, from smooth slabby outcrops to coarse blistered masses almost as rough as the gabbro of the Black Cuillins of Skye. They also include layers of slate, formed by compression of mud flows among the volcanic material and of the finest ash. Some yield attractive roofing material, notably the pale green slates of Honister, Elterwater and Coniston, their well defined cleavage enabling them to be split readily into thin uniform sheets.

A marked characteristic of the volcanic rocks is their distinct jointing, that is, surfaces of fracture within the mass of the rock caused by stresses during cooling and solidification of the lava. This gives a 'grain' to the rock, providing lines of weakness along which the forces of weathering and erosion can operate. Jointing very much affects the details of a climb, for on a small scale it furnishes incut cracks and sharp spikes, while on a larger scale it may define pinnacles and other protruding masses of rock. The Arrowhead on the Napes ridges is a beautifully regular diamond formed by two sets of intersecting joints, while the nearby Napes Needle (plate p 125), is the most famous natural obelisk in Lakeland; its top block is quite detached from the rest of the pinnacle by a horizontal joint, so that three climbers on top can make it move slightly, though this is not a practice to be recommended. A series of closely packed joints may cause the rock to fragment, rather like the shatter belt of a fault (p 16). Sergeant Crag in Langstrath is a mass of grey lava with distinct parallel joints sloping down at a high angle from left to right. On the right-hand face of the crag these joints are several yards apart and there the buttress is massive and slabby, but farther to the left they become closer, ultimately only a few inches apart. Along this zone the comminuted rock has been readily affected by frost and running water (in wet weather this climb becomes a waterfall), and the line of close jointing is thus deeply incised, forming Sergeant Crag Gully, a classic climb of its type.

Such varied volcanic rocks offer marked differences to denudation, the hard massive lavas forming buttresses, the softer ashes the gentler slopes, and as a result the mountains in the centre of the Lake District have strikingly rugged outlines as compared with the more uniform slate country to north and south. Most prominent crags, while seeming to be geological accidents, actually fit into a pattern; many are protrusions of resistant rock on the sides of valleys, some outcrop high on the breast of a mountain, others are on the back walls of combes (p 22). The important climbing crags included in this text are located on figure 13, shown in detail on the maps in the topographical chapters, and listed with their grid references in the table on p 200.

A further contribution to the structure of the Lake District was the forcing of igneous material in a molten state into the existing rocks, where it solidified; later denudation has in some areas removed the covering rocks and thus exposed the intrusions. They occur on various scales, the largest being the masses of granite in Eskdale, near Shap and to the east and north-east of Keswick, and of the fine-grained pinkish rock known as granophyre between Ennerdale and Wasdale. These large intrusions are not as a rule particularly striking elements in the landscape, except where they have been quarried, for the granite and granophyre tend to weather uniformly, rather like the Skiddaw Slates. One exception to this generalisation is a very complex mass consisting among other rocks of granite, gabbro and granophyre, which forms the rocky little Carrock Fell, in marked contrast to the nearby rounded moorland hills of Skiddaw Slate. Rarely are any of these intrusions sufficiently steep and defined to form climbing crags, though one notable exception is the granite Brantrake Crag in Eskdale.

Important contributions to the detailed relief are made by minor intrusions, notably *dykes* which occur in a more or less vertical plane relative to the existing beds, *sills* found in a near horizontal plane (Friar's Crag projecting into Derwentwater is a sill of the hard dark rock known as dolerite), and a multitude of thin irregular *veins*. If these are less resistant than the surrounding rock they may be etched out by the weather and by running water to form rifts, gullies, gorges and notches on the skyline, though if harder they may stand out as distinct steps, terraces or walls. Intrusions are commonly associated with mineral veins containing metal ores, which have been worked for centuries; they most frequently occur near the geological boundary between the Skiddaw Slates and the Borrowdale Volcanics, as around the flanks of Skiddaw and Blencathra, in Borrowdale and the Newlands Fells, to the north-west of Coniston and on the eastern flanks of Helvellyn; the OS map marks many disused mines and the walker should be wary of old shafts and workings in their neighbourhood. The minerals found in these intrusions are varied, the commonest being quartz; hillsides are sometimes pockmarked with its gleaming white fragments, and it may appear as thin bands or as clusters of crystals among the lavas and slates. The climber should treat these rather fragile crystals with delicacy should he need to use them, as on the second pitch of the *South-West* climb on the Pillar Rock where they provide indispensable holds.

The various rocks have been affected at intervals in the earth's geological history by movements of the crust. On a major scale they were upfolded into an elongated dome trending roughly from west to east, approximately through the position of Skiddaw. This dome has been so denuded that little trace of the folding can be detected, except for minor puckers and corrugations both in the ancient rocks and in the newer ones on the margins; excavations for the M6 motorway reveal some of the latter in section. This prolonged denudation removed great thicknesses of rock from the central axis of the dome, where the Skiddaw Slates, the oldest of the rocks, thus appear on the surface.

Also resulting from earth movements are numerous faults which form cracks and fissures in the solid rocks. Sometimes these are clean-cut single cracks, though more commonly the rock along the line of fracture is broken into angular fragments, forming a shatter belt, a distinct line of weakness similar to a zone of close jointing, along which the forces of nature can readily erode. Shatter belts are widely distributed and can be traced for long distances. An example on a large scale is the north—south line between the Helvellyn massif to the east and the Ullscarf—High Raise—Langdale Pikes upland to the west; emphasised by denudation, especially by glaciation, this cuts the Lakeland hills into a western and eastern group separated by a through-valley culminating in the col of Dunmail

Page 17 *(above left)* *Hailstorm*, Bowness Knott; *(above right)* *Green Gash*, Bowness Knott; *(below)* Ennerdale, with Pillar Mountain and Wind Gap on the left

Page 18 The Rib and Slab Climb, Pillar Rock

Raise at a height of only 782ft. Another example on a smaller scale separates Scafell and Scafell Pike; its weaker resistance has caused the formation of Mickledore, a col between Scafell Crag and Pike's Crag. On the northern face of Scafell Pike a fast-flowing torrent, Piers Gill, has taken advantage of several fault-lines intersecting almost at right angles to erode a zigzag course through steep-sided gorges. On the northern face of Crag Fell, overlooking Ennerdale Water, several parallel faults have allowed great slices of rock to slump downwards, producing a markedly stepped appearance on the hillside.

As in the case of an intrusion, a shatter belt is usually highly mineralised, most frequently with iron compounds which have percolated in solution through the broken rock; this accelerates weathering because the iron oxidises and so the rock decays readily. The iron imparts a distinctive pinkish tinge, hence the frequency of place names indicative of this: Red Pike, Red Crag in Newlands, Red Gully on Wallowbarrow Crag, Red Groove on Pavey Ark and several Red or Ruddy Gills. A belt of this iron-stained rock can be traced from the upper Ennerdale valley through Windy Gap between the Gables in a south-easterly direction and past Styhead Tarn towards Rossett Gill to the head of Langdale. At right angles to this a minor shatter belt has enabled Ruddy Gill to erode a steep-sided chasm in the crumbling red rocks.

These minor structural features—faults, veins, dykes and joints—have considerable effect on the detailed anatomy of a crag, hence on the possible climbs developed there. Gullies and chimneys not only form distinct lines for routes, but may divide a crag into individual buttresses and ridges; on the face of Great Gable the Napes gullies separate the Arrowhead, Eagle's Nest and Needle Ridges (figure 12); Moss Gill, Steep Gill and Deep Gill split the Scafell crags into a series of buttresses (figure 11); the black cleft of Walker's Gully divides Pillar Rock from Shamrock; and the buttresses of Dow Crag are demarcated by five prominent gullies (figure 8). One characteristic of both gullies and chimneys is that rocks become jammed across them as chockstones, forming obstacles in an ascent, though sometimes actually helping the climber.

A fault-crack may provide a line of ascent up an otherwise un-flawed impregnable rock face. Kern Knotts Buttress on Great Gable

B

is split right through by a vertical fault, creating *Kern Knotts Crack* on the eastern side, *Kern Knotts Chimney* on the west. A thinner hairline fault nearby forms the much more severe *Innominate Crack*, and yet another is responsible for a right-angled corner up which a strenuous layback movement is required to negotiate the first pitch of the *Sepulchre*. In Far Easedale near Grasmere a steep fissure between the main Deer Bield Crag and a huge detached buttress provides two climbs of great character, *Deer Bield Chimney* on the right and the much more difficult *Deer Bield Crack* on the left. Probably the most famous pitch of this nature in Lakeland is the Flake Crack (plate p 143), the key to climbing the *Central Buttress* of Scafell.

The Ice Age left a dramatic impress upon the Lakeland landscape. The margins of the area were affected by ice moving southward along both the coast of the Irish Sea and the Vale of Eden, while during the late stages the Lakeland mountains nurtured their own central ice cap from which glaciers moved downward and outward along the pre-glacial valleys. These glaciers at their maxima must have been of considerable thickness; distinct ice-worn scratches and grooves can be seen on outcrops on the Wasdale side of the Scafell range and on Helvellyn at a height of about 2,500ft. The ice caps and glaciers vanished about ten thousand years ago; today there is only a sporadic winter snowfall, which however contributes an attractive element to the scenery, especially as it picks out and emphasises the main features of the rock architecture. Occasionally there may be sufficient depth to allow skiing on the smoother fells; a portable ski lift is sometimes installed on the northeastern slopes of Raise in the Helvellyn range. North-facing hollows can hold snow for weeks, and alternate snowfall, partial thawing and refreezing produces ribbons of compact snow and ice in the gullies, so affording excellent winter climbing (p 43).

Many ridges, particularly in the east of the district, are smooth and rounded, even among the volcanic rocks, giving rise to some argument as to whether these areas were completely overridden by the ice at its maximum and were thus heavily eroded, or whether they are relics of a pre-glacial surface which the ice never covered. Whatever the cause, weathering has helped to emphasise this smoothness, both of the tuffs which form much of the High Street and Helvellyn ridges and of the Skiddaw Slates; large areas are covered with level sheets of gravelly material, the product of rock decay and disintegration *in situ* through frost action and the effects of melting snow. Ridges such as the Helvellyn—Dods range extending northwards towards Threlkeld and the long line of High Street to the west of Haweswater provide continuous high-level walking. By contrast, other ridges such as the Scafells are made of hard-jointed lavas, have a more jagged profile, and are strewn with large angular blocks, the result of frost action upon the strongly jointed rocks.

The profiles of the radial glaciated valleys tend towards a wide open U, with a flattish floor and steep walls. The valleys are fairly straight-sided, since a glacier tends to plane off projections to form blunted or 'truncated' spurs, as on the southern slopes of Blencathra, where the sharply projecting arêtes end suddenly in triangular facets. Other examples are the blunted ridges projecting north-eastward into Buttermere from the Red Pike—High Crag range, and the line of buttresses to the west of the Kentmere valley. This lateral erosion of the valley sides has emphasised masses of resistant rock as prominent buttresses; this is shown in Borrowdale and its lateral valleys, in upper Langdale (Gimmer and Raven Crags), Eskdale (Esk Buttress and Heron Crag), Grisedale (Eagle Crag), Thirlmere (the Castle Rock of Triermain facing Raven Crag across the dam at the foot of the lake), and Ennerdale (Bowness Knott and Angler's Crag).

Several glaciated valleys end abruptly at the head in a steep wall known as a *trough end* or a *back wall*; examples include the ring of crags surrounding Warnscale Bottom at the head of Buttermere, upper Ennerdale, the double trough end of Borrowdale (the Grains Gill and Styhead valleys separated by the spur of Seathwaite Fells), and Mickleden in Great Langdale. Many trough ends are surrounded by climbing crags: Gable Crag in upper Ennerdale, the impending mass of Dove Crag in Dovedale on the eastern flanks of the Fairfield—Hart Crag massif, and Striddle Crag, Warnscale Crag and Green Crag in Buttermere. The narrow though flat valley floors form small areas of lowland penetrating far into the heart of the mountains and help to emphasise their impressive quality; the tiny church at Wasdale Head lies at only 263ft and Rosthwaite in Borrowdale, nearly twenty miles from the coast as the crow flies, at 270ft.

The major lakes which lie in most, though not all, of these valleys are long and quite narrow, radiating from the drainage axis of the

Lakeland dome (figure 1). They owe their origin partly to glacial erosion, which formed narrow rock basins (the floor of Wastwater goes down to nearly 60ft below sea level), partly to the deposition at the end of each glacier of a terminal moraine, a crescent-shaped mound of clay and boulders forming a natural dam near the foot of the valley. The southern end of Windermere, for example, is enclosed by such a moraine, though it is partly cut through near Newby Bridge by the River Leven draining southward to Morecambe Bay, while Loweswater is impounded by such a considerable moraine that its outflow is forced to go eastward rather than directly towards the coast. The lakes vary considerably in depth, from Wastwater, where 258ft has been sounded, to the reedy Elterwater, at its deepest only 20ft, lying on the uneven clay-filled floor of lower Langdale.

Several valleys, including Eskdale, Dunnerdale and Great Langdale, do not contain lakes. At one time they probably did, but the former lakes have disappeared as a result of two complementary causes: the infilling of the basin with sediment laid down by inflowing streams, and the lowering of the water level by the downcutting of the exit river at the foot of the lake. This deposition of sediment can be seen as small deltas at the heads of most lakes, while some former large lakes have been cut into two, for example, Buttermere and Crummock Water, and Derwentwater and Bassenthwaite Lake.

Most glaciated valleys reveal along their flanks a pronounced break of slope, where the gently sloping tributary valleys and the shoulders or benches drop suddenly to the floor of the main valley; this indicates the height reached by the surface of the glacier, below which it eroded the valley sides. As a result the tributary valleys have been left 'hanging', so that their streams fall abruptly in cascades to join the main stream. Sour Milk Gill foams down from Bleaberry Combe above Buttermere, and the Watendlath Beck, rising on the northern slopes of Ullscarf, flows gently northward in a hanging valley before it spills over the edge of Borrowdale as Lodore Falls.

From high among the hills torrents issue from tiny sheets of water or tarns, of which there are alleged to be 463 named in the Lake District. They are usually contained in small basin-shaped hollows known as *combes* or *coves*, backed by steep crags such as Pavey

Ark above Stickle Tarn and Dow Crag overlooking the darkly brooding Goat's Water. A combe is the same feature as the French *cirque*, the Welsh *cwm* and the Scottish *corrie* or *coire*. Significantly the great majority of combes face between north and east, aspects which obviously favoured the accumulation of snow, leading during the Ice Age to the development of small glaciers and resulting erosion. The north-facing slopes of the Ennerdale and Buttermere valleys reveal a whole series of combes, while the south-facing sides, especially of Ennerdale, are smooth and even. The contrast between the uniform western slopes of Helvellyn and its eastern flanks dissected by several large combes is equally striking, as is that between the eastern side of the Froswick—Ill Bell—Rainsborrow Crag ridge in Kentmere and the uniform grass and scree-covered western slopes. Not all combes contain tarns, of course; many have swampy or peat-filled floors where a tarn obviously existed in the past; others, such as Birkness Combe above Buttermere, slope too steeply for a sheet of water to collect. The head of Deepdale, in the eastern fells, is divided into two upper basins, Sleet and Link Coves, by a rocky ridge terminating in Greenhow End; several climbing crags, including Hutaple in Sleet Cove and Scrubby in Link Cove, are found there. Gillercombe Buttress is on the back wall of Gillercombe, an elongated tarnless combe from which Sour Milk Gill cascades into Borrowdale near Seathwaite.

Since the glaciers and permanent snowfields disappeared, the forces of earth sculpture have continued their slow but inexorable operations. The main rivers which drain the Lake District flow more or less radially towards the Irish Sea and the Solway Firth, Morecambe Bay and the Vale of Eden. They wander along the flat floors of the valleys, often splitting or braiding their courses, as for example the Liza in Ennerdale, the Derwent in Borrowdale and the Great Langdale Beck, the last of which has caused such flooding that its bed has been regularised by straightening and dredging. Training walls and revetments of boulders have been constructed along the banks of many rivers to check erosion of the banks on steep curves which might threaten a nearby road; an example is along the River Duddon, whose flooding and resultant damage a few years ago caused the closing for some weeks of Wrynose Pass. The tributary gills, starting as springs high on the hillsides or issuing from tarns, have cut deeply into the slopes, and these torrents, with their boulder-strewn courses, rocky pools and foaming cascades, contribute much to the mountain landscape.

Mountain streams fluctuate greatly, the result of the rapid runoff over steep rocky slopes, and sudden heavy rain or rapid snow-melt can cause dramatic flooding.

A dramatic example occurred during the August Bank Holiday weekend of 1938, when nine inches of rain fell in thirty-six hours over the central Lake District. Lingmell Gill, normally a clear stream flowing down from under the Scafells, became a swollen raging torrent, coloured brown from the gashed and scarred slopes and with stones crashing along its bed. Two fields at the head of Wastwater were covered with sheets of stones and boulders, the load of the gill in spate, but within forty-eight hours or so it subsided and returned to its normal flow, having altered the landscape more in that short time than during the previous several decades. On August 13, 1966, a tremendous volume of rain fell over upper Borrowdale; this was remarkably local, as none at all fell in Grasmere only five miles away. Floods of fantastic energy poured down the valleys, washing away walls and bridges and bringing down boulders, pouring into houses, sweeping away cars and causing tremendous damage in the hamlets of Seathwaite, Seatoller and Rosthwaite. Scarcely had the rescue and clean-up operations made appreciable headway when three weeks later the same thing happened again; the bar in the Scawfell Hotel has two lines which indicate the water level on each occasion. Twice in a short time nature had cut loose, yet a local inhabitant more than eighty years of age could not remember a previous occurrence. The evidence of the two storms in the form of gashed slopes, bare rock outcrops and piles of boulders along the courses of the gills can still be seen.

Care should be taken when crossing flooded torrents; on occasions we have had to put on a rope and struggle thigh-deep across a stream which we had stepped across the same morning, and there have been several cases when walkers were drowned in trying to ford a stream in flood.

The work of the weather goes on relentlessly, especially the action of frost; water which has percolated into fissured or jointed rock freezes and expands, exerting a great shattering effect so that fragments break off and slopes of scree accumulate at a precarious angle below the foot of each buttress. Under the Napes ridges the reddish scree of Great Hell Gate streams down towards Wasdale, while lower down the valley the most impressive screes in the Lake District descend nearly 1,700ft from the broken crags of Illgill Head into Wastwater. The ascent of a scree slope should be avoided, unless the stones are large and quite stable, and if it must be crossed it is advisable to look for a sheep trod which contours the slope and has acquired a degree of stability. Some screes provide a fast descent to the valley, though running them needs experience and is hard on the boots. A well known scree run is from Dore Head, between Yewbarrow and Red Pike, into Mosedale but this indeed is so much used that sometimes steep bare earth or rock is exposed on which it is easy to take a toss.

Not only does frost loosen small fragments but large blocks may also break off, as evidenced by boulders lying around the floors and lower slopes of most valleys, and sometimes well-known landmarks are affected. The rock-steps of Broad Stand leading from Mickledore on to Scafell begin with several huge square blocks; during the winter of 1969–70 one of these masses split away and slid down the Eskdale side of the col. Under the west face of the Pillar Rock the *New West* climb starts, according to the current Guidebook, below a big embedded block; during the course of the same winter this block split vertically, half of it sliding a few feet down the gully.

The climber must be particularly careful to test crucial holds, especially in spring after the effects of winter frosts, for several accidents can be quite definitely attributed to loosened holds.

The central core of Lakeland is sometimes referred to as the high fells. The term *fell*, like others such as *crag, force* and *tarn*, is derived from the Old Norse and implies an open hillside covered with coarse vegetation used for the grazing of sheep, hence the 'fell pasture' and 'fell grazing'. To a farmer the fell is simply the upper part of his grazing land, though of course the term is also in general use as part of the proper name of some mountains, such as Bowfell and Scafell. The stony soil on the ridges and slopes consists mainly of coarse fragments, and in many parts bare rock appears on the surface. Between these outcrops and patches of scree develops a cover of grass, heather, ling, moss, lichens and bilberry (otherwise known as bleaberry). Badly drained, flat-topped ridges are covered with tussocky moor grass, and hollows and depressions are filled with layers of peat formed from sphagnum moss and cotton grass. Another common plant of the lower slopes is bracken, a menace to hill farmers since it spreads rapidly and so destroys the pasture. It can be unpleasant for the fell walker, unless he keeps to a defined path through it, since it can grow waist high, conceal hidden boulders and soak one's clothes. Stunted oaks, mountain ash or rowan, juniper and holly grow sporadically, especially along the sheltered courses of streams and near the crags where there is some protection from the wind. Trees cling to the face of cliffs, and on the crags more recently opened up by climbers, trees are sometimes integral constituents of a climb, providing belays and even direct assistance, though as a route becomes more popular the tree inevitably suffers and many degenerate into gaunt stumps or disappear altogether, in some cases making the climb harder.

Large blocks of conifers have been planted during the last fifty years by the Forestry Commission, notably in Ennerdale where the long straight lines of trees with their intersecting rides are a somewhat artificial element in the landscape, between Eskdale and Dunnerdale, in Grizedale between Coniston and Esthwaite Water, and on the fells to the west of Bassenthwaite. The Manchester Water Authority has also planted thickly with conifers the shores and lower slopes around Thirlmere. Fell walkers should plan their routes so as to use the rides provided through the forests and the stiles over the boundary fences.

Sheep farming has been directly responsible for a notable feature of the mountain landscape, the drystone walls which run for miles, sometimes ascending unbelievably steep slopes to the very summits. They separate the valley pastures from the fell grazings and demarcate the various properties, though today many are in a bad state of repair, largely because the art of their construction has almost died out. They can be extremely useful to the fell walker as guiding lines in misty weather, since they are marked on the 1:25,000 OS maps; coming back along the tops from Pillar to lower Ennerdale, for example, the walker can follow a wall almost all the way.

This then is the basis of the climber's Lakeland: an assemblage of bold ridges and deep valleys, smooth fells and prominent crags, long deep lakes and tiny high-lying tarns, gashed ravines and plunging mountain torrents, scree-strewn hillsides and heather-covered slopes.

2

THE MOUNTAIN WAY

THE Lake District with its unequalled assemblage of mountains, valleys and lakes is a precious heritage for all who seek peace and relaxation. Yet the attraction of this richly endowed area creates its own problems, since improvements in communications, especially the construction of motorways, have brought a stream of tourist traffic to the narrow lakeside roads and popular viewpoints. A National Park was established in 1951 '. . . to safeguard its beauty for the enjoyment of this and future generations . . .', and much is being done to avoid the destruction of the very qualities which people come so far to enjoy.

Much of the real Lake District is still the preserve of the walker and the climber, whether they prefer to traverse the dale-heads around the centre of the massif by inter-linked passes, to enjoy ridge walking, or to climb crags. Those of us who live in the Lake District and can climb on virtually any day of the year are fortunate in seeing the mountains in their splendour; on many expeditions we meet no one except perhaps an occasional group of Outward Bound students. A little thought and careful planning by the fell walker may be necessary on summer Sundays and Bank Holidays to escape being one of a caravan and by the rock climber to avoid queueing at the foot of the more popular crags. One aim of this book is to suggest some of the less well known possibilities for mountain enjoyment.

Over a hundred summits are at 2,000ft (610m) or more above sea level (more specifically above the Datum of the Ordnance Survey), including four which exceed 3,000ft (914m). But height alone is no real criterion; as was once said, we have elevated mere altitude to an unmerited eminence. The confidence of those who put their faith in the sanctity of numerical height was rather shaken when the 1970 edition of the 1″ Tourist Map of the Lake District appeared. The highest mountain in England, Scafell Pike, with its readily memorable height of 3,210ft, has shrunk by 4ft, while Helvellyn has fared even worse, having diminished by 5ft to

3,113ft. This is not the result of any *en masse* subsidence of the Lakeland dome; most peaks remain at their previous height and some have actually gained, including Skiddaw, Pillar, High Stile and High Street, though only of the order of a single foot. These changes are the result of refinements in surveying and computation methods.

FELL WALKING

Every Lakeland mountain can be ascended by a variety of routes, the most popular of which are scarred and blazened by the boots of generations of walkers and marked by lines of cairns. With the 1″ OS sheet, on which paths are shown by red dotted lines, the relevant volume of Arthur Wainwright (Bibliography, p 209), a compass and the ability to use it, the well-equipped walker has the freedom of the hills. One of the great pleasures is to get on to a ridge and string together a series of summits, for which the radial character of many Lakeland ridges gives splendid scope: the Helvellyn range from Grisedale Hause to Threlkeld; the fifteen-mile stretch northward from Garburn Pass above Kentmere over High Street to Pooley Bridge; the boulder-strewn line of Great End and the Scafells; and the shorter Red Pike—High Stile—High Crag and the Robinson—Hindscarth—Dale Head ridges, both readily accessible from Buttermere. One difficulty about this kind of outing is that it may begin and end some distance apart, thus requiring either a convenient bus service or a cooperative car driver.

For this reason, and also for its sheer satisfaction, a circuit route may be very rewarding. Examples of a modest character include the circuit of Grasmoor—Coledale Hause—Whiteside from Lanthwaite Green; the Mosedale round of Kirk Fell, Pillar, Red Pike and Yew-barrow from Wasdale Head; the Fairfield horseshoe of Heron Pike, Fairfield itself, Hart Crag and High Pike from Rydal; the circuit from Patterdale of the Red Tarn combe under Helvellyn, which includes both Striding Edge and Swirral Edge; and the Coniston round of Wetherlam, Swirl How and the Old Man.

If one is in good training and of the right frame of mind, much bigger circuits can be attempted, such as the tops enclosing the heads of Ennerdale, Eskdale, Great Langdale and Wasdale Head. The last can be expanded to make a complete traverse of the whole of Wasdale, beginning and ending at the village of Strands, a distance of about twenty-two miles and taking in Seatallan, Haycock, Pillar, Kirk Fell, Great Gable, the Scafells and Illgill Head. In the eastern fells the rounding of the upper Kent valley includes Kentmere Pike, the Nan Bield Pass, Mardale Ill Bell, High Street, Thornthwaite Crag and Ill Bell.

The strong walker can easily work out other routes with some logical basis, leading up to almost marathon efforts. An example is the annual event known as the Lakeland Three Thousands, which begins and ends at Keswick and includes Skiddaw, the two Scafells and Helvellyn; those who complete the course within twenty-four hours receive a well-merited certificate. Some are run on competitive lines, such as the Fairfield Horseshoe and the Ennerdale Horseshoe over known routes. Others, notably the Vaux Mountain Trial held each year at a different venue, involve an exacting kind of timed cross country cum orienteering over mountain country, linking a series of check points indicated to the participants only by grid references.

The most exacting form of mountain walking is a kind of supermarathon aiming to cover as many summits, miles of distance and feet of altitude as possible within twenty-four hours. Though not organised on any competitive basis, there is a hint here of a stimulating rivalry, of a successively expanding yardstick against which a fell runner can test himself. This goes back over a century, for some of the Victorians were powerful walkers, but it was after Dr A. W. Wakefield in 1905 covered a round involving 23,500ft of ascent and descent in twenty-two hours that the concept of a record unofficially crystallised. During the next sixty years this has been pushed to what must be very nearly the limit of human endurance by a succession of outstanding fell runners: Eustace Thomas, R. B. Graham, the Heaton brothers and Eric Beard. In 1971 Jos Naylor of Wasdale Head made a round involving sixty-one summits, a distance of ninety miles and an ascent of about 34,000ft within twenty-four hours. Some day!

As the hill walker acquires experience and learns to move safely over rough ground, he finds himself able to leave trodden paths up popular mountains and work out his own routes. Gradually the transition takes place from walking to scrambling, a difference only of degree and the first stage toward rock climbing. Scrambling can

be defined as making use of the hands in surmounting a rocky outcrop in balanced rhythmic movement, which can add much variety
and interest to an outing but which requires some caution. Worthwhile scrambler's routes include the Shamrock Traverse on the
eastern flank of the Pillar Rock; the crossing from Scafell Pike to
Scafell via Mickledore, Rake's Progress, Lord's Rake and the West
Wall Traverse; Jack's Rake across the face of Pavey Ark above
Langdale; the popular if a little hackneyed Striding Edge on Helvellyn; and the ascent of Sharp Edge on Blencathra. Under winter
conditions, of course, such scrambles may form a very different
proposition (p 45).

Those whose interests are primarily in rock climbing may be
obliged to include a fell walk in order to get to their chosen crag,
except where it lies near to the road. A few 'rock gymnasts' may
regard this preliminary walk as a necessary tedium before the real
work and interest of the day. But most climbers would regard this
and the return journey (preferably via the summit of the mountain
on which the crag lies) as an integral part of the outing; in fact
many of the best hill days comprise a balanced programme of fell
walking and rock climbing. Thus, for example, a good expedition
may be had from the Black Sail YH at the head of Ennerdale,
climbing on Boat Howe and Gable Crag via the intervening summit of Kirk Fell, and finishing the day over Great Gable, Green
Gable, Brandreth and the Hay Stacks to Scarth Gap. The Three
Pinnacles round makes a circuit of Wasdale Head, taking in Scafell Pinnacle, the Napes Needle and the Pillar Rock, an outing with
a certain artistic logicality.

The possibilities for unusual and original days on the hills are
infinite; we have found that rescue searches have taken us into
places of great interest which we would otherwise not visit. An
arduous kind of outing, regularly practised by one well-known
climber, is to contour strictly at mid-height some bulky mountain
such as Kirk Fell, taking any and every obstacle directly as it
comes. Streams can be followed to their sources (the ultimate in
this is an ascent of Piers Gill in Wasdale), a line of compass bearing can be strictly adhered to (try this in upper Eskdale), or a route
can be worked out from valley floor to summit taking in as much
scrambling on as direct a line as possible. Examples include the
ascent of Glaramara from the rocky Comb Gill valley via the notch

of Comb Door; of Red Pike directly from Mosedale to the north of
Black Beck; and of the northern flanks of Scafell Pike by a line
between the ravines of Piers and Greta Gills, giving a total ascent
of 2,700ft from valley to summit. Obviously such routes should be
taken only by the fairly experienced and in clear conditions, and
it is wise to leave at base some declaration of intent.

ROCK CLIMBING

It is hardly necessary to describe in any detail the evolution of
rock climbing in the Lake District; this has been done often enough.
It will be sufficient to examine the main features of development to
its present exacting standards, the interaction of three contributions:
(i) the periodic appearance of an exceptional climber, ahead of his
time, who pushed the standards of climbing well above the existing
ones, thereby stimulating others to emulate and in due course
surpass him; (ii) the progressive improvements in technique and
equipment; and (iii) the discovery and exploration of 'new' crags,
new, that is, in the sense that previously they had not been opened
up because of their apparent inaccessibility, insignificance or
vegetated appearance. The net result is that until the last few years
(when progress has been consistently rapid, even meteoric) the
story is one of periods when many new routes of grades more
severe than hitherto were worked out, alternating with phases of
pause and consolidation.

In 1936, the fiftieth anniversary of the first ascent of the Napes
Needle, H. M. Kelly and J. H. Doughty essayed a stocktaking of
Lakeland rock climbing and distinguished four main phases of
development. These they denoted as the periods of (a) the 'easy
way' (before about 1880); (b) the gully and chimney (1880 to 1900);
(c) the ridge and arête or rib (1890 to 1905); and (d) the slab and
wall (post 1905). These phases and dates are by no means exclusive
and there has been much overlapping, both of anticipation and
reversion, but they do indicate a broad evolutionary pattern.

THE GRADING AND NAMING OF CLIMBS
At this point it is necessary to examine two aspects of rock climbs
which contribute much to the esoteric character of the sport: their
grading (i.e. the classified degree of difficulty) and their naming.

The early climbers recognised in a vague sort of way that some routes were more difficult than others but in 1897 Owen Glynne Jones (p 38) produced *Rock Climbing in the English Lake District*, which achieved great popularity in its several editions. It is symptomatic of Jones's methodical approach that he included a list of seventy-five recommended climbs in order of technical difficulty, though his ranking involved only four categories: easy, moderate, difficult and exceptionally severe. Other grading systems have been used subsequently in climbing guidebooks, including combinations of letters and numbers (the practice in continental ranking), but the present method in the Lake District is really an expansion of Jones's. The major accepted standards are now Moderate (M), Difficult (D), Very Difficult (VD), Severe (S), Very Severe (VS) and Extremely Severe (XS); climbers commonly talk of 'diffs' and 'v-diffs'. Further modifications include qualifying adjectives, so we get such transitional grades as 'hard Very Difficult' and even such apparent contradictions as 'mild Very Severe'. These help to indicate fine shades, sometimes so fine that the differences become virtually subjective, the result of the variability of the personal factor, of fitness and mood. It is important to remember that this grading refers to dry weather conditions; damp, greasy or icy rocks will push up the standard of a climb by a grade or more. Nevertheless, the grading of a climb in the guidebooks published by the Fell and Rock Climbing Club, listed in the Bibliography, does give a leader an indication as to whether it is likely to be within his capabilities. This book for the most part follows the official grading.

The naming of a climb is a matter of great concern, since by that name it will be known thereafter. As there are now nearly two thousand rock climbs in the English Lake District, what was a simple matter in the early days has now become a problem. Many of the older climbs are eponymous, named after the leader on the first ascent, and as such represent honoured landmarks in the history of climbing. It is unlikely that these were the choice of the leader himself, who was probably no more nor less modest than the present-day 'tigers', but in the hotel smoking room others would talk of Jones's route up Scafell Pinnacle from Lord's Rake and thus it was perpetuated. So we have several *Jones's* and *Abraham's* climbs, a *Woodhead's* on Scafell and a *Woodhouse's* on Dow, a

Pendlebury Traverse on Pillar, and many more. These were all the successful leaders, though *Walker's Gully* on Pillar is a memorial to a distant relative of one of us, who fell down it in 1883. Occasionally the actual name is not used, as in the case of the *Keswick Brothers*' route on Scafell, but leaving us in no doubt that yet again the Abrahams had been there. The proper name has now been almost entirely eclipsed, though just occasionally it has been used; *Peascod's* route on Raven Crag in Great Langdale was led in 1945 by Bill Peascod, a fine climber who contributed many new routes, mainly in the Buttermere district, before emigrating to Australia. A few punning references creep in, such as the *Half Nelson* and the *Double Cross* climbs made on Eagle Crag in Birkness Combe in 1937 by a party including the well-known climbers Sid Cross and Alice Nelson (for so long the charming hosts of the Old Dungeon Ghyll Hotel, Langdale). Another example is *Cook's Tour*, a rather wandering climb on Pavey Ark led in 1943 by J. Cook. The left-hand ridge of Dove Crag in Dovedale under Fairfield was climbed in 1937 by a party who called it Wing Ridge, unaware that it had been led by H. Westmorland as long ago as 1910. It was therefore recently renamed *Westmorland's* route as a tribute to the contributions he has made to Lakeland climbing in general and to mountain rescue in particular.

Allied to the personal names are what might be called the vocational, as exemplified by the *Doctor's*, *Smuggler's* and *Engineer's Chimneys* on Gable Crag, *Professor's Chimney* on Scafell, *Doctor's Grooves* on Eagle Crag, Grisedale, and *Pedagague's Chimney* on Striddle Crag, Buttermere. A group of climbs on Pillar reveal the interests in atomic physics of their exponents: *Electron*, *Proton*, *Photon* and the like.

A third category is the alphabetical, called by Doughty '. . . the most arid, unimaginative and benighted of nomenclatures'. Thus there are the *A*, *B*, *C* and *D Gullies* on Pike's Crag, Scafell; the six Gimmer climbs in Langdale, *A* to *F*; and the *A*, *B*, *C*, *D* and *E* Buttresses on Dow (figure 8). Similar in concept are the routes on Green Gable crags, denoted by Greek letters from *Alpha* to *Fie*!

A large group can be classified as directional, and Pillar in particular is so covered with such climbs that it is almost possible to box the compass around the Rock; perhaps a crag with four major faces is doomed to such a nomenclature. Yet such is the power of tradition that the *North*, the *North-West* and the *South-West* climbs are classics, though as intervening routes were made the cardinal and ordinal directions were gradually used up and so arrived at *South-West by West*.

One of the most satisfactory groups is what might be called the topographically descriptive, and fortunately a large number fall into this category: the *Rib and Slab* and the *Grooved Wall* (Pillar); the *Arête, Chimney and Crack* (Dow); the magnificent *Overhanging Bastion* (Castle Rock of Triermain); the *Curving Gully* (Hutaple Crag, Deepdale); and the *Central Buttress* with its Flake Crack on Scafell. Surely these are the most evocative of names.

Lastly, the wit of modern climbers has added a vast and growing miscellaneous collection: imaginative, cryptic, punning and thematic. Sometimes the point behind the name is obvious; at other times it is the result of a joke coined in a tent or bar and understood only by the party concerned. One of the great climbs of the district, *Kipling Groove* on Gimmer, is said to have been so named because its exceptionally gifted leader, Arthur Dolphin, thought it to be 'ruddy 'ard'. *Scorpion* on Shepherd's Crag has its sting in the tail in the form of a good final pitch, while *Crescendo* becomes progressively harder. Sometimes the christening of a climb may be through the association of ideas. Thus the eastern buttress of the Napes on Great Gable, overlooking the scree slopes of Great Hell Gate, has *Tophet Bastion, Lucifer Ridge, Brimstone Buttress* and *Demon Wall*, and *Boat Howe Crag* has its obvious nautical terminology. After *Tia Maria* was climbed in 1954 on the East Buttress of Scafell, it was followed in sucession by *Tio Pepe, Chartreuse, Pernod* and *Absinthe*; on the Napes ridges are *Sabre, Scimitar* and *Cutlass*; on Seathwaite Buttress are *Snap, Crackle, Pop* and *Cornflakes*. When Red Crag, so called from the distinctive pinkish tinge in its rocks, was opened up in the Vale of Newlands, a whole string of names with Russian connotations was devised: *Kremlin, Capitalist, Tartar, Cossack, October* and *Bolshoi*. An apparent morbid obsession with death accounts for the necrophilic connotation of climbs on Black Crag and Greatend Crag in Troutdale. Finally, some of the XS climbs have been given ominous names indicative of their gravity, such as the *Tomb* on Gable Crag, the *Black Widow* on Pillar and *Armageddon* on the East Buttress of Scafell.

Page 35 Puppet, north face of Pillar Rock

Page 36 (above left) Winter ascent of *Central Gully*, Gable Crag; *(above right)* Kirk Fell and Pillar Mountain from Gable Crag; *(below)* Pillar from Red Pike (Buttermere)

EARLY EVOLUTION

During the first half of the nineteenth century a few climbs of a
scrambling nature were made, so infrequent that they have been the
subject of considerable historical research. Possibly the poet W. T.
Coleridge in 1802 visited *Broad Stand*, the rocky step on the western side of the Mickledore gap on the Scafell ridge; he describes
the narrow chasm between two massive blocks at its base, what
is now popularly known as *Fat Man's Agony*. In 1826 the first
recorded ascent of the Pillar Rock took place, appropriately enough
by an Ennerdale man, John Atkinson, who apparently climbed it
not as a shepherd would to rescue a crag-bound sheep, but because
of what has been termed the lure of the inaccessible. Wordsworth,
in his poem *The Brothers*, had earlier referred to the Pillar Stone
in a kind of morbidly curious way, which undoubtedly focused
attention on it.

As the century wore on, a growing number of climbers visited
Lakeland, mainly university dons, clerics, barristers and scientists,
those in fact who had sufficient leisure and means to spend time in
this still unusual and even eccentric way. Many were alpinists who
visited the Lake District during the winter, especially at Easter;
simple rock climbing and the ascent of snow-filled gullies were
merely a minor part of their greater mountaineering. If this can
be regarded as a first phase, the second was the emergence of
British rock climbing as an independent, self-contained and wholly
satisfying sport, so much so that its devotees were sometimes
patronisingly dismissed as 'rock gymnasts'. In modern times has
come the third phase, almost a reversal of the first, when British
climbers project their activities into the Alps, the Himalayas and
the Andes, applying the same highly skilled techniques in a wider
context. Most climbs before about 1900 belonged to the 'gully and
chimney' period, possibly because of the psychological factor of
some feeling of security within their safe if damp and gloomy recesses. A remarkable exception was the ascent by W. P. Haskett
Smith in 1886 of the Napes Needle (plate p 125), a pinnacle of striking aspect; now it has half a dozen alternative routes, one of them
a hard VS, and it is still an object of pilgrimage. This achievement
was undoubtedly a landmark, both for its own sake in that a
climber had deliberately courted a considerable degree of exposure
and also for the fact that it gained much publicity.

C

Though Owen Glynne Jones climbed in Lakeland only for a few years after 1890 (he was killed on the Dent Blanche in 1899), he raised dramatically the standards of climbing. While he brought the 'gully and chimney' epoch to a close with his ascents of *Kern Knotts Crack* on Great Gable and of *Walker's Gully* on the Pillar Rock, he anticipated later phases by his routes, climbing alone and in stocking feet up Scafell Pinnacle from Deep Gill and Lord's Rake; the latter was not repeated for fourteen years. He climbed much with the Abraham brothers of Keswick, who apart from their climbing competence had two great attributes: their eye for a route of quality and individuality, and their photographic skill. Admittedly they were early on the scene and had much untrodden rock from which to choose, but they left a series of fine climbs, including the *New West* on Pillar, *Abraham's* route on B Buttress of Dow Crag and the *Keswick Brothers'* route on Scafell. Their impressive action photographs, taken with unwieldy whole-plate cameras, illustrated their own and other books and sold in vast numbers as postcards.

Now the sport was becoming popular, no longer a strange mystique or rite practised by suicidally inclined extroverts. Gradually more crags were explored, and climbers left the safe recesses and ventured on to the more exposed arêtes, buttresses and walls. An exceptional effort was the lead by G. A. Solly on a bitter April day in 1892 of the steep and exposed *Eagle's Nest Ridge* on Great Gable, which is even today ranked as a mild VS route. Another remarkable *tour de force* was the ascent in 1903 by Fred Botterill of the ninety-foot slab on Scafell which now bears his name; even modern leaders find this distinctly thin, involving a long runout of great delicacy with little scope for protection. Three years later the same climber led the *North-West* climb on Pillar, a long route of great character. Mention must be made of Siegfried Herford, who during a few short years before he was killed in Flanders in 1916 applied to Scafell a technique so far ahead of his contemporaries that it would not be difficult to justify him as the greatest ever. His main achievement was the solution of the problems of the *Central Buttress* of Scafell, which remained the hardest climb in England for twenty years; the earliest F&RCC Guidebook described it succinctly as '. . . the most arduous ascent in the Lake District; unexampled exposure; combined tactics and rope engineering

essential . . .' Even now, when there are many climbs of much
greater severity, it retains its aura of a great route. He also worked
out a girdle traverse of Scafell and so initiated a type of climbing in
a roughly horizontal plane across the face of a crag, linking the best
pitches of existing routes; most cliffs now have their girdles, some
of a very exacting character.

LATER DEVELOPMENTS

For a few years after World War I there was an inevitable pause
in the development of climbing, but then came another vivid
acceleration, stimulated by the publication of a series of Guidebooks by the Fell and Rock Climbing Club. These, repeatedly
revised, have on the one hand led large numbers to the base of the
crags and indicated existing routes, and on the other have stimulated
the creation of new climbs to fill obvious gaps on the crags. Thus
the 1923 edition of the Guidebook to Pillar contained descriptions
of thirty-eight routes, that of 1968 included seventy-eight not
counting minor variations.

'New' crags included some already well known but which had
long been regarded as impregnable. One such was the East Buttress
of Scafell on the Eskdale side of Mickledore, which is in parts
overhanging and is usually extremely wet; the first climb to be
made, *Mickledore Grooves*, was climbed in 1931 and is still regarded
as the classic of the district, though now there are over thirty,
including five of XS standard. Other crags to be developed by the
'hard men' were the Castle Rock of Triermain at the southern end
of St John's Vale; the east-facing Raven Crag near the Thirlmere
dam; Heron Crag in Eskdale; Dove Crag and Scrubby Crag on
the eastern flanks of the Fairfield massif; Goat Crag near Grange
in Borrowdale; and Rainsborrow Crag in Kentmere, explored only
since 1967. Some of these are so impressive that earlier potential
leaders looked from a respectful distance and passed by, leaving
them to their brooding isolation. Others were so loose, wet and
rank with vegetation that they remained inviolate until a breed of
leaders evolved who, wearying of rock from which the only reason
for falling off was letting go, regarded these adverse qualities as
challenges to their technique. Still other crags appeared from a
distance as mere excrescences on the hillside, camouflaged among
broken outcrops, scree and heather until some determined enthusi-

ast of a pioneering frame of mind discovered that in reality they contained much continuous sound rock. Some crags were developed through the desire to escape from increasingly crowded areas to where they could perform in relative isolation. On pioneer routes leaders were sometimes equipped with trowels and other implements for the 'gardening' involved in clearing vegetation from holds and belays.

Inevitably many climbs on these 'new' crags are of a high standard, including most of the Lakeland XS's, but a large number of new routes of reasonable standard for the ordinary climber have also been discovered. A pioneer in this direction was Bentley Beetham, particularly in Borrowdale, hitherto a somewhat neglected valley, where he worked out over a hundred climbs on twenty or more crags; while some are hard, many were originally devised for the benefit of his parties of schoolboys. Another 'late developer' was Wallowbarrow (figure 9) in Dunnerdale, opened up in the 1950s by the Eskdale Outward Bound Mountain School. Its long neglect seems strange, since it has yielded climbs of considerable character from D to VS grading; moreover it faces south, is low-lying and sheltered, and dries off remarkably quickly.

THE MODERN CLIMBERS

Two reasons may be adduced for the increase both in the number of very hard climbs and of leaders competent to tackle them. One is the remarkable growth in the number of people who seek recreation in the hills, the other the developments in equipment and techniques, together with the corresponding psychological ability to apply them.

Until after World War II, while climbing was not necessarily a rich man's sport, it was not a poor man's either; as we have seen, many early climbers were mainly of the professional classes, with sufficient leisure to make the slow journey to the remote hills. There were a few local climbers; as youths we used to cycle from the coast of West Cumberland to a valley-head, climb all day and cycle back. But all this has altered dramatically, the result of greater leisure, longer holidays and perhaps most important of all easy access by road, so that a person one meets on Pillar on Sunday morning may be due back that evening in Bradford or Birmingham. The climber who is on the crags every weekend can of course operate at a consistently higher technical level than one who could perhaps come only at Easter and during the summer holidays.

It is noticeable that sometimes a group from a particular district gained a kind of lien on a specific crag. Local climbers are naturally at an advantage; West Cumbrians were responsible for the surge of new routes on Pillar in the 1960's and the Keswick climbers for high-grade exploration in Borrowdale and Thirlmere, almost, as it were, in their back gardens. But others come from farther afield; for example a group from Bradford did much to explore the eastern crags, and members of the Sheffield University Mountaineering Club concentrated on Eagle Crag in Grisedale, helped by the fact that their climbing hut, Ruthwaite Lodge, is only ten minutes away from the crag. Occasionally climbers habitually based in Wales, where the standards of the hardest climbs at one time were admittedly higher than in the Lake District, made forays north and added new lines of great severity. In 1953, for example, the incomparable Brown-Whillans partnership climbed the fierce *Triermain Eliminate* on the Castle Rock and *Dovedale Groove* on Dove Crag; the latter was unrepeated for nine years and achieved a kind of myth of inaccessibility, a most unusual occurrence in these competitive days. Another Welsh-based team repeated this climb in 1962 and went on to add a still harder, *Hiraeth*.

There has also undoubtedly been an educative influence at work, as an ever widening range of young people learn to appreciate the hills, coming with school parties or as members of organised courses at Outward Bound Mountain Schools and other training centres. A remarkable fact is the speed with which young climbers now progress, compared with earlier days when a novice worked his way through a list of carefully graded, progressively more difficult climbs. Now a naturally gifted young man, and there seem to be many of these, may be on routes of S and VS standard within a very short time.

Improvements both in climbing equipment and in the techniques to make efficient use of it have been major contributions to this rise in standards. A nineteenth century climber once wrote, describing his route, that no rope '. . . or any other artificial aid . . .' was used; now a leader and his second may be weighed down by their clanking armoury, each item of which has a specific purpose. The use of nylon rope, of various sophisticated safeguarding techniques involving the placing of running belays, and of lightweight rubber-soled footwear which can exploit frictional grip on tiny and indefinite holds, all contribute to safer high-standard climbing.

Few items of gear have been as controversial in the past as *pitons* (or *pegs*), spikes and blades of various shapes and sizes with a ring at the end, made of malleable steel or chrome-molybdenum alloy. Until after World War II they were unacceptable to most climbers in Lakeland, indeed, one can detect in the literature of the time an almost pathological prejudice against the use of 'ironmongery'. However, pitons were even then used occasionally on new climbs, and Maurice Linnell, one of the pioneers on the East Buttress of Scafell, employed them not only as a safeguard but to pull up on; in his account of one hard climb he is quite unashamed: '. . . those who prefer to climb the place unaided are cordially invited to remove the piton and do so'. Quite apart from so-called 'artificial climbing', where a route can only be forced with the direct aid of pitons, an increasing number of Lake District climbs involve their use, particularly on the first ascent or for sheer safety where a natural belay is lacking. But the indiscriminate use of pitons on a route which has already been climbed without their aid is to be strongly deprecated; this is a sign of weakness and inadequacy, of the lowering of the standard of a climb to the ability of a less than capable leader, and the party ought not to be there. The Guidebooks usually indicate where a piton is in place or should be inserted; for example, on *Gormenghast* on Heron Crag in Eskdale the first pitch ends at a niche which affords an adequate stance but has no belay, so a piton has been put there. Several are in place on the East Buttress of Scafell, as near the bottom of *May Day* and on the second pitch of *Overhanging Wall*. On these and other hard climbs their use is entirely reasonable, especially when the alternative is an indifferent or unsafe natural belay. The use of pitons is also reasonable under winter conditions when a real hazard may develop unpredictably, and in mountain rescue operations when safety is paramount.

Much of this account has been devoted to the achievements of the 'tigers' and the 'hard men' in the rock climbing world, but it will be appreciated that they are the pacemakers for the great majority of ordinary climbers, whose standards have risen accordingly. Twenty years ago the average climber could safely lead at

Difficult/Very Difficult level, his standard fluctuating around that margin according to his form on the day and with the conditions. Today the average leading standard has probably risen by a grade to mild Severe, and of course there are many more leaders who are competent to tackle the very hard climbs.

The net result of more than a century of effort and exploratory enterprise is that no less than 1,560 different Lakeland climbs are listed in the current Guidebooks, and since their latest editions at least a further two hundred new routes have been added. Out of this vast number we have selected one hundred: twenty-five from those of Very Difficult standard or easier, fifty from the most popular category of Severe and mild Very Severe, and twenty-five from the Very Severe group. These are listed in the Appendix (p 203) as our wholly subjective choice; the only qualifications are that each route has been climbed recently by one or other of us, usually by both, often together, and most important that we have enjoyed them. Bentley Beetham, a fine rock climber and alpinist and a member of the 1924 Everest team, once enunciated the eight requirements of a 'good climb' in order of importance: (a) sound clean rock; (b) leading to a definite summit; (c) adequate belays; (d) of reasonable length (ie not a mere 'boulder problem'); (e) affording continuous climbing uninterrupted by scree and grass slopes; (f) a southerly aspect; (g) variety of situation and detail; and (h) technical difficulty, ideally the hardest grade that a particular leader is just able to climb safely. Few climbs satisfy all these criteria, but we believe that our chosen hundred go some way in doing so.

WINTER CLIMBING

It is obviously necessary to draw a distinction between climbing in winter and climbing under winter conditions. The former simply implies being on the hills during the winter months, which at one time was fairly uncommon, partly because holidays were short and limited to a long Easter weekend and during the summer, partly because access for weekends and other short visits was difficult when people were generally not so mobile. Today many climb all the year round, on the one hand stimulated by greater leisure and much easier transport, on the other hand helped by the excellent clothing and equipment generally. Limited only by the shortness of daylight and by some degree of weather prudence, the well equipped fell walker, with the usual seven essentials in his sack,† can find great joy in roaming the winter hills. The views are commonly much sharper than on hazy summer days, the air is crisper and more invigorating, and mountain memories seem more vivid. On fine days, which are by no means rare, the rock climber may find dry and sheltered conditions on such low-lying crags as those in Borrowdale, Wallowbarrow in Dunnerdale, Bowness Knott in Ennerdale and Eagle Crag in Grisedale.

Winter climbing, by contrast, implies climbing with snow on the slopes and ridges and masking the holds on climbs, the rocks covered with ice crystals or glazed with water-ice and the gullies filled with long ribbons of compact snow. These conditions are more usually met with after Christmas and as late as March or even April, though early snowfalls are by no means unknown. Recently, we went to Dow to climb; there had been some snowfall during the week, but we were unprepared for thick snow on the ledges and glazed rock on the buttresses. After struggling lengthily up the first pitch of Easter Gully we abandoned the climb, roped off, and spent the day on the ridges in the sunshine.

While conditions are rarely as severe as on the Scottish mountains with their higher altitudes and more northerly latitudes, the Lake District in most years has cold spells and snowfall, and occasionally experiences winters harder than average, such as the splendid seasons of 1962–3 and 1968–9. Periodic snowfalls alternate with partial thaws, thus accumulating hard-packed snow and even ice in the gullies; long spells of anticyclonic weather bring clear skies, brilliant sunshine and keen frost. Then the climber has to cope with conditions as he finds them, to deal with problems as they arise; not for him are the well-known, even stereotyped grades of summer, and everything has a freshness, a novelty, a new challenge and stimulus. What are normally easy scrambles may become major propositions, and commonly the successful outcome of an expedition is in doubt to the very end. Always the climber is faced with the limiting factor of time, with the possibility of a chilly night on the hills.

† These are map, compass, whistle, torch with a spare battery and bulb, extra clothing, emergency rations and first aid kit; a polythene survival sack is a valuable addition for the lone climber.

Even to reach the foot of a climb can be unexpectedly time-consuming; sometimes this involves a heavy plod through deep powder-snow, especially trying when it is crusted so that the foot just breaks through and has to be lifted laboriously out. Then the climb may take longer than anticipated; to the leader, heavily engaged on a problem to which he is intensely committed and warm with exertion, the time passes too quickly, while his second, shivering on a cramped stance, becomes steadily colder. Large parties on gully climbs are a mistake, since there is so much waiting around in their chilly depths; ideally a party of two leading through makes best progress. Under winter conditions exposed faces, slabs and buttresses may be extremely difficult or even impossible; even if the rock is not actually iced or masked with snow, it is very cold and gloved hands cannot feel small holds. Up goes the standard of a moderate summer climb, as the leader sweeps away snow from the holds, or chips off a veneer of ice with his axe or hammer, perhaps putting in a piton where in summer it would be unthought of. Easy scrambles become worthy expeditions: the traverse of Striding Edge—Swirral Edge on Helvellyn, of Sharp Edge on Blencathra, of Crinkle Crags and Bowfell, and of the Scafells via Broad Stand or Lord's Rake. We make an annual pilgrimage on New Year's Day to the summit of the Pillar Rock, thus beginning the year well, usually by such easy routes as the *Old West, Slab and Notch* or the *Central Jordan* climbs; on occasion this has proved to be a considerable enterprise.

The best type of winter climbing is the ascent of a long well-defined gully, preferably leading to a summit ridge, which in summer may be so wet and loose as not to be worth a visit. Long slopes of hard-frozen snow, sometimes even of ice, may cover the boulders and scree in its bed, perhaps accumulating to such a depth that the vertical-walled pitches of summer, capped by great chock-stones, may be climbed by cutting steps or nicking in crampon points; sometimes these capstones are buried in snow. The bottom pitch of Deep Gill on Scafell affords an example of the differing conditions. In summer it consists of a rather damp cave formed by a huge boulder, which can be turned to the right on small holds. In winter it may be completely covered with a sheet of ice, necessitating delicate nicking of holds, or the cave may be filled with a huge snowdrift almost masking the boulder and considerably easing the ascent, or it may be only partially filled with a snow-cone, leaving a gap between it and the rock; each particular set of conditions requires its own solution and new techniques have to be applied.

The best prospects are in high-lying gullies on north- or east-facing crags or the steep back walls of the combes. One of the most popular venues is Great End at the north-eastern end of the Scafell range overlooking Sprinkling Tarn, to which an interesting approach can be made by way of the steep-sided ravine of Skew Gill; there are three gullies, the South-East, the Central and Cust's. As the foot of these gullies lies at about 2,500ft, the chances of good conditions are high. But they suffer from their popularity, since if a spell of settled weather becomes established, with a good forecast for the weekend ahead, hopeful climbers come from a distance and late arrivals may have to queue to ascend a staircase of steps already cut up the gullies. Then it pays to go off and visit a less well-known area and work out a route of one's own. Other possibilities include the high-lying gullies on the eastern side of the Helvellyn group, as on Tarn Crag and Falcon Crag on Dollywaggon Pike, High Crag on Nethermost Pike and on Helvellyn itself; *Central Gully* on Gable Crag (plate p 36); the A, B, C and D Gullies on Pike's Crag, Scafell, of which B is usually the hardest; and on Scafell Crag are Moss Gill, Steep Gill, Deep Gill and Lord's Rake. Moss Gill and Steep Gill possibly provide the best winter routes in the Lake District. Lord's Rake, combined with the West Wall Traverse and the upper part of Deep Gill, offers a good way to the top of Scafell itself under winter conditions. Another worthy climb may be provided by *Mickledore Chimney*, a hundred feet down from Mickledore on the Eskdale side of Scafell, which often contains hard ice and can give 300ft of climbing. In January 1969 we spent three days on this problem. Another climb can be made up the eastern side of Lingmell, the so-called *Continuation Gully* leading out of the last major right-angled bend of Pier's Gill; this can be followed almost to the summit.

MOUNTAIN RESCUE

It is inevitable that as more walkers and climbers go to the hills, the number of accidents has also increased, despite the fact that most people are better equipped and probably better informed about mountain conditions than ever before. But the law of gravity still operates as relentlessly as ever; a slip on what is normally an easy ridge walk, on an unexpected patch of ice possibly covered by innocent-looking fresh snow, or on slimy rock, may have tragic results. A sudden change of weather, to which mountains are peculiarly prone, may transform what was little more than a pleasant outing into a desperate struggle; this is particularly the case in spring, when valley sunshine may tempt walkers on to the tops where winter conditions still prevail. While the efficient use of map and compass should be part of every hill wanderer's training, people do get lost in mist or darkness; if they fail to return within a reasonable time, a search becomes necessary, sometimes involving a complex, highly organised effort. Contrary to general belief, accidents to rock climbers, practising their technique with great care on steep places, are comparatively rare. (In 1970 eight people died and ninety-three were injured on the Lakeland hills; of these only one fatality and eighteen injuries involved rock climbers.)

Before 1939 accidents were uncommon because relatively few people then had the inclination or opportunity to spend much time among the hills. When something did happen, an *ad hoc* collection of volunteers was assembled: police, shepherds, quarrymen and any available climbers in the vicinity. The clubs (notably the Fell and Rock, with its close Lakeland affinities) helped to establish rescue posts where first aid and other equipment was stored at hotels and climbing huts in the valleys and at various points in the hills.

Since World War II, and especially during the last decade, the whole aspect has changed; the Lake District is now served, probably more closely and intensively than any other mountain region in Britain, by a dozen voluntary teams, each based on a valley or small town and responsible for its own sector. Though organised as self-contained and self-supporting units, they come under the control of the Lake District Mountain Accidents Association, itself affiliated to a country-wide organisation known as the Mountain Rescue Committee. The teams are trained to carry out the dual aspects of mountain rescue: to search for a missing climber, and to bring down an injured person as safely, swiftly and comfortably as possible, or, in the last event, to recover the body after a fatal accident. Equipment has steadily become more efficient and sophisticated, including short-wave radios, powerful floodlights for night searches, specially designed stretchers and lowering harness, and winches with steel cables. First aid equipment, a stretcher and other necessities are kept in large metal boxes (painted blue and visible at a considerable distance) at strategic points in the mountains; their locations are marked on the 1″ OS Tourist Map.

A team responsible for a particular area will normally handle an 'incident' occurring in that district, called out by an elaborate system initiated by the police who should always be informed directly via the nearest telephone should action be required. In the event of a climber still missing after the initial search, a massive and coordinated effort, controlled by a search panel of LDMAA representatives in conjunction with the police, is put into effect; this may involve a number of teams, sometimes even drawn from beyond the Lake District, and such a search has been known to last for days, even weeks. This may seem surprising in such a limited area, but when one considers the rugged terrain, the cover of bracken and heather and the masking effects of bad weather, it may not be so surprising after all.

Mountain rescue teams turn out at all times, in all conditions of weather and do so willingly. Only one thing is really annoying: when they make a wearisome search for a person who has been reported missing, but who has in fact changed his plans without notification and is safe elsewhere.

3

ENNERDALE

ENNERDALE WATER is the most westerly of the English Lakes and is therefore less readily accessible to visitors from the south, especially as its approach roads are somewhat winding. Access for cars to the lake is limited to a narrow road leading to the site of the former Angler's Inn near the foot of the lake and another to Bowness Knott on its northern shores, where the National Trust has established a car park with superb views up the valley. Beyond this point a dirt road is restricted to the vehicles of the Forestry Commission and other authorised users. There is no road at all along the southern margin of the lake, a limitation which is largely responsible for the quiet nature of the valley.

Except for a few farms which take visitors, little accommodation is available, though there are two excellent Youth Hostels. One of these, attractively converted from two Forestry Commission cottages, is situated a mile above the head of the lake at Gillerthwaite, the other nearly four miles farther up at Black Sail, formerly a shepherd's cottage and one of the most finely situated hostels in the Lake District. But as its capacity is small, advance booking is essential during most of the season, for it is strategically situated near the foot of Black Sail Pass and Scarth Gap on the walker's highway around the centre of the Lakeland dome, and at the point of convergence of other tracks from several directions. Near the Gillerthwaite YH the old farmhouse of Lower Gillerthwaite has been converted into a field centre by the Leeds College of Education.

The Ennerdale valley extends for about nine miles from the foot of the lake to Windy Gap, a col between Great and Green Gable in the fine amphitheatre of peaks at the valley head (figure 2). From the scree slopes below the Gap issue headstreams of the River Liza, which wanders down the floor of the valley, joined by gills and becks mainly from the slopes on the southern side. For much of its length the river flows turbulently in its rocky bed with deep pools

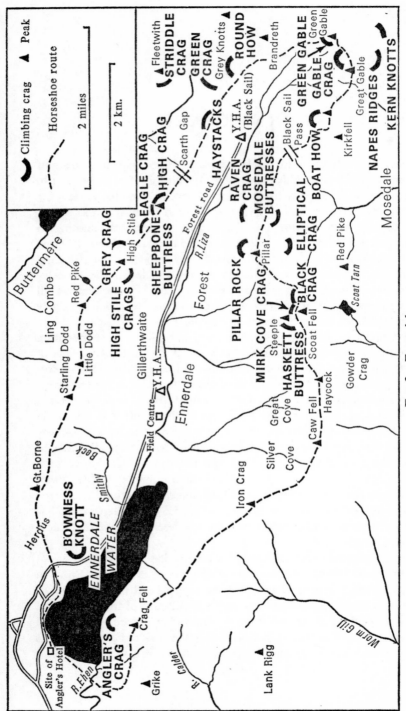

FIG 2. Ennerdale

and cascades, and in flood it may be impassable except at the bridge points.

The lowest is a wooden footbridge half a mile below Giller-thwaite; a mile beyond the Hostel is a slatted bridge with a wire handrail; then a solid stone and concrete structure built a few years ago for Forestry vehicles; and almost directly below a steep ride leading through the forest towards the Pillar Rock is a footbridge erected by the Cumberland County Council and the Fell and Rock Climbing Club as a memorial to members who lost their lives in World War II. A small bridge crosses the upper Liza just beyond the Black Sail YH on the route to Black Sail Pass.

As the Liza approaches the lake it flows among sheets of water-worn stones in braided channels which change in times of flood, and enters the lake through a marshy delta. At the lake foot the river emerges over a low weir which maintains the water level as a reservoir supplying Whitehaven and much of south Cumberland, and here changes its name to the Ehen, from a corruption of which Ennerdale is derived. A pleasant walk of about seven miles can be made around the lake. A footpath closely follows its southern shores, rounding the base of Angler's Crag, a rocky mass facing Bowness Knott across the water. At the lake-head it is advisable to keep along the edge of the higher land to the east to avoid marshy ground, and then cross the Liza by the footbridge below Giller-thwaite. The Forestry road leads along its northern shore almost to Bowness Knott, continued by a footpath past the site of the demolished Angler's Hotel, still marked on the 1970 edition of the 1″ OS map to the fury of thirsty walkers when they discover that it no longer exists.

Before the 1930s most of the valley formed part of the grazing lands of Gillerthwaite Farm, but nearly 9,000 acres were acquired by the Forestry Commission and much has been planted with coni-fers. Ennerdale Forest thus forms a dark swathing carpet over the valley floor and sides up to about 900ft, and seen from the ridges the straight-line boundaries and rides appear somewhat alien, though with the passage of time some trees have died off and the tree-line has become irregular and more natural. The walk up the valley along the forest road through the pine woods, with glimpses of ridges and crags between the trees, is attractive, and the uniformity of the conifers has been modified by the planting of deciduous trees along the margins; the beeches between the lake-head and Gillerthwaite are especially colourful in autumn.

FELL WALKS

The Ennerdale valley is bounded on the north and south by a remarkably continuous ridge line. The south-facing slopes are quite smooth though steep and scree covered. By contrast, the wave-like curve of the opposite ridge (plate p 17), is deeply dissected by a whole series of crag-rimmed hollows known as *coves*: Green, Hind and Pillar Coves to the east of the Pillar Rock; Windgap, Mirk, Mirklin, Great and Silver Coves to the west, rarely visited except by shepherds engaged in gathering sheep from their rocky fast-nesses; here the snow lies late and there is a great feeling of remote-ness. Between the coves and on their back walls buttresses stand out prominently, the most striking being the Pillar Rock on the northern slopes of Pillar mountain and Boat Howe high under the summit of Kirk Fell, while the head of the valley is dominated by the gully-seamed cliffs of Gable Crag.

This whole bounding ridge-line is sometimes known as the Ennerdale horseshoe (figure 2), and an annual race is held in early June around it, though omitting the summit of Great Gable, a distance of about twenty-three miles and a total ascent of about 7,000ft. This route, preferably including Great Gable since it is the logical culminating summit on the circuit, makes a worthy day of nine to ten hours of reasonable going, though it is worth re-membering that Jos Naylor, a Wasdale farmer, holds the record for the race, an unbelievable 3 hours 35 minutes.

The more attractive way round is in the clockwise direction. Starting up Great Borne, whose southern scree slopes are known as Herdus, one ascends either the grass and heather-covered west-ern ridge or more interestingly a well-defined path which leaves the road just short of the Bowness Knott car park, through the bracken to the col between the mountain and its little spur of Bowness Knott. A steep path through the heather beside the deeply cut Rake Beck gully leads to Great Borne's extensive plateau-summit, covered with peat, heather and boulders, a mountain with several tops, one crowned with a large cairn overlooking the lonely Floutern Tarn beneath broken crags, another bearing the OS

Page 53 *(above left) Waterfall Buttress,* Newlands; *(above right) Quantral,* Ling Crag, Crummock Water; *(below)* Buttermere and Fleetwith Pike

Page 54 Seathwaite and Borrowdale from Taylor Gill

triangulation column. The walker then strides off for about two and a half miles in a direction just south of east over a broad grassy ridge, crossing the humps of Starling Dodd and Little Dodd before heading for the graceful cone of Red Pike. This mountain can also be climbed by a gentle gradient from just beyond the Gillerthwaite YH (this affords a very fast descent), and also from Buttermere (p 75). From its summit a path leads over smooth turf, boulders and rock outcrops along the fine ridge of High Stile and High Crag; on the left (north) Chapel Crags drop steeply into Bleaberry Combe, Grey Crag and Eagle Crag into Birkness Combe. A rapid descent can be made down the south-eastern ridge of High Crag, known as Gamlin End, where what was not long ago a smooth, grassy hillside has been scarred by countless boots into a scree slope, leading to Scarth Gap at about 1,400ft, the walker's pass between Ennerdale and Buttermere.

The next section of the horseshoe climbs up to the Hay Stacks, a complex ridge with a maze of rounded craggy outcrops, low cliffs, boulders, small tarns, peat bogs and stretches of heather and bilberry. The path wanders its eastward way for almost a mile to the broad ridge running southward from Brandreth, where it joins the much scarred track between Honister Pass and the Gables, crossing Windy Gap at a height of about 2,460ft. After gaining the plateau-summit of Great Gable (p 197), the descent is made by the north-western ridge to Beck Head, a broad marshy col with two small tarns lying in peat hollows. Ahead lies the bulky hump of Kirk Fell (p 176), with its twin tops separated by a good half-mile of grass and boulders, also with several small tarns; the path here is not very well defined and in thick mist it is easy to stray, especially as the remains of a fence does not cross the higher summit. A steep descent is made among easy broken crags and scree to Black Sail Pass at about 1,800ft.

The third section of the horseshoe lies ahead and the remains of either fence posts or a wall can be followed almost all the way. so that one can stride on in thick mist with confidence. Pillar mountain is easily attained by its long eastern ridge, mostly grassy though with three stony rises and with crags dropping away on its flanks, especially impressive to the north in the coves. The mountain is of course named after the Rock and is not itself shaped like a pillar; rather it is a broad plateau, with an OS column and

D

several piles of stones erected as windbreaks; from its northern edge the top of the Rock can be seen 500ft below.

From the summit of Pillar the route zigzags down among boulders and scree in a south-westerly direction to Wind Gap (plate p 17), at about 2,600ft, another crossing point in the main ridge from which rough descents lead north-westward into Windgap Cove and so into Ennerdale, south-eastward into Mosedale and thence Wasdale. From this gap the long ridge of Scoat Fell is ascended, with its several tops (oddly enough, Great Scoat Fell is lower in altitude than Little Scoat Fell, though more extensive in area), craggy outcrops and steep boulder-strewn slopes; its highest point is a cairn perched on a massive wall. Here it is worth branching northward from the main ridge to scramble easily across a rocky notch on to Steeple, a craggy little peak defined by the rugged fastnesses of Mirk Cove on the east, Mirklin Cove on the west; a quick descent into Ennerdale can be made from Steeple along its northern ridge.

The rest of the horseshoe consists of about seven miles of easy going over grassy and boulder-strewn slopes, with gentle rises and descents over Haycock, Caw Fell, the long ridge of Iron Crag and Crag Fell, and down the boulder-strewn gully of Ben Gill to the foot of the lake.

Between Ennerdale and Wasdale lie rolling hills separated by the broad valleys of the River Calder, its main tributary Worm Gill and the River Bleng. These moorlands and sheep grazings, with great tracts of tussock grass, heather and peat bog, afford good walking, with fine views of the high fells to the east; rarely does one meet anybody other than an occasional shepherd. The most prominent summit is Lank Rigg, marked by an OS column, a tiny tarn and numerous tumuli and other prehistoric remains. When approaching this hill from the Ennerdale—Calder Bridge road over Cold Fell, the Calder can be crossed either by a ford or by a superb example of a pack horse bridge known as Matty Benn's or the Monk's Bridge. Several long though easy walks lead over to Wasdale, notably over Crag Fell, Caw Fell and Haycock, then striking south over Seatallan and so down past Greendale Tarn to the Gosforth road about three miles from Wasdale Head. Particular care is needed in mist among these rather lonely and indeterminate hills, especially as the presence of iron deposits (there are many traces of haematite mines) renders the compass unreliable in places.

ROCK CLIMBING IN ENNERDALE

LOWER ENNERDALE

Although only a little above 1,700ft in height, Crag Fell is a mountain of considerable character; its north face descends in shattered rock-steps towards Angler's Crag dropping steeply into the lake. As on its westerly neighbour Grike, frequent outcrops provide short pitches of interest, though the slaty rock should be treated with caution, and several scrambling routes can be worked out which take in small buttresses where practicable and traverse along grassy ledges below impossible sections.

Angler's Crag (1) provides a variety of short climbs, mostly starting near the lake shore, and as it is only about three-quarters of a mile from the Gauge-house at the end of the lake it affords a handy practice ground for an afternoon or summer evening. Though consisting of Skiddaw Slate, the rock is on the whole reasonably sound. Several steep buttresses are separated by rather lichenous grooves and square-cut chimneys; the routes usually land rather unexpectedly on to sizable grass and heather ledges where sheep, tempted down by the luscious grass, are frequently marooned. A characteristic feature is the presence of holly trees growing from steep cracks, sometimes useful for belaying purposes.

Several grades of difficulty can be found from D routes to four quite exacting VS's. The climbs are situated on several separate outcrops, the buttress on the left (east) which almost reaches the edge of the lake being the most popular and extensive. From left to right the first route of note is *Forgotten Wall* (mild VS), which takes the longest section of clean rock near the edge and involves some exposed moves up a series of shallow grooves. *Phantom Groove* (VD) follows a clearly defined groove to a clump of trees on a ledge, and after a short traverse to the left finishes up a pleasant wall. *Like It or Lump It* (D) is a little slab climb starting a few feet left of the lowest point of the crag, with the nearby *Midge Arête* (VD) circumventing an obvious overhang by a neat, slightly awkward move to the right. The most worthwhile routes are on a higher buttress to the west, reached by a short walk up a grassy embayment. These include *Angel's Step* (mild VS), an excellent climb, steep in its upper portion and including a distinctly awkward mantelshelf; the exposed *Hook, Line and Sinker* (VS), which requires several pitons both for belaying and for aid; and *Crystal Groove* (mild S), away to the right of the buttress, involving a sloping gangway and an open groove under an overhang. Above the climbs an easy scramble leads to the top of the Crag and so to the grassy saddle between it and the mountain.

About 500ft above Angler's Crag can be seen the Pinnacles, the grotesquely serrated edge of a wall-shaped outcrop. These provide interesting scrambling, though the rock must be treated with care, especially where it is spattered with quartz crystals, and the exposure is considerable on the northern face. Most of the short routes (only 20 or 30ft), are on the southern side, though *Magog* (mild S), gives a steep and quite exposed 80ft pitch up the long side of the largest pinnacle.

Bowness Knott (10), its lower slopes swathed in larch plantations, projects boldly south of Great Borne towards the lake, where the road from the west runs round the foot of the Knott to a car park, making the climbs very accessible. They vary in length, some as much as 250ft, providing excellent climbing when the high crags are too cold or wet, and since they face south-west they are delightful on a quiet afternoon or summer evening in the sunshine. Though the face of the Knott is shattered, with extensive slopes of pinkish scree and patches of dense heather and bilberry, there are several prominent buttresses of clean rock.

The first buttress on the left is Long Crag, from whose lowest point starts the attractive *Black Crack* route (S) which includes seven varied pitches: a wall, several slabs and ribs, and the right-angled chimney of the Black Crack itself. Some 60ft to the right the very good **Hailstorm* (hard S), merits this grading mainly from its second pitch, a vertical wall with a thin crack up the centre (plate p 17). A more exacting route starts about 15ft up the scree from Hailstorm, called the *Marriage* (VS) because its original leader merged the better portions of his two previous routes into a single really good one; on one wall the use of a piton for protection is advisable and the top pitch, a very steep groove behind a tree, demands considerable effort, including some use of the tree itself. Though this route is but 160ft, it has the feeling of a much bigger

climb. The rock is of excellent quality and the situations are very
fine.

A slanting descent across scree leads to Bowness Crag, marked
by a prominent cleft known as the Green Gash, bounded on its
left-hand edge by the *Skyhook* (VD) which provides over 80ft of
slab climbing. *Green Gash* (mild VS) is a fine climb (plate p 17),
though it should be noted that the description in the F&RCC
Guidebook seems to be in some error; after climbing the first 15ft
of the groove from a rowan tree at its base, step out *left* to Kestrel's
Corner and continue over a 'cannon stone' to a small slab, which is
then crossed leftward to a corner with a piton belay. A diagonal
move to the right over slabs leads back into the Gash itself, which
is climbed almost to the top where the crux is met; a steep wall has
to be crossed to reach a good foothold on the right edge.

Several short climbs have been made on the next two buttresses
to the east, Oak Grove and High Crag; the *Garden Wall* (hard S),
takes a line up the centre of the vertical wall on the latter. The last
buttress is Hollow Gill Crag, reached by a slightly tedious scramble,
though providing as a reward the enjoyable *Holly Tree Wall*, a
VD climb of about 130ft.

HIGH STILE CRAGS (59)

Several small and apparently insignificant outcrops lie high up on
the southern face of High Stile, only about 200ft from the summit
ridge. They repay a visit on a fine day, either as an interlude during
the Red Pike—High Crag ridge-walk or for a party which has toiled
up the Red Pike path from Gillerthwaite en route to Birkness
Combe (p 79). On a misty day the crags can be baffling to find
unless one happens to come across a striking 20ft rock pinnacle
known as the Spearhead; the climbs mostly lie east of this. Except
for the possibly offputting effects of the tedious ascent from the
valley, this is an excellent place to bring a beginner, since there are
numerous ridges, buttresses, cracks and slabs which dry off quickly;
the rock is rough and sound; belays are plentiful; and there is plenty
of scope for variants. The *Chrysalis Arête* (VD) and the *Outside
Edge* (D) can be recommended. Rather harder is *Butterfly Crack*
(mild S), which is really a series of thin fissures running steeply
up the centre of the most prominent buttress to merge higher up
into a single better defined chimney groove.

THE PILLAR ROCK (78)

The Pillar is the most magnificent mass of rock in the Lake District, with an identity all its own; standing remotely far up Ennerdale (plate p 17), a day's climbing here represents quite an expedition. Its first recorded ascent was made as long ago as 1826, and today there are no less than seventy-eight different climbs (not counting variation pitches and some very recent new routes), including half a dozen of the élite XS category; the last are the result of an intensive assault mainly by West Cumbrian climbers during recent years. Several routes are long, continuous and logically straightforward, with splendid situations; they possess that rare quality and individuality of a climb which is a true and memorable line up a significant topographical feature. Yet Pillar is not just a crag for the expert; there are numerous D and VD routes, especially satisfying when they finish on the very top of the Rock. It is, however, high lying, its summit attaining almost exactly 2,500ft, and as such it can be very wet and cold; following a prolonged spell of rainy weather the rocks acquire a green, almost slimy, quality, which pushes up the standard of the easy climbs and may make the hard ones impossible. In recent months there have been several rescues of climbers stranded overnight on the Rock because of bad conditions. On the other hand, in fine weather the bold rhyolite slabs of the west face, in places as rough as gabbro, take on a warm comforting glow when the sun comes round in the afternoon and severities seem mitigated. On one lovely June day we counted twenty-five climbers dotted around the west face on various climbs, their white helmets giving an impression of a sudden crop of mushrooms.

The most direct approach is naturally enough from Ennerdale, for it is practicable to drive with permission from the Forestry Commission along the dirt road past Gillerthwaite, crossing the Liza by the stone bridge to a turning circle directly below a ride leading up through the forest. From the top of this ride a path climbs to the right (west) of a small waterfall into the boulder-strewn cove under the north face of the Rock. A rather ill-defined path continues left of the Rock to reach the start of the Shamrock Traverse and so to the east face, while to get to the west face the quickest and safest route (especially on the descent), is to diverge to the

right (west) of the steep basal rocks on to the fell side, and then
work back over the scree to the start of the climbs. An easy approach from Gillerthwaite is to cross the Liza by the slatted bridge,
follow a rather boggy ride through the forest to a stile and strike
up the grassy north-western ridge of Pillar mountain. A short
distance below a prominent little rock mass (White Pike), traverse
to the left (east) when the west face of Pillar comes strikingly into
view. This route provides a rapid descent and in mist the remains
of an old wall and a line of fence posts can be safely followed. The
approach from Buttermere involves a walk over Scarth Gap, then
a slanting descent through the forest to the memorial bridge over
the Liza. From Wasdale follow the Black Sail path, striking off up
the slopes of grass and scree of Looking Stead until at a height of
about 2,100ft a cairn marks the start of the High Level Route. This
traverses with slight undulations the spectacular northern face of
the mountain through Green and Hind Coves and makes for the
prominent Robinson's Cairn, a memorial to a late-nineteenth
century pioneer climber from Lorton who was particularly associated with Pillar. When returning to Wasdale an enjoyable end to
the day is to scramble from behind the Rock to the summit of the
mountain and wander back along the ridge of Mosedale Red Pike
and Yewbarrow.

The Rock consists of a broadly conical mass, once described as
resembling a great cathedral front, rising in a series of walls and
gullies from the prominent Green Ledge at its base to its lower
summit (Low Man) and then more gently up broken rocks to the
true summit (High Man), an overall vertical height of about 750ft.
The opposite southern side is short and steep, falling to a gap with
a floor of chaotically piled boulders and rising again equally steeply
to a rocky mass leaning against the mountain side. The early
climbers, who must have been Biblically inclined, called this mass
after Pisgah from which Moses viewed the promised land across
the Jordan, hence the name Jordan Gap for the notch between
Pisgah and the Rock proper. The western side of the gap is formed
by the deeply cut *West Jordan Gully* (S), which gives a good climb
culminating in a steep-walled pitch under the huge capstone.

Thus the northern and southern sides of the Rock are markedly
different in character, and so indeed are the eastern and western
aspects. The east face, rather a confusion of ledges, terraces and

chimneys, is complicated by the fact that it is flanked by another rock mass known as the Shamrock; early references call it the Sham Rock, since it partially masks Pillar Rock when seen from the east. The lower sections of the two are separated by the dark cleft of Walker's Gully, above which is a scree-filled, funnel-shaped amphitheatre and the broken east face of High Man. The Shamrock Traverse, reached from the path from Robinson's Cairn and the High Level Route, provides an easy scrambling line scarred by generations of nailed boots across the upper flanks of the Shamrock to the gap behind Pisgah.

The west faces of Low and High Man rise impressively some 300ft from a slope of scree and boulders which continues into a steep gully of rotten, iron-stained rocks leading to the gap between Pisgah and the mountain; this gully affords a quick descent from Pisgah as long as a party keeps close together to avoid the dangers of stone fall. The west face of High Man (plate p 18), has some fine walls, slabs, ribs, a long prominent groove on the left and several chimneys, for the most part well supplied with stances and belays. The west face of Low Man is characterised by steep walls with little vegetation, which helps it to dry out more quickly than any other section of the Rock. These two faces are separated by a distinct line of weakness known as the *Old West*, which rends diagonally leftward to the top of Low Man; this was probably the route of the 1826 ascent. It forms a convenient line of descent since it is normally little more than a scramble, but it is exposed and when wet or under snow or icy conditions it can be quite difficult.

It would be tedious and impracticable to describe all the seventy-eight routes on this crag, a number which current exploration is still extending; we can merely mention a few of our favourites. On the west face of High Man three climbs are outstanding in their respective categories: the New West, the Rib and Slab and the South-West, all reaching the top of the Rock. The *New West*, so called in contrast to the Old West after it was climbed in 1901 by a party led by George Abraham, is regarded by many as the best D climb in the Lake District. Few routes of that standard offer such continuity and sense of comfortable yet exhilarating exposure and such a variety of pitches: a staircase, a rib, several lower traverses, a deeply cut chimney and a fine exposed traverse to a long slab finish, in all 290ft of superb rock. It is also an excellent climb to descend. However, it can become quite hard under greasy conditions, especially the 30ft of the chimney, in the back of which a reassuring thread runner can be fixed. The slightly longer *Rib and Slab* (S) starts to the left of the New West, crossing it twice; the most striking pitch, though by no means the hardest, is a neat traverse to the right with fine incut holds on to and up the 70ft of the huge slab which is a major feature of the west face (plate p 18). The *South-West* (mild VS and scarcely that in PA's) follows delicately the sweep of slabs immediately to the left of West Jordan Gully, where the climber balances up on small but always adequate holds, using with care occasional embedded quartz crystals. For long the two hardest climbs on the west face were known somewhat prosaically as Route 1 and Route 2 (both VS), led on the same day in 1919 by H. M. Kelly, the editor of the earlier editions of the Pillar Guidebook. In the 1968 edition the names were changed to *Sodom* and *Gomorrah*, which, it is alleged, were suggested by Kelly's companion but at the time were not regarded as quite suitable. Neither is really hard; Gomorrah, starting from the Old West, follows a long well-defined groove; Sodom takes a line farther to the right and finishes up a black unprepossessing chimney, the upper part of the same chimney on the New West which the climber leaves by a traverse to the right. In recent years a hard VS (*Vandal*) and an exacting XS (*Gondor*) have been added on this face.

The western side of Low Man offers several extremely enjoyable climbs up clean walls and grooves. The *West Wall* climb (VD) is steep and continuous, strikingly so for its standard, finishing up a fine ascending traverse and an exposed groove; belays are small though adequate and stances a little cramped. The neighbouring *Ledge and Groove*, of slightly harder standard (S), crosses the West Wall climb by descending the same traverse. The *Nook and Wall* (mild S), the longest (280ft) on this face, and the *Appian Way* (S) both afford this same satisfying succession of exposed though safe situations up walls, ribs and slabs.

The western flank of Low Man is sharply defined by the cleft of the West Waterfall, which can be crossed below the fall by an awkward looking though not really difficult descent on rather rounded and usually slimy rock into its bed, from whence an easy scramble leads leftwards to the Green Ledge. A possible direct route to the foot of the west face of Low Man involves climbing the rocks to the left (true right) of the Waterfall, though this is quite an exposed line of D standard and should not be treated lightly.

The Green Ledge marks the start of the climbs on the north face, for the considerable mass of rock below it is more broken and grassy than would appear from a distance. Only one climb has been made there, the *Pedestal Wall* (S), a series of slabs, greasy except in quite dry weather, separated by grassy ledges. The north face is dominated by several steep walls, and its usually sunless aspect is somewhat dark and offputting, especially as the many grassy ledges hold moisture and the rock is often greasy. Yet several very hard climbs have been made here in recent years, notably the XS *Puppet* (plate p 35). Perhaps the best route for average climbers is the *North-West* (mild VS), over 400ft in length and characterised by some steep, shallow, groove-like chimneys; it was first climbed in 1906 by the man whose name is perpetuated in Botterill's Slab (p 122) on Scafell. The *North* climb has been for eighty years a traditional wet weather, nailed-boot climb with named pitches beloved of the pioneers: the V-Chimney, the Stomach Traverse and the Split Blocks. It is only of D standard until the last pitch is reached, but this Nose (S), a little buttress projecting to the left and seemingly little more than a slightly awkward balance problem over the void, often gives good climbers pause for thought. A neat alternative is the Hand Traverse which lands one on a rocky platform above the Nose; though the hands can grasp a sharp flake the 20ft of traverse is quite strenuous, especially as halfway along it is necessary to transfer to a second flake a couple of feet higher. The North climb finishes up Stony Gully on to Low Man. The *Grooved Wall* (VS) is a fine climb on the right wall (true left) of Walker's Gully, linking a series of steep grooves, while more modest climbers may get the flavour of this wall by an ascent of the *North-East* climb (hard VD, though appreciably more serious under wet conditions). This starts at the top of the third pitch of the North Climb and traverses leftward across the face to enter one of the grooves which is climbed for 80ft before leaving it, where it steepens to form the final pitch of the Grooved Wall, by a little wall on the right.

Those who are keen on gullies will find *Walker's* (hard S) really satisfying, though after much rain it can become literally a water-

fall. It was first climbed in 1899 by Owen Glynne Jones on a cold
January day in falling sleet, with snow and ice on the rocks and
'. . . a strong jet of ice-cold water coming down the gully'; his lead
(the last pitch in socks) was a remarkable *tour de force*. Apart
from one section of scrambling up the deeply cut bed of the gully,
the pitches are short but continuous. On the eighth it is vital to get
the arms through a hole before the head and shoulders or the
climber will become a fixture. The last pitch is a deep cave under
a capstone with an exposed finish, though the leader can fix at
least one runner to assist the final move up the right-hand wall and
so pull over on to the scree.

The east face of High Man, reached by a scree path from the
top of Shamrock, provides a number of easy, well-scratched routes
to the summit: the *Slab and Notch* (M) with its variant the *Pendlebury Traverse* (allegedly first climbed a century ago by a Cambridge don in carpet slippers), the *Curtain* and the *Arête* (D); the
last two taken in conjunction provide nearly 180ft of steep rock
well endowed with holds. For long, Shamrock was not well regarded
as a climbing ground, largely because of its vegetated character;
Shamrock Gully, for example, though rated S, is a messy climb.
However, a number of very hard climbs have recently been made.

On the short south side of the Rock are about half a dozen
interesting climbs; indeed, *Jordan Bastion* provides a strenuous
single-pitch hard S climb, extremely trying on the fingers. The most
speedy descent from the Rock is on this side of the Jordan Gap,
either by roping down the Bastion or by sliding down the rectangu-
lar corner of the *Central Jordan* climb (D) from one chockstone
to the next and over the right-hand edge of Pisgah on to the mountain.

The Pillar Rock provides a girdle traverse of about 1,300ft,
starting near Walker's Gully up the *Grooved Wall*, taking in fifteen
good pitches and finishing up the top part of the *South-West*. For
those who revel in long continuous climbing of a less exacting
nature, preferably with two climbers leading through, the Rock
lends itself to the stringing together of linked ascents and descents;
one excellent expedition we made in 1969 started up the *North-
West*, continued down the *North*, climbed the rocks up the left-
hand edge of the Waterfall, up the *West Wall*, down the *Old West*,
up the *South-West* and finally down the *New West*: in all, nearly

1,500ft of climbing in warm, dry, sunny conditions; a memorable day.

THE OUTLYING CRAGS ON THE PILLAR RANGE

Though Pillar Rock is such a dominating attraction, the neighbouring high coves are well worth exploring. While much is inevitably of a scrambling nature, pitches can be strung together up the scattered outcrops to the summit ridge, providing interesting pioneering outings, especially in winter. Several buttresses split by gullies form prominent features in Hind Cove, reached by scrambling about 250ft upwards from the High Level Route, and in the Great Doup (the cove east of Pillar Rock). In West Cove on its western side *Wide Gully* (S) has some good cave pitches ending in a section of steep rock best climbed by a prominent crack in its right-hand wall. At a much lower level, just above the Forestry fence and east of the stream spilling down from the cove below the Rock, a whale-backed outcrop of rough sound rock, seamed with thin cracks, is known as Raven Crag (82). This provides several neat slab climbs, notably *Centipede* (S) which begins at the lowest apex of the buttress and gives nearly 350ft of climbing, and the easier *Scarab* (VD) on its right flank; one or other can be taken by the enthusiast as an aperitif on his way to the Rock above.

An impressive area of crags can be seen in Windgap Cove, the high-lying rocky basin between Pillar mountain and the ridge projecting northward from Scoat Fell. Immediately to the west of Wind Gap is Black Crag (3), where a dozen climbs have been made, including *Main Ridge* (D) which follows the left-hand edge of the crag and gives a mountaineering route of about 300ft. Several slab climbs of S standard, very much harder when damp because of their mossy character, can be found farther to the right.

The upper part of Windgap Cove is separated off by a rocky spur to form the high-lying Mirk Cove in the angle with the Steeple ridge. Mirk Cove Buttress (70) on its back wall is split by a prominent gully which has been climbed, though somewhat slimy and mossy. The buttress on the right has two obvious ribs forming the *Twin Ribs* climb (S), erroneously stated in the F&RCC Guidebook to be on Haskett Buttress, which is actually in Mirklin Cove.

Steeple itself throws down some impressive crags into Mirk

Cove, but these are deceptively limited from a climbing point of view. *Steeple Buttress* (VD) (101) is not easy to find or to follow and involves much scrambling in its overall 500ft, though it has several sections of wall, crack and groove and it lands satisfactorily on the summit of the mountain. Haskett Buttress (52) projects from the western side of the Steeple ridge overlooking Mirklin Cove. Some very exacting climbs have been made, with such names as *Ductile Slant*, *Devious Slash* and *Dolorous Stroke*, the last of XS standard and, in the words of the account of the first ascent, '. . . a magnificent crack line, bristling with overhangs'.

BOAT HOWE CRAGS (7)

The rugged northern flank of Kirk Fell can be reached from either Beck Head or the top of Black Sail Pass, between which a faint path traverses the scree under the crags, whose base lies at about 2,100ft. These were formerly known as Kirk Fell Crags, but when T. Graham Brown began his explorations in 1925 he decided on Boat Howe, partly because this was a local name but mainly because the central rock pillar has some likeness to the prow of a boat. This choice has therefore stimulated an obvious nautical terminology for the climbs. The right-hand edge of the East Buttress gives a pleasant slabby route called the *Sea Wall Arête* (D), and to its right a 90ft sweep of rock forms the single-pitch *Breakwater Slabs* (S), which can be continued up a pinnacle logically referred to as the *Lighthouse*. The central pillar is flanked on the left by a squarish chimney, the *Hatchway*, succeeded by a rock tower known as the *Rigging* (D), on the right by the not very attractive *Starboard Chimney* (VD). This central part of the crags provides some attractive climbs, of which the *Larboard* and *Starboard Arêtes* (both mild S) may be recommended; the last provides 200ft of good rock and utilises near the top a magnificent belay-block which had to be called the Capstan. The left-hand side of the *Prow of the Boat* was climbed in 1940 by that outstanding 'mixed doubles' team, the Hargreaves and the Crosses, a hard VS climb involving some steep grooves and corners and several delicate traverses. In recent years there has been renewed interest in this somewhat lonely crag, culminating in 1969 with a more direct route up the very centre of the Prow called *Fanghorn*, of XS category and requiring several pitons for the climb.

GABLE CRAG (32)

For every hundred climbers who visit the Napes ridges on the sunny south-western side of Great Gable, perhaps one finds his way to the crag on its northern face which dominates the head of Ennerdale, rising above the scree slopes of Stone Cove. Admittedly it is high-lying with its base at about 2,500ft, it carries much vegetation, it is usually wet, and it has a rather gloomy and at times even an uninviting effect. Yet to penetrate its dark-shadowed recesses can be very rewarding and in winter, when it long holds the snow, it can provide miniature 'Nordwand' conditions (plates p 36). The crag is easily accessible in spite of its apparent remoteness, for the crowds who follow the well-beaten routes up Gable from Honister or Seathwaite pass only a few yards beyond its eastern wing through Windy Gap, from which a well-defined scree path skirts its base; this is the North Gable Traverse (p 178).

The first impression of Gable Crag is of a series of parallel deeply-cut chimneys and gullies slanting upwards to the left, separating some rather broken-looking buttresses. By contrast, almost in the centre of the Crag a stretch of impressively steep slabs is the scene of most of the recent hard climbs, including an XS gloomily called the *Tomb*. The *Central Gully* splits the crags at their right-centre to the very top; this route involves much scrambling and though some quite hard rock pitches can be found (notably the top direct crack), it is really a winter route on which alternatives have to be selected according to the prevailing conditions (plate p 36).

For the chimney-minded there are several good examples of these damp recesses: *Oblique* (VD), cutting deeply high up to the left; *Engineer's* (hard S), a strenuous effort involving in its upper section a backing-up movement until a thin crack in the left wall is attained; **Smuggler's* (VS), even more strenuous inside its narrow depths, where it is so easy to jam that one despairs of future progress; and *Doctor's* (D), a less strenuous effort on the far right of the crag. An expedition of no great difficulty, yet affording a continuous line among impressive rock scenery, is the 500ft *Barney Buttress* (D), an improvement on the original so-called Bottle-Shaped Pinnacle Ridge. Starting from almost the lowest point of the crag, it links up a series of buttresses of good rough rock, then slants up to the conspicuous 'bottle', sitting on whose 'cork' the climber gets an impressive view into the green depths of the Oblique Chimney on the right, then finishes up a broken ridge to the summit plateau.

GREEN GABLE CRAG (46)

When walking from Black Sail YH towards Windy Gap, a rather insignificant outcrop of rock can be seen under the summit of Green Gable, but after one arrives at the Gap and skirts left it becomes more outstanding and in fact yields a dozen routes of up to 140ft in length on clean, sound rock and from D to VS in standard. It is doubtful whether anyone would make the trip solely to climb here, but the crags are well worth an incidental visit, particularly on a fine summer evening, and provide an agreeable contrast after climbing in the gloom of Gable Crag. The climbs are named after Greek letters, from *Alpha* (D) away on the left to the punning *Fie!* (a VS with a single 90ft pitch) on the right. Most were ascended by Dr Graham Macphee in 1927–8 and named, as one description put it, 'in a surge of Hellenic inspiration'. The really keen climber can link the best pitches into a neat girdle traverse of almost 600ft.

4

BUTTERMERE AND NEWLANDS

THE verdant Vale of Lorton extends southward for about seven miles from the little market town of Cockermouth, so called because the River Cocker, which takes the drainage of the Buttermere valley, here joins the Derwent, the master-stream of western Lakeland. The vale is sheltered on the east by the imposing fronts of the Whiteside—Grasmoor mountain group, on the west by the long ridge of Low Fell, and at its southern end leads into a narrow valley about ten miles long, doubly blessed in that it encloses two charming lakes, Crummock and Buttermere. A little to the west is a third lake, Loweswater, unique in that it drains inward towards the centre of Lakeland; from it the small Dub Beck wanders across the valley floor to enter Crummock near its foot. Loweswater is only a mile in length and bordered by fields, woodland and grassy fells giving it a soft pastoral quality. There is no village of Loweswater, merely scattered farms and a small nucleus of church and inn at Kirkstile.

Crummock and Buttermere lie in a narrow, steep-sided valley, connected by a stream known oddly as Buttermere Dales, which flows languidly as there is only eight feet difference in their surface levels. Crummock is inconspicuously controlled by a weir, for it is the main reservoir of the West Cumberland Water Board supplying Workington and neighbouring parts of the county. Possibly the two lakes once formed a single sheet of water, but inflowing streams deposited sediment as deltas which ultimately converged to form an isthmus cutting the original lake in two. Buttermere has been much reduced in length through deposition at its head by streams flowing down from the surrounding hills, forming an alluvial flat known as Warnscale Bottom; some of this former marshy land has been drained, providing rich grazing for Gatesgarth Farm.

Unlike Ennerdale, Buttermere is a motorist's through-valley and the road from Cockermouth skirts the eastern shores of the lakes; at Hause Point, where Rannerdale Knott protrudes into Crummock,

Page 71 (above) Stages in the traverse, *Kransic Crack*, Shepherd's Crag, Borrowdale; *(below)* Langstrath and Eagle Crag

Page 72 *(above left)* *Communist Convert*, Raven Crag, Thirlmere; *(above right)* *Kestrel Wall*, Eagle Crag, Grisedale; *(below)* Hart Crag and Fairfield

the road had to be blasted out of solid rock. From the little hamlet of Buttermere there is a choice of exits from the valley; a steeply winding road to the north-east crosses Newlands Pass at a height of 1,096ft, hence to Stair and Keswick, while another continues past Buttermere to Honister Pass (1,176ft) and so to Borrowdale and Keswick. The two passes provide an extremely popular motoring circuit from Keswick. Much of the valley and all three lakes are owned by the National Trust, who in cooperation with other landowners have done much to cope with problems of parking and camping. The valley offers a certain amount of accommodation, with several hotels and guest houses in Buttermere and at Scale Hill near the foot of Crummock. A Youth Hostel occupies the former Buttermere Hotel just outside the hamlet, and another is finely situated on the crest of Honister Pass near the slate quarries. The Fell and Rock Climbing Club have an attractive hut at Hassness on the shores of Buttermere.

Several groups of uplands surround the Crummock—Buttermere valley: the Loweswater Fells in the north-west, the massive Brackenthwaite Fells east of Crummock, and the Buttermere and Derwent Fells north-east of Buttermere. Each group is dissected by deep valleys into a pattern of smooth summits, well defined ridges and scree-covered slopes. Most are of Skiddaw Slate and only the amphitheatre at the head of the valley and the imposing line of Red Pike—High Stile—High Crag are of the Borrowdale Volcanics. Near the geological boundary at the valley-head are many abandoned workings where copper and other metals were mined for centuries, and here too the great mass of Honister Crag is still quarried for the attractive pale green slate. This forms part of Fleetwith Pike, which pushes its sharply angled north-western ridge into the main valley, dividing its head into two (plate p 53). To the north Gatesgarthdale rises to Honister Pass, enclosed by vast stretches of rock debris, both natural and man-made (from the quarry waste dumps) and enormous boulders lie chaotically around the lower slopes and valley floor, down which the turbulent Gatesgarthdale Beck flows in its rocky bed. To the south of Fleetwith the Warnscale trough end is surrounded by a rim of shattered crags.

E

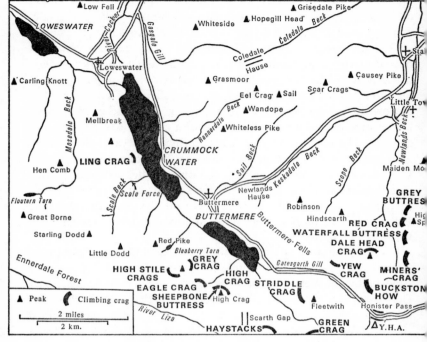

FIG 3.   The Buttermere and Newlands district

FELL WALKS IN BUTTERMERE AND NEWLANDS

Buttermere is one of the best Lakeland valleys for varied walks; delightful excursions may be made around each of the lakes, following footpaths through fields and woodland, with occasional shingly bays and rocky promontories. The gentle grass-covered Loweswater Fells form the hill country between Loweswater and Ennerdale and several walks link the two valleys. The ridge-lines of Carling Knott —Blake Fell, Black Crag—Gavel Fell and Hen Comb (the last a prominent ridge forming the 'comb of a hen', not a hollow, like the Buttermere combes), are separated by flat-floored valleys. The most prominent hill is Mellbreak, sharply defined whether viewed end on beyond Loweswater or in profile across the foot of Crummock. Though made of slate, its northern prow consists of a series of steep crags with several prominent gullies flanked by slopes of pale scree and dense heather, through which a scrambling route can be made to the summit ridge. From its south top the walker can follow a fence down the grass and bracken of the south ridge, cross the little knoll of Scale Knott and then visit Scale Force, where a beck makes a leap of 156ft through a dark, fern-draped cleft, Lakeland's highest single fall. The return to Buttermere hamlet can be made down the side of Scale Beck and along the shore of the lake, though this is usually extremely boggy.

The southern wall of the Buttermere valley, the line of Red Pike —High Stile—High Crag, has been described as part of the Ennerdale horseshoe (p 55). But in fact this ridge is traversed much more frequently from the Buttermere side because the hamlet forms a convenient start and finish to the circuit. Undoubtedly too this side of the range is more impressive, for instead of the monotonous slopes on the south (p 23), three fine combes are separated by buttresses and surrounded by craggy rims. From the north-west these are Ling Comb, well named as its floor is thickly carpeted with heather, Bleaberry Combe containing a tiny jewel of a tarn, and the boulder-strewn Birkness (sometimes called Burtness) Combe on whose back wall are two of Buttermere's best climbing grounds, Eagle and Grey Crags. From each combe a stream spills down, notably Sour Milk Gill which issues from Bleaberry Tarn, foaming and tumbling among the bare rock slabs on the hillside. The main ridge can be reached either from the Scarth Gap track on the east, cutting off to the right well before the top of the pass, or by paths through Bleaberry or Ling Combes; an easy line ascends from the tarn to the Saddle on a ridge projecting from Red Pike. The scrambler can follow the course of one of the gills up the hillside or make his way up one of the broken buttresses between the combes.

The walker may begin a traverse of the head of Buttermere by climbing the long north-western ridge of Fleetwith Pike (plate p 53), from behind Gatesgarth Farm, passing low down a cross to the memory of a girl killed there almost a century ago. Several outcrops make this ridge an interesting scramble, though for those who prefer it a distinct path leads through the heather and grass, so avoiding the rock. From the summit either continue south-eastward past old quarry workings to the rocky summit of Grey Knotts, thence to Brandreth, or curve round at a lower level to the Hay Stacks and so to the Scarth Gap track and back to Buttermere.

The Brackenthwaite Fells, enclosed by Crummock and the Vale of Lorton on the west and the Bassenthwaite—Newlands valley on the east, are deeply dissected by scree-lined valleys. Those containing Gasgale Gill flowing west and Coledale Beck flowing east provide a walker's through-route across the massif by way of Coledale Hause at about 1,900ft, which overlooks the abandoned workings of the Force Crag mine. These tops, linked by well defined ridges, can be traversed by three circuits of great charm.

The first is the round of the Gasgale valley from Lanthwaite Green, taking in Grasmoor, the highest of the group, Hopegill Head and Whiteside. Grasmoor can be climbed by several routes: an easy scramble through the heather, scree and broken crags which form the angle between the north and west faces; from the south by a path through bracken, steep grass and the pinkish scree of Red Gill or up the gentle Lad Howes ridge; and best of all directly up the west face, a bold triangle of broken crags and screes, by way of the prominent Y-shaped gully, though this is actually a modest rock climb. The summit is an extensive plateau covered with turf and occasional plaques of slate, and with half a dozen large cairns and windbreaks. From the top a path leads towards Coledale Hause, skirting the curving rim of the shattered Dove Crags which bite into the northern edge of the plateau; a few hard climbs have been made up some of its unsafe and unattractive gullies. From the Hause the route strikes north past old mine shafts where caution is needed in mist and on to the sharply defined pyramid of Hopegill Head, sometimes called Hobcarton Pike after the crumbling buttresses and rickety pinnacles of Hobcarton Crag below its summit. This area has been acquired by the National Trust, mainly because of the flora which flourish on the mineral-rich soil derived from the fragmented rock in the gullies and on the ledges. Due west lies the mile-long ridge to Whiteside, at first sharply defined, with quartz-pocked slabs, flat plaques of slate and scrambling rock-steps, and though it broadens towards Whiteside the shaly slabs still drop away steeply as Gasgale Crags on the left. From the summit of Whiteside, with its superb views towards the Solway Firth and the Scottish hills beyond, the easiest descent to Lanthwaite Green is a clearly defined path down the south-western edge of Gasgale Crags through scree and heather to the little knoll of Whin Ben.

A second circuit also takes in Grasmoor, ascending the pyramid of Whiteless Pike either from Buttermere or Rannerdale and then following a distinct path to the Saddlegate depression some 500ft below, past the cairn of Thirdgill Head Man (an odd name, but logical enough since it is the peak at the head of the third tributary of Sail Beck) and on to Wandope. To the north-east below the summit of Wandope is Addacomb Hole, a deep basin rimmed by crags and scree, tarnless but with a headstream of Addacomb Beck spilling over its lip in a fine cascade. The path continues to Eel Crag (named Crag Hill on the 1″ map) and cuts across by a clearly cairned line to the eastern end of the Grasmoor plateau.

A third circuit starts from Braithwaite, where a path slants gently up grass and bracken to Sleet How, the eastern ridge of the popular and shapely Grisedale Pike. The route continues over the Pike to Coledale Hause, then up to Eel Crag and eastward over the grassy hump of Sail to Sail Pass, a col on a walker's crossing between Braithwaite and Buttermere via the valleys of Coledale Beck and Sail Beck. From here the path leads to Scar Crags and the knobby ridge of Causey Pike, so down Rowling End to the village of Stair in the Vale of Newlands.

The Buttermere and Newlands Fells form a distinctive group between Newlands Pass and Borrowdale, in pattern resembling a gridiron with its base formed by the north wall of the Buttermere—Gatesgarth valleys, from which three prong-like ridges taper north-ward. Between them are lonely valleys, down which flow the Keska-dale, Scope and Newlands Becks, with waterfalls and deep pools. This base-ridge can be traversed from Buttermere hamlet to Honister Hause, crossing in turn Robinson, Hindscarth (though this top actually lies a little north of the ridge line) and Dale Head with its crags overlooking the head of the Newlands valley. A more attractive way to visit these summits is from Little Town in New-lands on to the Cat Bells—Maiden Moor ridge, which is followed southward over High Spy to Dale Head. The return to Little Town can be made from Robinson down its broken north-east ridge which is prolonged towards the valley as High Snab Bank; this descent is mostly along a path through the bracken, with easy scrambling on some step-like outcrops.

ROCK CLIMBING IN BUTTERMERE AND NEWLANDS

For long, Buttermere was regarded mainly as a walker's valley with only limited prospects and opportunities for rock climbers; in fact the F&RCC Guidebook of 1937 referred to it as the Cinderella of the climbing valleys of Lakeland but '. . . unlike Cinderella her charms are not very obvious even on better acquaintance'. This judgement was made largely because most of the mountains around are of Skiddaw Slate and the outcrops are shattered, heavily vegetated and unreliable for climbing, though there are a few exceptions. One is the prominent forked *Y* or *Lorton Gully* (D) on the western face of Grasmoor, which provides a route almost to the top of the ridge known as Grasmoor End. A series of short chimney and slab pitches with water-worn rock of surprisingly good quality leads to the fork in the gully; slant left at this point and then follow a rock staircase rather than the unstable wall between the fork, where one of us once nearly came to grief. Another Skiddaw Slate outcrop of some merit is the recently explored Ling Crag (63).

At the head of Warnscale Bottom on the flanks of the Hay Stacks some big crags, impressive from a distance, are split by a series of black gullies (the *Y Gully*, *Warn Gill* and *Stack Gill*), where the rock is of poor, even dangerous, quality. While Stack Gill was climbed as long ago as 1900 and Warn Gill seven years later, the Y Gully, with its big 80ft pitch likened to an inverted funnel of rotten rock with an almost total absence of belays, only succumbed in 1941 after a desperate assault, and as far as is known this has not been repeated. While the rock is said to be sounder in Stack Gill, it is doubtful whether anyone now visits this family of evil gullies, though some very hard routes have been made recently on the intervening buttresses.

For many years attention was devoted almost entirely to the two major crags on the back wall of Birkness Combe: the cheerful welcoming Grey Crag (49), still by far the most popular in Buttermere for the ordinary climber, and the dark imposing Eagle Crag (25) across the Combe, touched only by the early morning summer sunshine. In addition, a number of short though hard climbs were made on Sheepbone Buttress (97) situated on the High Crag wall of the Combe.

Since World War II, however, several hitherto neglected possibilities have been explored. One was developed on the south-eastern flanks of Dale Head, known to the Honister quarrymen as Drum House Crag, though it has now been renamed Buckstone How (14). Attention was paid later to the buttresses along the eastern side of the Vale of Newlands under the ridge of High Spy and on the northern face of Dale Head, an area near the boundary between the Volcanics and the Slates so that the outcrops partake of the quality of both, something less reliable than the andesites but appreciably better than the slaty rocks of the Brackenthwaite Fells. Other 'new' crags include Striddle (102) on Fleetwith Pike and the wet Green Crag (45) on the north-western side of Hay Stacks, which after much gardening to clear away vegetation has yielded a crop of VS routes on steep rhyolite outcrops. High Crag (57), on the north-eastern buttress of the mountain of the same name projecting towards the head of Buttermere, is hardly distinguishable among many broken outcrops, but it has yielded half a dozen very hard climbs on sound rough rhyolite which have gone into the expert's repertoire. The most notable is *High Crag Buttress* (hard VS), which takes a straight line up the centre of the face, following a series of steep cracks and grooves.

Thus Buttermere now has many worthy possibilities and the current Guidebook lists about 180 routes; despite the great advance of standards nearly a third are of Very Difficult or easier grades.

THE CRAGS IN BIRKNESS COMBE

It is an easy walk to the Combe from Gatesgarth, leaving the Scarth Gap track near its foot and slanting up among the boulders through great patches of bilberries and finally up a steep path over the scree to the foot of Grey Crag (49), three tiers of rocks high on the eastern face of High Stile. Its silvery-grey rock is delightfully rough and sound, dries quickly after rain, may be in the sun for most of the summer day and offers a wide range of standards from M to VS. It is a good place on a rainy day, for wet rock does not make an appreciable difference to the standard of much of the climbing, while in summer many a jaded climber has regained his confidence on its welcoming rock; its only real disadvantage is its high and exposed situation which makes it vulnerable to strong winds. *Harrow Buttress* (D), which starts from almost the lowest point of the bottom tier, *Mitre Buttress Ordinary* (M) and the well scratched *Chockstone Ridge* (M) on the second tier are all short with excellent stances and belays, and are so well graded that beginners can make good progress. In due course they can move on to the classic VD and S climbs: the *Mitre Direct* (VD) with its steep walls and cracks, the *Slabs West* route (S), a beautiful climb with two long pitches on the left-hand side of the second tier, and the two *Oxford and Cambridge* routes on the top tier. The *Ordinary* (D) traverses left from the prominent right-angled arête, the *Direct* (mild S) follows the arête itself, involving one or two delicate balance moves; this is not a place for a windy day. If a leader is confident in his PA's in the warm sunshine, he may feel like trying a group of climbs up a steep wall on the right-hand side of the second tier, where the rock consists of compact banded lavas with delightful incut holds. The most notable are the popular *Suaviter* (S) and *Fortiter* (mild VS), almost parallel and a few feet apart; the former involves a short ascent to a ledge (the Balcony), and a traverse across the face into and up a steep thin crack. The latter is an excellent wall climb, its longest pitch of 70ft containing a crux which involves surmounting an overhang by a semi-layback move on to a small mantelshelf; it is advisable to fix a runner before leaving this shelf to gain a thin crack by a somewhat exposed move. Another mild VS climb, *Spider Wall*, takes a direct line up the centre of Harrow Buttress, starting a few feet to the right of the Buttress climb. It involves surmounting an overhang by a thin, strenuous crack and a top very smooth wall on which one ascends diagonally to a little bracket, finishing up another crack to the top. The hardest route on Grey Crag is *Dexter Wall* (VS), the final feet of the last pitch being climbed on small and not too obvious holds. In the event of a sudden break in the weather on this high-lying crag, good shelter can be found in a snug little cave at the top of the first pitch of the Mitre Buttress Ordinary Route.

Eagle Crag (25) is a dark wedge-shaped mass nearly 500ft high and almost reaching the summit ridge. Split by vertical chimneys and gullies and with a grassy terrace slanting up right at about two-thirds of its height, it drops steeply in front to the floor of

Birkness Combe, its wings decreasing in height as they fall back into the scree-covered hillside. It is slow-drying and the longer climbs of 400 to 500ft are serious propositions.

Birkness Gully (VD) and *Birkness Chimney* (S) provide traditional routes; the latter is quite exacting and we have no compunction in using combined tactics on the fourth pitch, difficult both to enter and to ascend. The other deeply cut line is *Central Chimney* (VS), one of the most continuous and exacting chimneys in Lakeland; it was not climbed throughout until 1948 after several previous attempts.

The dozen face climbs on the crag are all of S or VS standard, steep and exposed, culminating in *Eagle Front* (VS) and *Carnival* (hard VS). *Eagle Front* is a classic face route, once considered among the best in Lakeland; in spite of the interruption by a 25 yard descending walk leftward along the Terrace, it is still the most direct practicable line up the face of the crag, and as it is almost 500ft in length it provides a worthy day's climbing. One pitch of *Fifth Avenue* (VS) involves a runout of 140ft; one of us on its first ascent climbed this steep wall after it had been greasily plastered with earthy material dislodged by the leader, Bill Peascod, who of course had his own worries. Two excellent routes for average climbers are *Easter Buttress* and *Western Buttress Ordinary*, both of hard S category, though they seem of much lower standard if climbed under rare dry conditions. Easter Buttress is the shorter, starting well up the crag to the left of Central Chimney, but Western Buttress begins at its very base a few feet right of Carnival and Eagle Front; as it continues beyond the Terrace it provides a fine route of over 400ft.

OTHER BUTTERMERE CRAGS

It is not surprising that little was known of Striddle Crag (102) until 1956, for it is a retiring and insignificant mass camouflaged by broken rocks, scree and heather on the south-western flank of Fleetwith Pike. But it is low-lying and can be reached in about forty minutes from Gatesgarth by the track round into Warnscale, then striking up the boulder-strewn hillside. The crag actually forms the left-hand containing wall of the prominent *Fleetwith Gully*, which contains one hard pitch surmounted by a massive chockstone. As a climbing ground Striddle has several advantages: some surprisingly sound and rough rock, it is quick drying, has a south-westerly aspect ideal for a quiet afternoon in the sunshine and a charming feeling of seclusion; even the noise of traffic on Honister Pass, so palpable on Buckstone How, is lost around this corner.

Striddle Crag Buttress (VD), starting at some large blocks to the left of the main arête, takes a fairly natural line up the edge of the crag with no great difficulties, in fact it deliberately avoids them; but it is well worth doing and makes a good expedition if continued up the broken rocks to the top of Fleetwith. *Gradus Wall* (hard VD) is distinctly better, with several walls, cracks and grooves. The most memorable, even unique, climb is *Pedagogue's Chimney* (hard S), an excellent wet-day climb with short protected pitches, except for a rather artificial and easily avoidable 40ft crack at the top which if really wet requires a fierce struggle up slippery green rock. The main section of the climb consists of a flue-like chimney enclosed by a wedged mass of rock, which entails a strenuous squirm, then a bridging technique up its dimly lighted interior (though good protection can be gained from thread runners), from which the climber emerges triumphantly if breathlessly through the well named 'Manhole' into the daylight. The rest is in the open air; another memorable pitch is a wall climbed by a neat move up a thin corner-crack. Several other climbs on Striddle include four VS's and at least two good S's, so that a very rewarding day can be spent. Visitors for the first time should note that a safe descent to the foot of the crag after completing a route is not easy to find, especially in the dusk, since all the obvious ways seem to end at sudden drops. However, a trodden line off is gradually developing, using a section of Fleetwith Gully.

Buckstone How (14) can be reached by a gentle stroll along a quarry track from the top of Honister Pass, skirting the side of Dale Head. It is a mass of metamorphosed slate, presenting a series of steep curving ribs and grooves, and its rather brittle quality in some places gives uneasiness; the sharply intersecting joints produce prominent spike holds but it is wise to treat them with caution. There are now a dozen climbs, some of VS or harder standard, notably *Cleopatra*, the best of all Buckstone's offerings, *Caesar* and *Sinister Grooves*; these generally negotiate some remarkably steep and exposed grooves. The most enjoyable of reasonable standard is *Honister Wall* (hard S), first climbed in 1946. It is nearly 300ft in length and includes several exposed walls with well spaced and nicely incut holds, a groove, some slabs and traverses, one involving a dainty move leftward around a nose using to maintain balance a sideways crack into which the fingers gratefully sink.

Farther down Gatesgarthdale an outcrop known as Yew Crag (109) is split by a distinctive gully; the 1" OS tourist map, it should be noted, bestows this name on some crags much higher up the valley. The gully provides a long expedition of VD quality, though its central section is as yet unclimbed and has to be avoided by leaving its bed and scrambling up heather-covered slabs on the left. Several very hard climbs have been made on the buttress, though the worthwhile pitches are rather contrived among the loose and vegetated outcrops.

Just behind a peninsula projecting into the western side of Crummock Water is a small outcrop called Ling Crag (63) on the lower slopes of Mellbreak. Recently explored, it has yielded half a dozen hard though short climbs, and also a slab route at its southern end of only D standard. We climbed the mild VS *Quantral* (plate p 53), on a damp January day; its top pitch includes a superb traverse across a steep little wall.

THE NEWLANDS BUTTRESSES

From Little Town in the Vale of Newlands a track leads south up the valley past the Carlisle Mountaineering Club Hut towards the bold crags which dominate the northern face of Dale Head. Just beyond the rocky spur of Castle Nook a path leaves the main track and makes a rather laborious rising traverse across the scree to a line of buttresses under the ridge of High Spy. An alternative approach, leaving the car at Honister Pass, follows the north ridge of Dale Head for about half a mile, then bears right over a grassy shoulder and drops down past Dalehead Tarn into the Newlands valley.

Though known collectively as Eel Crags, four distinct buttresses have been named and explored, in order from north to south: Grey Buttress, Red Crag, Waterfall Buttress just opposite the prominent fall in the Newlands Beck below, and Miners' Crag. From a distance these are most impressive though when one gets nearer they seem to degenerate into disappointing broken vertiginous sections separated by grass and heather ledges; then when one actually sets foot on them the quality of the rock is mostly pleasing and some routes are remarkably continuous. In fact more than forty climbs have been made here, some of VS standard, while several long mountaineering routes almost attaining the summit ridge are available. The chief disadvantage is their frequent interruption by large ledges on which grow holly trees, though these can be used both for direct assistance and for belaying. The rock consists of metamorphosed slates and lavas, for the most part sound, though in places the holds have a flaky quality which demands care, as do some of the prominent belays. Even more than at Striddle, there is a problem if one is not going to the summit ridge of finding a route off, especially from Red Crag; it is easy to get stuck and be obliged to retrace one's steps, though as the crags become more popular the best descent lines are becoming evident.

On Grey Buttress (48) the four-pitch *Pinnacle Wall* (S) starts just left of the centre of the crag and includes several cracks, a steep wall and a finish either up an arête to the left or by a fine exposed slab on the right. The extreme right edge of the Buttress is followed by *Grey Slab* (mild VS), with short safe pitches and delightful holds.

Red Crag (86), so called because the rock has a distinct pinkish tinge, consists of an upper and lower buttress separated by a broad heather-covered terrace. *Kremlin Grooves* (hard S) goes up to the left of a prominent gully to the terrace, above which a continuation has been worked out almost trebling the length of the original climb, though the quality of the rock on the upper section is in places poor. The most popular route on the upper tier is *Cossack Crack* (VS), a very direct thin groove with quite good rock, while *October Slab* (VD) takes an easier line up the slabs on the left of the lower tier, with a harder continuation possible above.

The routes on Waterfall Buttress are long and interesting (plate p 53), the two main climbs, the *Waterfall Buttress Ordinary* (VD) and *Direct* (S), starting to the left and right respectively of a grassy gully near the base of the crag; they maintain close contact with each other, crossing halfway up and meeting again higher. Each is of the order of 400ft in length and provides an assortment of pitches, though occasionally interrupted by short walks along heathery ledges, and variants between the two climbs, or pitches from either, can be taken according to the conditions and mood.

On Miners' Crag (69), where the rock is of slightly more dubious quality than in the others, the deeply cut *Newlands Gully* (VD) provides a series of steep chimney pitches crowned as usual with chockstones. On this crag can be found one of the best climbs in the valley, **Newlands Buttress* (mild S), which takes a satisfying line of 235ft up the buttress from its lowest point near the right of the gully. Holds are plentiful and belays adequate; the most interesting moves involve a clean-cut ramp sloping up right, followed by a steep wall. A more exacting route is *Rope Walk* (hard S), which starts a few feet higher up the hillside, involving several hard cracks, a steep gangway and a groove which to enter necessitates an exposed move followed by a difficult pull-up. Still farther right and higher is *Corkscrew* (hard S), so called from its twisting line on good rock, saving its most sensational moves for the final pitch up an exposed arête. *Double Slab* (VD), a few feet right of Corkscrew, provides a modest but pleasant line up two clean slabs with an intervening groove.

The northern face of Dale Head is steep and rocky, though somewhat broken; among the outcrops one continuous mass is known as Dale Head Crag (19), where half a dozen climbs have been made, mostly of a very hard nature. An exception is the short *Gable End* (VD) on the arête bounding the right-hand edge of the crag, which includes four varied pitches culminating in a steep groove on the left of the now overhanging arête; after a strenuous effort the upper part of the groove relents and a series of good holds leads to easy ground above. *Dale Head Pillar* (mild VS), feels a big climb with considerable exposure, taking a line up a subsidiary buttress to the left of the main crag. The overhanging central wall of Dale Head Crag is crossed by the magnificent *Mithril* (hard VS), the most serious route in Newlands.

5

BORROWDALE AND THE KESWICK DISTRICT

BORROWDALE extends in a northerly direction from the central mountain group of Great Gable—Great End—Bowfell. This well defined valley is the drainage line of the upper Derwent which issues from Sprinkling Tarn high up under the north face of Great End, flows through Styhead Tarn to spill out of a hanging valley as Taylorgill Force and continues through the fastnesses of Borrowdale (plate p 54). The largest of its many confluents, Langstrath Beck, flows in shingle-lined curves down Langstrath, a curious though well-merited intrusion of a Scottish place name; its steep-sided, flat-floored valley seems endless at the end of a long day. This beck merges with Greenup Gill and as Stonethwaite Beck joins the Derwent just below Rosthwaite, a small village lying in a meadow-floored basin. This is a remarkable drainage focus and since it is a very rainy area (Seathwaite is reputed to be the wettest inhabited place in England), the rapid runoff sometimes causes flooding; the boulders bordering the streams and the gashed and scoured hillsides still bear witness to the effects of the floods of 1966 (p 24). The main valley then narrows between tree-covered crags with Grange Fell to the east and Castle Crag to the west, forming the 'Jaws of Borrowdale' beloved by the early guidebook writers and engravers who revelled in its horrific quality. Then the valley walls fall back and the Derwent wanders over marshy flats, much prone to flooding, before entering the reedy shallows of Derwentwater through a rapidly extending delta. This lake, a mile broad and quite shallow (71ft at its maximum), is linked with Bassenthwaite Lake by the Derwent, which wanders over an area of flat, marshy land with reed beds and lines of willows and seamed with drainage channels known locally as soughs. Bassenthwaite has more the character of a ribbon lake, enclosed on the east by the Skiddaw massif, on the west by the thickly wooded edge of the Thornthwaite and Lorton Fells.

Keswick, situated on slightly higher land away from flooding

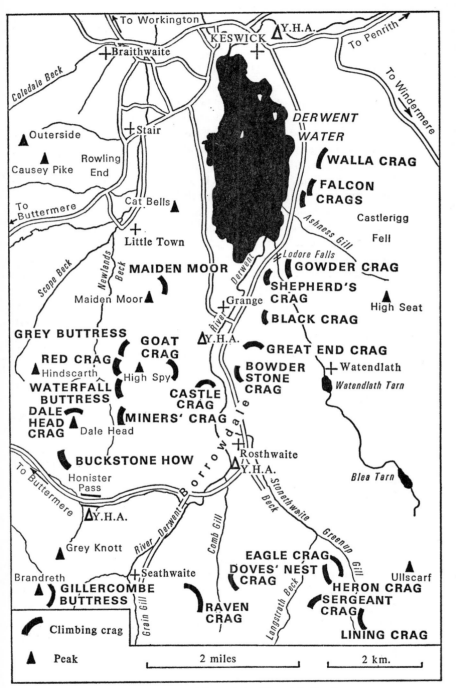

FIG 4. Borrowdale and the Keswick district

at the convergence of several valley routeways, became a market town and then a focal point for tourists, stimulated by the arrival of the railway in 1864 and by the advertisement given to the Lake District by poets, writers and artists. The rail link to Workington has now gone and that eastward to Penrith just survives, but cars and coaches arrive during the season in ever greater numbers. Hotels, boarding houses, restaurants and hostels abound, and the familiar places of beauty and interest (Friar's Crag, Lodore Falls, Watendlath, the stone circle at Castlerigg, the Bowder Stone and many others) are more popular than ever.

To the north of Derwentwater rises the rounded bulk of Skiddaw and the elegant curves of Blencathra's saddled summit. On the west of the lake the long ridge of Catbells—Maiden Moor— High Spy forms the eastern 'prong' of the Derwent Fells 'gridiron' described on p 77. In the east another north-south line of uplands extends from Castlerigg in the north to High Raise; this may be regarded as the central axial ridge of Lakeland, separated from the parallel Helvellyn—Fairfield range by the Thirlmere trough (p 106). The head of Borrowdale is surrounded by ridges of the Volcanic rocks, dominated by Great End at the heart of the Lakeland dome.

The Skiddaw Slates are interrupted by several igneous intrusions. One type consists of dolerite, usually hard and resistant; it appears, for example, as the prominent little hill of Castle Head just south of Keswick and in Friar's Crag projecting into Derwentwater. Carrock Fell to the north-east of Skiddaw is formed of a mass of complex igneous rocks, including the pinkish-white Skiddaw granite and grey gabbro which have been exposed by denudation, so that the summit stands out from the rather dreary moorland of the Skiddaw Slate hills.

FELL WALKS IN THE KESWICK DISTRICT

Since Borrowdale forms a line of access into the heart of the central mountains of Lakeland, several tracks cross the passes to adjacent valleys. From Seathwaite a route leads up Styhead Gill past the rocky ravine of Taylorgill Force and so by Styhead Tarn over into Wasdale. The lengthy walk from Stonethwaite up Langstrath crosses Esk Hause and drops down through the wild solitudes of upper Eskdale, while a path branching off left from this Langstrath track

Page 89 (above left) Hutaple Crag, Deepdale; (above right) Dove Crag,
Dovedale; (below) Overhanging Bastion, Castle Rock of Triermain, Thirlmere

Page 90 (above left) The north-western face of Gimmer Crag; (above right) Kipling Groove, Gimmer Crag; (below) the Langdale Pikes from near Elterwater

crosses the Stake Pass (1,576ft) into Mickleden at the head of Great Langdale. A popular way from Stonethwaite ascends the valley of Greenup Gill to cross the Ullscarf—High Raise ridge at Greenup Edge practically on the 2,000ft contour, from which the walker can either descend the valley of the Wyth Burn to the head of Thirlmere, or continue into Far Easedale and so to Grasmere. Two walks farther north also link Borrowdale with Thirlmere, both by way of the attractive little hamlet and tarn at Watendlath. One strikes due east over the grassy summit of High Tove and descends beside the Fisher Gill, the other continues south-east to Blea Tarn and after crossing the ridge just north of Standing Crag goes down through the trees past Harrop Tarn. These tracks are thronged in summer with walkers.

The smooth grassy slopes of Skiddaw are possibly ascended by more walkers (though by fewer climbers) than any other Lakeland summit, for its tracks are well defined and the views from the top are superb. The usual ascent from Keswick is by a track which skirts the western side of Latrigg and rises gently over the grassy slopes of Lonscale Fell and Jenkin Hill. The most interesting way from the west is up a grassy ridge over a mile in length known as The Edge to the conical summit of Ullock Pike, thence over Longside Edge; to the left, scree slopes and broken crags fall steeply into the secluded valley of Southerndale, rarely visited except by shepherds. A short descent is made to the broad grassy saddle of Carl Side and so by scree slopes to Skiddaw's south top, some 20ft lower than its main summit where the OS column is situated, nearly half a mile away along a broad ridge almost paved with flat slaty plaques. Another walk traverses the mountain from Bassenthwaite village; after following the Dash Beck and visiting its attractive waterfalls, the walker strides up the ridge past a deeply cut combe with its rocky back wall of Dead Crag, and follows a fence all the way to the north col, hence to the north top. This route can be extended eastward to Lonscale Fell and down the valley of the Glenderaterra Beck, while more enterprising walkers can continue to Blease Fell and then traverse Blencathra.

The summit ridge of Blencathra consists of a series of wave-like crests almost three miles in length; while its gentle northern slopes stretch away over the grass and heather moorlands of Mungrisdale Common, its scalloped southern face consists of a succession of

F

scree-choked ravines alternating with spurs which near the top are narrow and rocky, but lower down blunt, grassy and heathery and falling almost to the Keswick-Penrith road. This is a rare example of a peak with its northern slopes less steep than those on the south. Though it can be ascended from either end it is more interesting to scramble up one of the projecting spurs or up the rocky bed of one of the intervening ravines. At the eastern end a combe containing Scales Tarn is enclosed by Sharp Edge, a small-scale version of Striding Edge on Helvellyn, giving an easy but enjoyable scramble on to the broken Foule Crag, the northern end of Blencathra's saddle. In winter Sharp Edge may be quite a climb, sometimes accumulating considerable cornices; under snow Blencathra looks magnificent, especially when seen from the south between the enclosing walls of St John's in the Vale.

To the north of Skiddaw and Blencathra extend the moorlands, upland grazings and peat bogs of Skiddaw Forest and the Uldale and Caldbeck Fells, John Peel's hunting territory. The most prominent summit is Carrock Fell, projecting eastward within a right-angled bend of the River Caldew; on its flanks appear the only outcrop of gabbro in the Lake District and its southern and eastern slopes are steep, strewn with boulders and broken crags among which dwarf juniper grows in profusion and white heather is commonly found. Several short climbs have been made on the east-facing crags, mostly one-pitch routes, and there is a good deal of pleasurable scrambling. Long walks can be made over these rolling hills, starting for example from Carrock Fell along a grassy ridge to High Pike, then south over Great Lingy Hill, the turf-covered Knott and the stony pyramid of Great Calva, returning along the Caldew valley.

The undulating upland to the east of Borrowdale has some rather undistinguished summits covered with heather, grass and marshy peat, so that rarely does anyone walk its full length. It becomes better defined and the going of more interest south of Ullscarf along Greenup Edge to High Raise and so into the more rugged country of the Langdale peaks (p 131).

Of much greater character and interest is the ridge of Glaramara and Allen Crags, which provides a rough high-level walk from Stonethwaite to Esk Hause. The route between Glaramara and Allen Crags wanders over grassy ridges among outcrops and patches of bog, with several secluded little tarns, including the rock-girt High House and Lincomb Tarns which may be surprisingly hard to find even in clear weather.

The western margins of Borrowdale provide an excellent walk between Keswick and Wasdale, divided into two sections by Honister Pass. That to the north, from Maiden Moor to Dale Head, has been described earlier (p 77). The southern section forms a popular route to Great Gable; leaving the car at Honister gives a starting height of nearly 1,200ft, and a track first follows the line of the old quarry tramway, then skirts Grey Knotts and Brandreth before crossing Green Gable into Windy Gap and so up the north-eastern edge of Great Gable and down into Wasdale.

ROCK CLIMBING IN BORROWDALE

To the rock climber Borrowdale for long was merely a convenient avenue of approach from Keswick to Great Gable and Scafell; it had no famous challenging cliffs and little attention was paid to the occasional outcrops visible through the trees. There were, it is true, a few products of the 'gully era' of activity, including the steep clefts which split Raven Crag in the Comb Gill valley and Sergeant Crag in Langstrath, both first climbed within the same week of 1893. One or two buttresses yielded lines which have become classics of their kind; *Gillercombe Buttress* on the face of Grey Knotts and *Troutdale Pinnacle* on Black Crag in Troutdale are still two of the most popular mild S climbs. In 1921 Bentley Beetham was walking back from Wasdale to Keswick when he saw a rib of rock through the trees overlooking the head of Derwentwater. He and his companion Claud Frankland, who was later killed on the Chantry Buttress of the Napes, climbed this *Brown Slabs Arête*, the shape of things to come, but by 1936 there were still only twenty-two climbs in Borrowdale. Since then the number has dramatically increased, the result of two distinct phases of activity. Responsibility and credit for the first lies entirely with Bentley Beetham, who diligently searched almost every outcrop of rock. We have a vivid memory of him on Raven Crag in the Comb Gill valley; we were belayed at a stance during an early ascent of the *Summit Route* when some distance to our right a hand holding a brush appeared over the edge, daintily swept it

clear of earth and moss and withdrew, to be followed by two hands
and then by Bentley's cheerful though somewhat grubby counten-
ance. He was engaged in 'gardening' a new route, equipped with
the brush, a saw and other implements. Throughout the '40s and
into the early '50s his accounts of new routes poured out, culminating in the 1953 edition of the Borrowdale Guidebook. In this,
however, he stated '. . . All the same, Borrowdale is not a good
hunting ground for the tigers of our sport . . .', which in due course
proved to be a rapidly accepted challenge by the 'hard men' of
Keswick and elsewhere.

Since then several outcrops of tremendous steepness have been
opened up, including Walla, Falcon, Greatend and Eagle Crags,
and fiercest of all, the buttresses known collectively as Goat Crag
on the western side of the valley about a mile above Grange, which
for a time was shrouded in a veil of competitive secrecy. At first
sight many of these crags are distinctly unwelcoming in appearance,
dark, profusely vegetated, usually rather damp and with prominent
bulges and overhangs alternating with broken rock. But they have
yielded, and continue to yield, numerous impressively serious routes,
including a dozen of XS and fifty of hard VS category; on some of
these the use of pitons is essential, both for security and for aid
on artificial sections.

But Borrowdale has also much to offer the ordinary climber with
over eighty VD or easier routes and a number of attractive and
amenable S climbs. The low-lying sylvan surroundings of the crags,
their generally quick-drying rock of good quality, popular routes
which are climbed so frequently that the rock is now clean and
sound, the fact that one so often visits them on a sunny afternoon
or evening, all combine to give a visitor a feeling that he is a better
climber than he imagined. At the same time a note of caution should
be sounded; there have been more accidents on these crags than on
any other group in recent years, an obvious indication of their
accessibility and popularity but also at times the result of the over-
confidence of the inexperienced.

THE DERWENTWATER CRAGS

For two miles along the eastern shores of Derwentwater several
outcrops project from the hillside among the woods, providing a
series of low level climbing grounds. The first of note after leaving
Keswick is Walla Crag (105), of a steeply impending character. The

vegetated gully splitting the crag was climbed in 1892 by the Abraham brothers, probably the first recorded ascent in the Keswick district. The severity of the half-dozen routes which have been made is manifest by the fact that the earliest was not climbed until sixty-five years later; this was *White Buttress* (mild VS), a three-pitch effort up a groove on the left-hand buttress. The climbs are steep and strenuous and in almost every case it is necessary to use pitons for belaying.

Falcon Crags (30), the next outcrop half a mile up the valley, provide not only a range of VS climbs but also five short but fierce XS's, several involving artificial moves of a strenuous character on pitons. The crags include an upper and a lower section, the latter being more popular and offering a greater range of possibilities. Their steep bulging nature necessitates exposed traverses to avoid impossibilities, and the climbing is therefore almost as demanding for the second man as for the leader. *Hedera Grooves* (mild VS) and *Spinup* (VS) are usually the earliest routes to be attemped by newcomers. The first pitch of the former is ivy covered, but this soon gives way to traverses, first right, then left, on good clean rock to a prominent holly used as a belay. The crux move follows as a groove to the left somewhat hard to enter, and then a pleasant sloping ramp leads leftwards to the top of the crag. *Spinup* goes up the left-hand rib of the lower crag, a two-pitch climb of sustained interest yet of a not too exacting character. An introduction to the more serious routes is provided by *Illusion* (hard VS), a choice name as the climber will discover as he resolves the mysteries of its moves; it consists essentially of a difficult pitch involving a runout of over 100ft separating much easier introductory and concluding sections. After a very steep groove the leader makes a mantelshelf move on to a prominent flake, followed by a long and difficult traverse into another groove; nuts and slings should be used for protection. A short descent from the groove leads to a swing out right, with a step-down using a high handhold, then continuing up to a grassy ledge and a final easy wall.

Gowder Crag (40) is a fine buttress of rock rising among the trees on the left-hand side of Lodore Falls and reached from the road by the tourist path behind the hotel and through the turnstile or by following a footpath leaving the road north of the hotel. *Fool's Paradise* (VS) properly starts at the lowest point of the buttress up a rather broken-looking arête. Unfortunately the latest edition of the Guidebook has shortened the route as originally climbed in 1951 (the first party, incidentally, was in nailed boots) and has given the first and second pitches up the arête to *Gowder Buttress* (mild VS), a rather poor climb. The correct route, nearly 450ft in length as described in the 1953 edition of the Guidebook, is one of the best climbs of its grade in Borrowdale. It crosses the crag from bottom left to top right; its problems are varied and delicate, and the situations looking down through the trees are superb. The best pitch of nearly 70ft is a long traverse rightward beneath the overhangs, helped by fixing a high runner near the start, and followed by a poorly protected scoop. Though this pitch is the crux, the climb is by no means over since a steep chimney follows, its ascent complicated by a constriction which forces the climber briefly on to a slab to the left before he thankfully resumes his safe back and foot ascent of the top of the chimney.

Across the foot of Derwentwater on the eastern slopes of Maiden Moor (68) some broken but in places surprisingly steep outcrops are split by several gullies. They are mentioned not because the quality of the climbing justifies the plod there, but because in 1897 the Abraham brothers forced a direct finish up Mouse Gill, the left-hand of the three most prominent gullies. This is classified as mild VS, a remarkable standard for a climb of that time and the first of its category in the valley. The outcrop was not explored again until 1968, when another route of the same grade was made to the left and christened *Mouse Gill Grooves*, the two thus covering a remarkable span of climbing history.

SHEPHERD'S CRAG (98)
It is even more difficult than usual to do justice to the wealth of climbing riches provided by the group of outcrops known as Shepherd's, considerately situated only five minutes easy scramble from the Borrowdale road over a tree-shaded slope of mossy boulders and furnished with an hotel at either end; clearly climbing here is hardly of the character of an expedition. This accessibility is in some ways a disadvantage, for one may have to queue for a popular climb; the best time to visit Shepherd's is on a fine midweek day in winter. The base of the crag is covered with trees, which give climbers some privacy; otherwise the situation would be similar to that of the Llanberis crags exposed to the public gaze. Though

much gardening was necessary in the early days, the routes have been so frequented that most rock is now very clean. Some trees which once grew out of niches on the crag have gone, others still cling on determinedly, sometimes offering convenient belays. Descent lines, originally difficult to locate, are now so well blazened that there is no real problem in getting back to the base of the crags; incidentally, several routes are well suited for practice in climbing down. After a climbing day it is well worth going to the top of the crag at only about 700ft, which provides a view point of great charm and remarkable solitude.

The outcrops at Shepherd's can be divided into three: the Brown Slabs section in the north, the North Buttress group rising in the centre above a scree-covered bay and the Chamonix group in the south. The warm-looking, south-facing Brown Slabs offer several parallel lines of D or VD standard, excellent for tuition in climbing and abseiling and hence liable to be monopolised by large groups under their instructors. On the left of the Slabs *Brown Crag Wall* (hard S) provides an excellent introduction to steep wall climbing; starting at the lowest point of the crag, it ascends a scoop to the left of the corner overhangs, followed by some nice slabs and grooves. Several other hard climbs, including the single-pitch *Conclusion* (hard VS) with its strenuous groove and *P.T.O.* (VS), have been put up the fierce angle between Brown Crag Wall and the Slabs on the right.

Moving some fifty yards south (right) through the trees, the next prominent crag is North Buttress. *Ardus* (hard S) first takes a steep gully and then traverses left quite sensationally before ascending a thin slanting crack; on a recent visit we saw a leader come off the crack, but fortunately he had fixed a nut and runner, so that instead of a tremendous pendulum back into the gully he merely slithered, slightly distraught, down the slab to a dangling halt and accepted our rope end. The nearby *Eve* (mild VS), reputedly named after an attractive barmaid at one of the nearby hotels, is a fine climb, involving a traverse across a bulging slab and a top rib provided with exactly the necessary holds. As an obvious partner, *Adam* (VS) takes a somewhat harder line to the right.

Crossing a scree-fan to the south brings the climber to the popular Chamonix group of climbs; they were so called because they are '. . . so shapely and clean cut, so aiguille-like and distinctive . . .' The lower pitches of *Chamonix* (S) are a shade contrived, but they give neat climbing on excellent flake-holds; this is popularly known as Big Cham in contrast to *Little Chamonix* (VD), which takes an easier line to the right to reach the photogenic top pitch with its magnificent holds, common to both (frontispiece). The rocky belvedere above Chamonix and its neighbours, well equipped for belaying with stoutly established trees, is a favourite consorting place. If a leader wants a harder showpiece for his technique than Big Cham, he can try *Kransic Crack* (mild VS) to the left, which includes a steep 30ft crack climbed by jamming and a rightward traverse, safeguarded by a runner around a lassoed spike (plates p 71), to join Chamonix. Farther to the right, *Crescendo* (VD) starts up a little chimney near a large rock pillar which stands against the main buttress. Farther right still, just beyond the start of Little Chamonix, is *Scorpion* (hard S), taking a gently diagonal line leftward across the crag; it too has some rather contrived though interesting pitches, but the final one is really excellent, starting from a belay shared with Chamonix, branching off left below a prominent overhang and following first an undercut groove then leftward up a steep slab with very small holds. This requires delicate footwork, though protection can be arranged with a jammed nut before starting the slab. Above this, an overhanging block is climbed by bridging two cracks with the feet.

Several routes take the wall to the right of the projecting prow of Chamonix, including *Derision Groove* (mild VS) which provides a strenuous bridging effort. *Shepherd's Chimney* (S) is a good climb, not really a chimney at all but a wide overhanging corner; the crux at mid-height is a difficult wall with tiny holds, though the exposed top wall has some gratifying holds. *Rogues' Gallery* (VS) makes a mini-girdle traverse of this section of the crag; one descends left from Shepherd's Chimney by a spectacular series of moves, crosses into Derision Groove by means of excellent flake-holds and finishes up the last pitch of Scorpion. Finally, on the right-hand section of the crag the ever popular *Donkey's Ears* (VD) includes a semi-hand traverse across a slab, an ascent between two prominent rock spikes (the donkey's ears) followed by the famous traverse, the key to which is a niche for the left fingers, leading to a finishing crack. *Monolith Crack* (mild VS) is distinctly awkward to start, quite steep and strenuous and poorly protected.

TROUTDALE

Black Crag (5) is situated at the head of Troutdale, a short lateral
valley reached from the Keswick road by a walk over pleasant
meadows, then briefly up a tree-covered hillside. So conveniently
located is this crag that a party can start its chosen climb within
half an hour of leaving the road, and being sheltered and low-lying
it forms an excellent venue for a winter day.

Black Crag is a steep, squarish, clean-cut mass of rock, divided
into two buttresses by a tree-choked gully. The very steep left-hand
buttress, usually rather wet because of the prevalence of moss, has
been the scene in recent years of some very exacting climbing which
has produced VS routes with such offputting names as the *Shroud*,
the *Coffin* and the *Wreath*. Several of these involve artificial techniques, in fact *Vertigo* (VS) requires half a dozen pitons for belays
and as direct aid in the ascent of a strenuous wall pitch, while the
inelegantly named *D.T.*'s (VS) needs four pitons and a wedge to
overcome a large overhang. By contrast, the right-hand crag, despite
its initial appearance of overhangs and steep grooves, offers several
amenable routes. One climb of outstanding quality is **Troutdale
Pinnacle* (mild S), otherwise known as Black Crag Buttress; this
begins near the lowest point of the crag and provides a delightful
route with excellent belays and positions. After working rightward
up some awkward walls, grooves and slabs, a descending traverse
across steep slabs under a great overhang leads left into a corner
where a runner can be fixed, followed by a pull up a steep wall on
good holds to the prominent pinnacle which gives the climb its
name; an exposed rib and groove provide a good finish. A harder
version of this climb, *Troutdale Pinnacle Direct* (mild VS), takes
a line to the left of the ordinary route, and a still harder variant,
the *Superdirect* (hard VS), goes up left from the top of the third
pitch of the Direct.

Troutdale Ridge (S) is another pleasing climb on the slabby
right-hand edge of the crag, giving over 200ft of clean slabs and
walls with several neat yet awkward movements. *Holly Tree Corner*
(mild VS) works out a line between the Pinnacle and Ridge climbs,
using the fourth pitch of the former (the one preceding the slabs
traverse) and the top part of the ridge; this makes a fairly straight
and logical line up the right-hand section of the crag. As an introduction to the hard climbs, **Obituary Grooves* (VS) may be recom-

mended; starting up the initial slab of the Direct, it keeps to a series of grooves and corners, never desperate but never really relaxing until it finishes up parallel cracks.

Also in Troutdale, about half a mile from Black Crag, is Great-end Crag (43) which should be mentioned because some VS climbs have been made there, mostly named with the death wish evident in some of the harder routes on Black Crag, including the *Undertaker*, *Charon* and *Styx*. It is an unattractive crag, damp and gloomy.

THE BOWDERSTONE CRAGS (8)

A small group of outcrops in the neighbourhood of the Bowder Stone provide some quite good routes not far from the road. Near the National Trust car park and rising above the mounds of quarry waste is Quayfoot Buttress, where for such a small crag a few surprisingly hard climbs have been worked out, though the *Ordinary* route (VD) takes a pleasant slabby line up its left-hand edge. On the left of the path from the car park to the Bowder Stone the Woden's Face buttress offers three good climbs on sound rock: the *Original* route (hard VD), which after a short wall moves left into a groove; the *Direct* (mild S), more or less up the central wall; and *Woden's Cheek* (hard S), following a steep shallow groove to the right.

Higher up the fellside several more outcrops are reached by a faintly defined path. The lowest, on the left, is *Woden's Needle* (D), so called after a prominent pinnacle reached by a little wall climbed on good holds; it is preferable to put a runner on the tip of the pinnacle and continue up the shallow groove, so making a single pitch climb. The **Bowderstone Pinnacle* (D) on the main crag may seem rather easy but it is well worth doing; after following the front edge of the buttress, one steps across on to the tip of a pinnacle formed by a deep cleft separating it from the main mass. The usual descent is by roping down the gully, though if other parties are about care is needed since the line of abseil is directly above the start of the climb; an alternative is to step back across the gap on to a narrow ridge and so reach the hillside. Other routes include *Thor's Exit* (VD), a rather contrived method of attaining the gap behind the pinnacle up a smooth strenuous crack, and *Balder's Crack* (S) which leads steeply into the cleft on the Pinnacle Route.

THE LANGSTRATH AND GREENUP CRAGS

When walking up the Stonethwaite valley, the view ahead is dominated by the giant rock-step of Eagle Crag (26) (plate p 71), projecting from the eastern side of the spur between Langstrath and the Greenup Gill valley. On the western side of this spur, looking out across Langstrath, are Heron Crag and farther south Sergeant Crag.

Eagle is unexceptionally a crag for the top climber; of its eleven climbs three are XS (one of these, *Post Mortem*, is said to have the finest single pitch in the valley, a steeply overhanging crack), and only one is as modest as hard S. This, *Postern Gate*, at the right-hand end of the crag, gives an excellent climb involving a steep ascent into a deeply cut overhanging chimney, a rather desperate effort to get up this overhang and out on to the left wall, and a finish up the easy top section of the chimney. Another good route with remarkably varied pitches is *Falconer's Crack* (VS), which includes an exacting crack, a groove followed by a steep wall, and a nice finish up a clean rib on the right of a prominent chimney.

In contrast, Heron Crag (56) has more possibilities for the average performer, though the continuity of its routes suffers from its step-like formation, with steep riser walls separated by grassy terraces and ledges. In the centre the broken and shallowly defined *Heron Crag Gully* (S) is usually wet and sometimes a cascade. To its right the *Pinnacle* route (VD) starts up a groove behind a prominent pinnacle, landing the climber on to a series of heathery ledges from which some scrambling and a steep corner leads to a groove with an awkward exit, followed by a short traverse and a wall finish; despite this lack of continuity it is a good route. The best line is *Heron Crag Buttress* (hard S), which gives a climb of over 300ft up the ribs to the left of the gully; though its continuity likewise is broken by a heather ledge, the steep sections of the buttress make an enjoyable climb.

The base of Sergeant Crag (96) at about 1,400ft is reached by a slanting traverse from the Langstrath Beck up the steep hillside over bracken and scree. The crag is split by *Sergeant Crag Gully*, one of the good old classics, first ascended by O. G. Jones in 1893. As it is usually wet and in places slimy it is ranked as S, but it makes a fine expedition either in nails or in socks over rubbers (as we climbed it on a recent damp January day), though after heavy rain it becomes a waterfall. It offers an assortment of steep chock-stone pitches, the walls on either side providing plentiful holds which however should be carefully tested by the leader as the numerous close joints induce a certain friable quality. The fourth pitch provides an exacting move up its left-hand containing wall on small greasy holds, though a thread can be fixed rather strenuously round a chockstone. There are several other climbs, the *Redoubt* being of VS standard, but the crag is much interrupted by grassy ledges. The *West Face* route (D), alleged to be over 800ft in length, is so broken and interrupted by traverses over heathery and grassy ledges that there may be doubt as to whether the correct line has been followed. However, like the Gully it ends near the summit of Sergeant Crag, from which a party should slant down the fell beyond some steep slabby outcrops to return to the base of the buttress.

THE CRAGS IN COMB GILL

From a group of cottages on the Keswick—Borrowdale road about a mile from Seatoller a track leads into a short valley between the spurs of Thornythwaite and Rosthwaite Fells, known as Comb Gill after its stream. It is a hanging valley with slabby flanks excellent for scrambling, and several short climbs have been made up its ice-scarred walls. But these are not easy to find and it is more enjoyable and less trouble to work out one's own line to the top of the oddly named Bessyboot, then follow the ridge in a south-easterly direction towards the slot of Comb Door en route to the summit of Glaramara.

Two larger outcrops face across the head of the combe, Doves' Nest on the east and the dark mass of Raven Crag on the west, each reached by a path traversing the hillside. Doves' Nest (23) has been formed by the detachment along a fault line of a buttress which has slumped bodily down the slope and remained leaning against it; a series of interlinked passages, cavities and fissures has thus been created, well worth an exploratory visit. Various routes include the *Face* or *Outside* route (D) which makes its way from the lowest point of the rocks, ascends the prominent Central Chimney and reaches a recess known as the Attic Cave, from which exploration of the inner passages can be launched. An inside route is possible, though not easy to find or to follow and strictly for the

lean climber; it leaves the Outside route at the top of its second
pitch, ascends the North Chimney, squeezes through a black slot
on the right about ten inches wide known as the Rat Hole, and
higher up enters the Central Chimney.

The most obvious feature of Raven Crag (80) is the deeply cut
gully towards its right which gives over 500ft of climbing, though
it includes much scrambling up its stony bed. The way up each
pitch depends on the amount of water flowing down; should a
direct pitch under a chockstone be a waterfall it can usually be
turned by a groove or staircase on one side. Near the top a steep
crack rises from a kind of amphitheatre, making a hard finish which
can be avoided under too wet conditions.

The crag provides two other recommended climbs of about 500ft.
Over to the left, beginning up some grey slabs at almost the lowest
point of the crag, is *Corvus*, of only D standard but a very worthwhile, well worn, all weather sort of climb. It includes several
varied pitches—slabs, ribs and scoops, a semi-hand traverse on the
mid-section wall along a line of flakes and finishes near the top
of the crag. The *Summit* route (mild S) starts up just to the right
of the gully and takes a line of grooves and cracks to a big grassy
terrace below the final wall. Here it is necessary to walk thirty
yards to the left to a point overlooking the gully, from which a
slightly awkward scoop leads to a leftward traverse and a steep
finish up a crack and groove, in all a very enjoyable climb, especially
above the terrace where the rock is of remarkable quality with a
gabbro-like roughness. Just to the right of the start of the Summit
Route begins *Raven Bastion* (D), long and rather broken, but with
some pleasant pitches. The big overhanging wall near the extreme
left was climbed in 1959 by a route known as the *Pendulum* (hard
VS); on the crux pitch near the top seven pitons were required.

GILLERCOMBE BUTTRESS (35)

A prominent buttress projects from the south-eastern face of the
Grey Knotts—Brandreth ridge overlooking the hanging valley of
Gillercombe, from whose tarnless though marshy floor foams Sour
Milk Gill to join the Derwent near Seathwaite. As the base of the
buttress is at about 1,700ft it is quite a long plod; if the path from
Seathwaite is taken alongside Sour Milk Gill the walk can be
enlivened by disporting on the Seathwaite Slabs near the valley

and on easier angled slabs higher up. A lazier approach is from Honister Pass, traversing diagonally on to the eastern ridge of Grey Knotts and contouring across the slope to the foot of the buttress.

The crag is more impressive from a distance than at close quarters for though massive it is rather broken, the rocks lean back and there are many grassy terraces. A prominent forked gully splits the buttress, the right fork providing a VD route of no great merit. To its left is *Gillercombe Bastion* (mild VS); its upper part rather fades out into scrambling steps interrupted with grassy ledges, but the lower consists of steep slabs giving delicate climbing.

The most popular route is the nine-pitch **Gillercombe Buttress* (mild S) on the right of the gully, starting with a steep wall followed by a neat upward traverse to the left. Climbed as long ago as 1912, it was later given a more direct finish up a grooved slab and steep rocks to the right of a chimney. On one occasion we so enjoyed this route in the sunshine that we climbed straight down again. At a celebrated F&RCC meet long ago, the President led a rope of twenty-one people up this climb; it is alleged that he was sitting down to tea in Seathwaite before the last man started. Farther to the right is *Grey Knotts Face* (just VD) up a subsidiary buttress where ends the fence across the floor of the combe. This is rather a discursive and rambling expedition, markedly inferior to the Buttress, but it includes a memorable pitch known as the Letter Box, a squarish hole through which one wriggles before rather strenuously climbing a slit behind it. Several very hard and exposed climbs have been worked out on the steep Right Wall at the northern end of the crag; these include *Eyrie* and *Tiercel Wall* (hard VS), the latter involving a piton move.

GOAT CRAG (37)

Of all the recent discoveries of 'new' crags, especially in Borrowdale where it might seem that all the good rock had been developed, the exploration of Goat Crag is outstanding. Though handily situated near Castle Crag on the western side of the valley above Grange, part of the long broken escarpment under the summit ridge of High Spy, it had been passed by for years behind its camouflage of trees, grass and moss; an early reference simply stated that it was not worth a visit by climbers. There was no concept of the actual amount of rock; who could have envisaged a lately discovered crag yielding routes of up to 370ft and a girdle traverse exceeding 600ft? Of course, it has required much gardening, a process still in operation; we read in the accounts of early ascents of efforts by leaders involved in '. . . hurling down occasional landslides of earth on our ungrateful heads from a steep scoop . . .' and who '. . . padded up moss to a swing on tatty heather to finish'.

It is a complex crag, with several distinct sections. The Southern Buttresses are broken and offer only wandering lines on indifferent rock, and away to the right the small outcrop of Steel Knotts has two short routes on good quality rock. Farther north and higher is the extensive, dark looking Northern Face, with its overhangs, roofs, grooves and bulging walls up which run all the big climbs. Les Brown began developments in 1965 with *Praying Mantis* (hard VS) on the right-hand side of the crag, which rapidly attracted other parties so that vast quantities of vegetation were removed and the route much improved. This has become an established climb, generally regarded as the best on the crag; its initial pitch which follows a steep groove is especially fine. Above this the route bears left up steep grass and a groove until a traverse to the right is possible to an exposed piton belay below the long top pitch; later the leader of the original first ascent made a short XS link-pitch to the stance below the final pitch, thus forming an alternative more direct climb and raising its standard. While Goat Crag has yielded only VS and harder grades for the expert who is a connoisseur of such rock, more than a dozen routes have been made, including several XS and artificial lines. The *Great Buttress* (hard VS) involves some artificial climbing, where skill in the placing of bolts and pitons is imperative; this so far is the only route to negotiate the extremely steep wall on the right side of the North Face.

Higher up to the right is Knitting Needle Gully bounded by a wall; the name of the gully has been derived from a steep flake called the Knitting Needle, though there appears to be some confusion, possibly of a punning kind, with the name Nitting Haws marked on the OS maps. On this wall several climbs have been made, one of which, *King Rat* (VS) deserves mention; it has an exceedingly steep and problematical start leading to a groove with a hard corner near the top, but once started the holds on this climb prove to be much better than elsewhere.

6

THE EASTERN FELLS

To the east of the Keswick—Ambleside—Windermere road lies a complicated area of broad ridges and deep valleys, splaying away south-eastward to where the Shap and Howgill Fells form an upland link between the Lakeland hills and the Pennines. This link is crossed at Shap by the main railway line from Crewe to Carlisle, by the A6 trunk road and farther to the east by the recently opened section of the M6 motorway. Though the pattern of the valleys and their streams seems confused, a main watershed can be traced eastward from Dunmail Raise to the summit of the Kirkstone Pass and so to Shap. To the north of this line the waters converge on Ullswater and Haweswater, hence via the Rivers Eamont and Lowther which meet near Penrith and in due course join the Eden, the master stream of the long trough between the Lake District and the North Pennines. To the south of the main watershed the drainage finds its way into Morecambe Bay via Windermere and the River Leven, by the River Kent flowing through Kendal, and in the extreme south-east by the River Lune.

Three major lakes are included in this section. Thirlmere lies in a deep trough between the broadly parallel lines of the High Seat—Ullscarf and the Helvellyn ridges, Ullswater and Haweswater over to the east. The thirsty demands of Manchester and south Lancashire generally have involved all three lakes, Thirlmere and Haweswater by the construction of dams to raise the level of the water. In the case of Thirlmere this has involved the demolishing or submergence of several farms and the construction of a new road along its western shore, while the surrounding slopes to about a thousand feet were thickly planted with solid masses of conifers. Access to its shores except at a few authorised viewpoints is strictly forbidden, though in recent years official policy has been somewhat relaxed and several walks and nature trails have been opened. The dam across the foot of Haweswater almost doubled its length and depth, submerging the head of Mardale with its village, church and inn.

Page 107 (above left) Revelation, Raven Crag, Great Langdale; (above right) the Gordian Knot, White Gill, Great Langdale; (below) the Eskdale face of Bowfell

Page 108 (above left) The Trident Route, A Buttress, Dow Crag; (above right) The Plumb, Wallowbarrow Crag; (below) view across Grey Friar to the Scafell range

Ullswater in the opinion of many, including William Wordsworth, is the loveliest of the Lakes, partly because of its three
distinct reaches which offer changing vistas of tree-bordered water,
deep side valleys and bounding skyline ridges, partly because of the
frame of bold summits which appear to enclose its head. The valley
projects deeply into the heart of the eastern fells, so that Patterdale
and Glenridding are convenient bases for visitors. The south-eastern
shore of the lake in every way is more attractive than the much
frequented opposite side. A quiet road leads from Pooley Bridge
to Howtown and continues to Sandwick round the southern slopes
of little Hallin Fell which attains only 1,271ft, though from the foot
of the lake near Pooley Bridge it dominates the eastern panorama.
From Sandwick, where the becks draining the steep-sided Martindale valleys enter the lake, a track continues near the shore to the
hamlet of Rooking and over Grisedale Bridge into Patterdale; it is
particularly attractive around Silver Point, with its little bays and
headlands. The peace of this walk is emphasised by the constant
roar of summer traffic on the A592 across the water.

The main road continues south from Patterdale past little
Brothers Water, curiously square in shape and liable to increase
in area after heavy rain, then crosses the Kirkstone Pass at a height
of almost 1,500ft and down into Windermere. The road divides this
part of Lakeland into two distinct sections: that to the west is
dominated by the Helvellyn—Fairfield ridge, that to the east by the
long spine of High Street. While the summit ridges and their western
slopes are almost invariably smooth and grassy, their eastern and
south-eastern flanks are deeply dissected by long valley-troughs
ending at their heads in combes backed by crags; the east-facing
tendency of these combes (p 23) is here strikingly evident. Several
contain tarns, notably Red Tarn under Helvellyn enclosed between
the rocky arms of Striding and Swirral Edges, and Blea Water
under the summit of High Street, claimed to be the deepest Lakeland tarn (207ft has been sounded). The main valleys include the
roughly parallel Grisedale, Deepdale and Dovedale, extending from
under the crest of the Fairfield—Hart Crag ridge towards the Ullswater—Brothers Water valley; then the long straight south-eastern
valleys of Kentmere, Long Sleddale, Bannisdale and Crookdale;
in the east are the remote and infrequently visited Wet Sleddale
and the Mosedale—Swindale valley; and opening into the southern

G

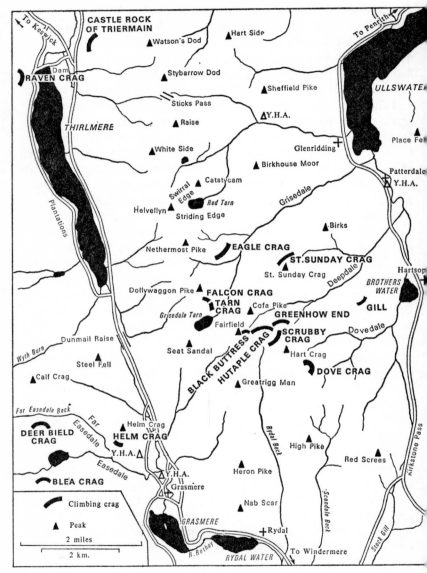

FIG 5. The Eastern Fells

shores of Ullswater are Boardale (spelt Boredale on the 1" map), Bannerdale which is a sanctuary for the Martindale red deer, and Fusedale.

FELL WALKS IN THE EASTERN UPLANDS

Helvellyn and High Street are merely the best known summits of this considerable upland area; Arthur Wainwright describes no less than thirty-five individual mountains in each of the sections to the west and east of the Kirkstone Pass road. This is country for the strong walker, though he can cover most of the main tops in a couple of well planned circuits; while he will find tracks crossing the passes and ascending the popular peaks, much of the area is rarely visited.

Several walker's routes cross the main ridges by high passes. The Sticks Pass, second in height in Lakeland only to Esk Hause, climbs up steep grassy slopes from the Keswick—Threlkeld road junction, crosses the ridge at a height of 2,420ft between the rounded summits of Stybarrow Dod and Raise and descends past the disused Greenside mine buildings to Glenridding. Grisedale Hause forms a popular way from either Grasmere or the top of Dunmail Raise past the large tarn and down Grisedale to Patterdale. In the south-east a path ascends the slopes on the east of the Kentmere valley to the Nan Bield Pass on the 2,100ft contour, descending past Small Water under Piot Crag to Haweswater.

Long Sleddale is a secluded valley, in its lower reaches strikingly reminiscent of a Pennine dale, with its flat, lush floor, prosperous farms strung out along the valley sides, and the River Sprint, crossed at intervals by stone-arched bridges, flowing alternately in winding curves over the level sections and through short stretches of rocky gorge. Beyond Sadgill, the last settlement up the valley, the road changes into a track which served the Wrengill quarries, and this can be followed up to a col at over 1,300ft. The valley sides steepen and become rugged, the tributary gills descending in rocky rifts and the Sprint cascading in a series of fine falls; on the right is the imposing Buckbarrow Crag. Beyond the col, where the track swings left into the abandoned Wrengill quarry, lies an extensive marshy hollow; a path continues north over Gatescarth Pass to Mardale, another, rather faint and marshy, crosses a low col into Mosedale and Swindale. From the Long Sleddale track several peaks can easily be reached, notably Kentmere Pike and the grassy dome of Harter Fell with its summit cairn disfigured by old fence posts. If the walker has left his car at Sadgill, the return from Harter Fell can be made south along a grassy ridge to Kentmere Pike, continuing over Goat Scar and the oddly named Shipman Knotts, then down the rough hillside to the valley.

Helvellyn exemplifies the pattern of many Lakeland peaks, its western slopes falling steeply and uniformly towards the plantations bordering Thirlmere, its eastern flanks deeply dissected by crag-girt combes. Its ascent is immensely popular, though its flat shale-strewn summit is dull unless one goes to the eastern edge to look down at Red Tarn; the view over central and western Lakeland is a further compensation, and it is a splendid point from which to await the glories of the dawn. Helvellyn is pre-eminently a mountain to be climbed in winter; it is then relatively peaceful and under favourable conditions Striding Edge may afford an interesting route.

Half a dozen paths plod up Helvellyn from Thirlmere. The best way is from near Wythburn up the Whelpside Gill, whose source is a spring bursting out from the scree at about 2,400ft, one of the highest sources of running water in Lakeland. What might well be called the classic ascent of Helvellyn takes a path from Patterdale over the grass and heather of Birkhouse Moor to the easy, near-horizontal Striding Edge, which is apt to be exceedingly crowded on a fine day, ending with a mild scramble to the summit. The round of Red Tarn can be completed by descending Swirral Edge, thence by a good track down to the old Greenside mine buildings now used as a climbers' hostel, and so to Glenridding. A longer circuit from Glenridding follows the valley of the Glenridding Beck to a marshy hollow which once contained Keppelcove Tarn, a reservoir serving the mine; in 1927 a rainstorm caused flood waters to cut a new outlet from the tarn and a few years later the dam itself was breached. From this point the fine looking but deceptively easy north-western ridge of the shapely Catstycam (variously called Catstyecam and Catchedicam) can be followed to its summit, thence across a col to Swirral Edge. From the summit of Helvellyn a heavily scarred track goes south over Nethermost and Dollywaggon Pikes, though missing their actual summits, and by a series of zigzags down to Grisedale Hause. Like Helvellyn, the eastern sides of these two peaks reveal steep-sided coves, crags split by gullies, slopes of scree and boulders, and cascading becks; several scrambling routes to their summits can be worked out on this flank.

Beyond Grisedale Hause scree slopes rise steeply southward to the massive bulk of Fairfield, with its broad top of smooth turf and grassy ridges descending amiably towards Grasmere and Rydal. The horseshoe from Grasmere encloses the soft green valley of the Rydal Beck, traversing several tops on each leg and taking in the three main summits of Dove Crag, Hart Crag and Fairfield itself; this is a gentle excursion except on the occasion of the annual 'horseshoe fell race'. The horseshoe can be extended to the east by continuing along the ridge to the rocky twin-topped summit of Little Hart Crag, crossing Scandale Pass at 1,750ft and so on to Red Screes, a bulky mountain with pinkish scree slopes from which it is named, overlooking the Kirkstone Pass.

Fairfield is yet another example of a double-faced mountain; many a walker rambling along its grassy summit plateau has no concept of the great cliffs below the ridgeline. This aspect of the mountain is best appreciated by an ascent from Patterdale up the lovely Deepdale (plate p 89) into Sleet Cove at its head, to the col of Deepdale Hause and over the shattered little summit of Cofa Pike. An alternative approach from Deepdale keeps to the left of Greenhow End into Link Cove and under Scrubby Crag to the ridge. An enjoyable eastern horseshoe can be made from Patterdale up the grassy spur of Birks and along the shapely ridge of St Sunday Crag with its steep scree and rocky buttresses falling away northward into Grisedale; the route continues by way of Deepdale Hause and Cofa Pike as before. The return journey can be made via Hart Crag and down its north-eastern shoulder, following the ridge for three miles along a faint but well cairned path to Hartsop above How, grassy or boggy sections alternating with rocky outcrops; the last two-thirds of the way follows one of the finest drystone walls in Lakeland, and drops off through the steep woodland of Deepdale Park to reach the main road at Bridgend about a mile from Patterdale.

The fell walker who really wishes to extend himself on a good high-level route should try the fifteen-mile Helvellyn—Fairfield

ridge from Threlkeld to Grasmere. The first section over the several Dods and Raise is a gently undulating stroll, an area little
visited except when skiers come in search of adequate snow, which
they are more likely to find here than anywhere else in Lakeland;
indeed a ski club has erected a hut on the north-eastern slopes of
Raise. The way leads south over Helvellyn, Nethermost and Dollywaggon to Grisedale Tarn, steeply on to Fairfield and down one
side or the other of the horseshoe to Grasmere.

The summit of High Street is marked by an OS column at a
height of 2,719ft, but otherwise it is a featureless grassy plateau
with a few slabby stones and a tumbledown wall, merely the highest point of a quietly undulating ridge of which more than eight
miles is above 2,000ft. Its uniform directness led the Romans,
who always had an eye for a good line, to use it for their road
from *Galava* near Ambleside to *Brovacum* in the Eden valley near
Penrith; this road is marked on the 1″ map and sections of its
paved surface can still be distinguished.

Several possible routes lead to the summit of High Street, of
which three can be recommended. From the head of Mardale an
easy rocky scramble ascends the ridge of Rough Crag and Long
Stile with the steep-walled Riggindale on the right, the haunt of
red deer and fell ponies, returning either by way of Blea Water or
northward to The Knott and then along the ridge of Kidsty Pike.
From Patterdale a pleasant walk ascends from the hamlet of Rooking by way of Angle Tarn, if desired, visiting the twin Angletarn
Pikes en route, and follows the ridge to The Knott; an alternative
though more tedious way is from Hartsop by way of Hayeswater.
Perhaps the most enjoyable route is from Kentmere, either by way
of the Nan Bield Pass or over Lingmell End to Mardale Ill Bell,
a summit of smooth turf with two massive cairns; from there it is
an easy stroll to High Street. The return may be made by following
a wall south to Thornthwaite Crag with its tall slender cairn, and
along the Froswick—Ill Bell—Yoke ridge whose craggy flanks bor-
der Kentmere on the west; on the side of Yoke is the imposing
Rainsborrow Crag. From Yoke a grassy ridge descends to the
Garburn Pass at about 1,750ft, from which paths lead south-west-
ward to Troutbeck and Windermere, eastward to Kentmere village.

ROCK CLIMBING IN THE EASTERN FELLS

The 1938 edition of the F&RCC Guidebook to Dow Crag and Langdale contained an eighteen page addendum expansively entitled *Outlying Crags*. This included some routes on Dollywaggon Pike, Buckbarrow in Long Sleddale and a few other scattered locations, mostly described with no real enthusiasm. There were, it is true, hints of things to come. Dr Graham Macphee and others had seen something of what the Castle Rock of Triermain had to offer and had made some routes on the milder South Crag. R. J. Birkett near the start of his long and immensely productive climbing career, had set foot on Dove Crag in 1937 to work out a route known as the *Tarsus*. On the same crag the name *Inaccessible Gully* was belied in the same year and a complete line was made up *Wing Ridge*, now renamed *Westmorland's* route (p 33). While these remote crags appeared to have little to offer, such statements as '. . . Although this crag presents such a bold face to the east, nothing was found worthy of description as a climb . . .' implied a challenge which in due course was accepted by a new generation of climbers. One can readily understand this neglect. Some of the big, remote and rather rambling cliffs were of course known, but they had no instant visual impact other than of an offputting character; to some extent they were camouflaged both by the scale of their surroundings, so that they appeared as mere excrescences on the headwall of a combe, and by their heavily vegetated nature. The uplands east of Thirlmere were left as the domain of the fell walker, fine free-striding country but not, it was believed, for the rock climber.

Just before World War II R. J. Birkett made his earliest big climbs on Triermain, *Overhanging Bastion* and *Zigzag*, while J. W. Haggas put the first major route up the main face of Dove Crag, the VS *Hangover*, a climb which more than thirty years later retains its considerable reputation. These were indeed breakthroughs, though their follow-up was inevitably interrupted by the War. As early as 1946 one of us led some new routes on Gouther Crag in Swindale. The pace then accelerated and not only were fresh routes worked out on the newly explored crags but standards were pushed up; the present list of almost 250 climbs on thirty-eight different crags includes more than a dozen of XS category. With the exception of Castle Rock and Raven Crag, handily situated near the main road at the foot of Thirlmere, and a few low-lying outcrops near Patterdale, most eastern crags are reached by lengthy walks and a climb forms part of a day's expedition. Thus after a stroll up Deepdale, followed by a long route on Hutaple or Scrubby, it is logical to continue to the summit of Fairfield and complete a satisfying day along the ridges back to Patterdale.

THE THIRLMERE CRAGS

The Castle Rock of Triermain (17) guards the southern entrance to the Vale of St John. It is an elongated mass rising from swathing trees, with a steep almost overhanging North Crag (plate p 89) separated by a tree-filled embayment from the lower and more broken South Crag. As it offers steep sound rock within ten minutes of a main road, it is hardly surprising that despite, or perhaps because of, the obvious severity of its routes it is extremely popular.

Though the climbs on the South Crag are short, from 80 to 140ft, they include three nice slab climbs of VD standard away to the right: the *Slab* itself, the *Gangway* and the *Yewtree*. The *Via Media* is also a good VD climb (with an alternative VS start), involving some attractive slabs and a leftward traverse. The best climb on the South Crag is the *Direct* route (mild VS), which provides a hint of the exposed and strenuous character of its northern neighbour. Halfway up the second steep wall the climber finds himself in a square niche or 'sentry box' and an awkward move is required to leave it for a steep crack above.

The North Crag is clearly a place for determined climbers; on a fine day a few of the routes may appear to relent, but never the half dozen formidable XS climbs. There are however three excellent possibilities for ordinary climbers. *The Barbican* is of mild VS standard, ranked the easiest on the North Crag; on its lower pitches the climber makes his way, albeit steeply, through lush vegetation, belaying in turn on an oak, a yew and an ash, while its upper section works out exposedly above the great main wall with its XS climbs. Since this route involves a long traverse followed by a short descent and an awkward step to the right, the second man should be competent, since in this instance he is less well safeguarded than is his leader. The best finish is a move right on to the usual top pitch of Overhanging Bastion. *Zigzag*, though officially in the VS category, gives a much less exacting impression than does the allegedly milder Barbican, possibly because its rather wandering line, interspersed with some short walks, minimises the feeling of exposure and technical difficulties seem to occur near the belays. Since Zigzag crosses three of the hard climbs and shares with them some stances and belays, it is an excellent route for getting the feel of the crag and it finishes satisfactorily up a fine stretch of slabs.

The fine 250ft route *Overhanging Bastion* (VS) must be a serious contender for the title of 'Lakeland's best climb'. It takes a line up the crag's most obvious feature, a long gangway which curves across its face (plate p 89); this pitch looks sensational from the road and feels just as sensational on it. The lower pitches are steep, the bottom one much harder now that a once helpful tree has disappeared. The fourth pitch is the crux; after stepping airily from a pinnacle on to the gangway, one just keeps going on technically not very difficult rock, though increasingly conscious of the overhang below. It is advisable for the leader to arrange several runners, not just for his own protection but for that of his second who, should he lose contact, will make a big pendulum and dangle well clear of the face. The gangway is interrupted at an overhang where the climber moves left into a recess containing a yew, a fantastically exposed move on good flake holds, to finish either up a slab on the right or less attractively up the topographical continuation of the gangway through some scrubby vegetation.

The massive east-facing Raven Crag (84) rises sombrely for about 300ft above the Thirlmere dam, peering down through its swathing trees. It is an intimidating crag for several reasons, not the least being its lack of obvious lines of weakness and its rather gloomy atmosphere. The earliest routes (*Genesis* and *Exodus*) were not made until 1952 and the first two XS climbs until 1964 (the *Medlar* and *Totalitarian*); the Medlar takes, according to the Guidebook, '. . . a malevolent and improbable line . . .' The crag now has a dozen routes, though so far it has not attained the popularity of the Castle Rock across the way.

Valedictory (mild S) is a reasonable climb on the left (south) end of the crag; it starts quite high up from the base following an unpleasant approach over steep earth and rocky ledges, sharing the first two pitches with the neighbouring *Exodus* (mild S). After a short walk right, the route ascends a wall recessed with grooves, involving an awkward move around a bulge beneath an overhang from one groove to the next. The last pitch, a corner-crack surmounted by a tree, is a nice problem; the main difficulty is to gain sufficient height to reach some good exit holds high up on the left.

Away to the right of the crag is the amenable *Genesis* (S); it goes up a buttress to an obvious squarish overhang negotiated by excellent holds on the right, followed by a corner-crack climbed by bridging and a wall whose main difficulty lies at the start up rather sloping footholds. After some scrambling the route finishes up a short chimney well supplied with chockstones.

The best of the reasonable climbs is *Communist Convert* (VS), which has become quite popular (plate p 72); after a steep slabby pitch it takes a diagonal line right across the face, with some delicate moves to a grassy ledge where a piton may justifiably be inserted for belaying or for a runner. It finishes by stepping off the crag just below the final overhangs on the XS route *Totalitarian*.

THE GRISEDALE CRAGS

The Grisedale valley forms a steep-sided trench enclosed on the north by the ridge projecting from Helvellyn, on the south by the long line of Cofa Pike—St Sunday Crag—Birks. Apart from the little outcrops of Elm How, Thornhow and Harrison's Crags low down on the southern side of the valley and worthy of a casual visit, three climbing grounds are in Grisedale: the small though excellent Eagle Crag, the long line of broken outcrops under the summit ridge of St Sunday, and Falcon and Tarn Crags on Dollywaggon Pike.

Eagle Crag (27) is situated on the south side of a spur between Nethermost and Ruthwaite Coves, only a few minutes walk across the hillside from Ruthwaite Lodge, a former shooting-box now a university mountaineering club hut. The outcrop is quite low-lying, its base at about 1,200ft, and easily reached from the Grisedale track. There are actually two crags; that to the north is vegetated and broken, but the one to the south has such good rock that it has become very popular. It is about 200ft high, with a grass belvedere known as The Pasture at just over half its height, and has a south-easterly aspect; on one occasion we visited the crag in late December and found it so clean, dry and inviting that despite cold hands two S climbs went very comfortably. On the left *Kestrel Wall* (S) is a delightful route of steep cracks and walls with sharp incut holds exactly where the fingers drop into them (plate p 72). Round to the right *Doctor's Grooves* (hard S) is an interesting climb of unusual variety: a long corner, a rather greasy groove for which we pulled on socks over our rubbers, a delightful semi-hand traverse across a slab, a steep rib with a delicate move over to an arête on good holds and a final chimney climbed by a neat layback. A very worthy route is *Sobrenada* (VS), taking a steep and delicate line up the front of the buttress to reach The Pasture; the 75ft pitch above involves two thin traverses, a shallow chimney which is extremely awkward to leave and a slab finish.

It is hardly surprising that potential climbs on St Sunday Crag (89) were neglected until 1954–6; probably nobody had noticed them or they had baulked at the tedious ascent from Patterdale since their base lies along the 2,000ft contour. Yet the crags exceed half a mile in length, forming a fringe of rock 100 to 200ft high under the summit ridge; small outcrops of continuous rock are separated by gullies, not recommended except under winter conditions or as convenient lines of descent. In spite of the long grind over scree and steep grass, it is preferable to walk about one and a half miles up the valley, locate and line up the main features of the crags, notably the easily identified Y gully in the centre, and then strike straight up to the objective. On one occasion in mist, we approached from the east along the Birks ridge and as a result never really located ourselves; all day we messed about on rock that at first seemed to fit the Guidebook description and then higher up clearly did not. Numerous routes have been made, some never recorded, though more than a dozen are listed in the Guidebook. Away to the east beyond the first major gully (the East Chockstone Gully) is the *Slab* route (hard D), which provides 100ft of clean rock; if the party scrambles up some distance to a higher buttress the *Continuation* route more than doubles the length of this worthy slab climb. A much harder proposition is the *Nose Direct* (S), a three pitch sequence of slabs and an exposed arête between the branching arms of the Y gully.

Falcon (31) and Tarn Crags (103) project boldly eastward from the ridge running south from the summit of Dollywaggon Pike; the base of Tarn Crag can be reached by a short scramble up the scree from the Grisedale track, while the other lies about 200ft higher to the north. Several steep buttresses provide three or four climbs of VS standard, and some deeply cut gullies can give excellent winter climbing.

THE DEEPDALE CRAGS

From the main Ullswater—Brothers Water road the crags at the head of Deepdale stand out in the morning sunshine (plate p 72), especially in winter when they may be picked out in snow. The path wanders for about three miles up the valley among morainic mounds and scattered boulders, keeping well to the right of several marshy depressions. Ahead rises Greenhow End (named The Step on the 1″ map), a spur separating Sleet Cove on the right (north) from Link Cove on the left. It is advisable to keep up the right-hand headstream of Deepdale Beck until just below a slabby outcrop under Greenhow End; for Scrubby Crag in Link Cove strike left up a grassy rake, for Hutaple and Black Buttress make a rising traverse up steep grass and scree under the base of the cliffs.

Greenhow End (47) is a striking, even dominating mass from a distance, but closer acquaintance reveals it to be extremely broken, with steep and mossy, sometimes dripping, slabs separated by grassy and heathery ledges and with a profusion of stunted trees. *Deepdale* (VD) and *Central* (hard D) *Gullies* provide possible lines on the Sleet Cove side, but their ascent involves much scrambling on loose vegetated rock separating a few pitches of interest.

Beyond the deeply recessed East Hutaple Gully the Sleet Cove face steepens up to form Hutaple Crag (60), a big mass almost 500ft in height, though much broken up by grassy ledges. The dominating feature is *Curving Gully* (hard VD), extending the full height of the crag and providing an interesting continuous route (plate p 89). It is admittedly loose in some parts, mossy and lichenous in others, but it gives a climber a good impression of what the real 'gully epoch' (p 31) must have been like. It was not climbed until 1952 and when we were there recently it gave little evidence of frequent usage, so that we removed, with due discretion, a considerable amount of loose rock and vegetation. Chimneys, caves, chockstones and mossy walls succeed each other, with some short intermissions up scree; after passing a ledge sloping from the right a third of the way up there are no more escape routes and the party is committed to the climb. Nearly twenty routes have been made on Hutaple, some very hard, not always easy to follow and interrupted by a good deal of vegetation and ledges cluttered with loose stones. In places the mossy and lichenous slabs have an uncomfortable greasy feel except after a prolonged dry period. Probably the best climb is *Sleet Wall* (S) on the buttress well to the left of Curving Gully; its start can be recognised up a steep gangway trending left and it then takes a satisfyingly direct line to a large terrace where several other routes end. This gives over 300ft of quite continuous climbing, succeeded by a further 200ft of scrambling up little walls from one ledge to another to the top of the crag.

To the right of Hutaple Crag, separated from it by an easy-angled scree shoot (which can be used for a safe descent from the ridge), is the prominent Black Buttress (2), on which a couple of climbs have been made; *Portcullis Ridge* (hard VD) goes up the right side of the face and provides a continuous series of ribs, walls and grooves, with nice short pitches.

Link Cove is almost enclosed by a prominent rock bar, up which one can take a scrambling line beside a little tumbling rill; from its crest is obtained an awesome view of the walls and grooves of Scrubby Crag (94), a cliff on the south-eastern face of the combe with its left wing resting on the summit screes of Link Hause. A path skirts the base, from which broken grassy ledges and walls lead to the foot of the climbs. For much of its length the crag is crossed at above mid-height by a remarkably well defined grassy terrace known as Long Ledge. As a result the hard direct climbs, of which the most attractive are *Beowulf* (VS), *Grendel* (mild VS), taking a very well marked V-groove up its centre and *Hrothgar* (VS), have distinct lower and upper sections separated by this ledge, which is fortunately well supplied with belays, though one or two stances require the insertion of pitons for security. An impressive introduction to the crag, visiting virtually all the climbs, is provided by a route known as *Long Ledge Entry and Exit* (VD), which gives what might fairly claim to be the most exposed walk in Lakeland. Near the left of the crag a prominent right-angled corner leads into the steep *Juniper Crack* (S); after climbing its initial pitch an awkward little rightward traverse, involving some slabs and a short up and down move, ends on Long Ledge, where a thread belay can be fixed in a crack at the back of a shallow cave. Long Ledge is then followed sensationally but easily right across the crag, using a runner at suitable intervals for peace of mind when rounding corners and for the ascent of a little chimney, until its right-hand edge is reached above a shallow bay. A short descent and traverse to the right leads to an easy scrambling exit leftward to the top of the cliff. It must be emphasised that climbing on Scrubby is a serious undertaking; its base lies at about 2,300ft and with the plentiful vegetation it does not dry easily. One fine day in January we arrived to find the rock cold and wet and after abortive attempts at several bottom pitches we abandoned it.

THE DOVEDALE CRAGS

Dovedale is the third and most southerly of the sister dales, opening out into the main valley just above Brothers Water; access to traffic along the side road to Hartsop Hall, owned by the National Trust, is now closed, so a car should be left in the park near the foot of the lake. The path leads along its western shores past the Hall and through the trees on the lower slopes. An ascending traverse to the right leads up to a sweep of ice-worn slabs known as Gill Crag (34) or in earlier days simply as Deepdale Slabs, situated on the southern flanks of Hartsop above How at about 1,700ft, only about an hour from the road. These south-facing outcrops with their rough texture form a delightful practice ground for a summer's day and an excellent place for beginners, since the friendly reassuring feel of the rock inspires confidence in the use of small footholds; on occasions we have here dallied the day away pleasurably in the sunshine rather than move on to more strenuous things. There are three or four slab climbs on clean rock, 150ft or more in length, though the climber can in several places work out his own variants, as the scratched rocks indicate. One climb, *Main Slab* route, goes right up the slabs to a prominent pinnacle known as The Perch; it has a second pitch with a runout of 110ft with no possibility of fixing runners, so that although it is only of VD standard it cannot be regarded too lightly. The hardest route, *Corner and Wall* (hard S), though somewhat contrived, is useful in that it extends the climber while he is on this friendly little outcrop.

Dovedale is of course dominated by Dove Crag (22) and one feels its presence looming ever more largely during the walk up the valley (plate p 89) and into the boulder-strewn basin of Hunsett Cove. A steep ascent over scree leads to the base of the crag at about 2,000ft. Its right-hand buttress, fiercely overhanging by about 12ft from the vertical, was first climbed in 1970 by artificial methods after years of abortive attempts, while its left-hand buttress contains six hard routes of which four are of XS category.

Dove is bounded on the left by the scree-filled South Gully, into the right wall of which at half-height opens the overhanging cleft of *Inaccessible Gully*; this provides a difficult problem of mild VS standard, usually involving combined tactics for the second pitch. The *Tarsus* (hard S) takes a line up the wall of South Gully, with several distinctly awkward moves and situations involving some blocks and flakes of dubious quality; such is the unrelenting steepness of the rocks that the route is compelled to finish up the last two pitches of *Westmorland's* route. The latter, of hard VD category, is the only route on Dove for ordinary climbers; it starts near the lowest point of the rocks and follows an obvious line up the left-hand side of the buttress; several variants are possible and the exposure at certain points is appreciable. The rock in some places is suspect, and on our last visit the second man, while intentionally disposing of a loose block after the leftward traverse on the sixth pitch, started a large rock fall which crashed alarmingly and sulphurously into the gully below. The climbs ends at the top of the crag and a short scramble leads to the summit plateau.

OTHER EASTERN CRAGS

For low level enthusiasts in the Ullswater area, Gowbarrow Crag (39) is visible from the road just past Dobbinwood Lodge and is situated a mile east of Aira Point. The crag rises prominently above the wooded lower slopes of Green Hill, the southern flank of Gowbarrow Fell, whose summit gives a fine view of the head of the lake. The approach is along a path winding upwards past some small outcrops, the second of which provides a two-pitch climb named the *Whistler* (hard S). A short ridge leads from the lowest point of the crag to an obvious overhang, surmounted by a pull over to the right on superb holds, followed by a diagonal leftward traverse; the second pitch after crossing some blocks takes to the arête. The main crag is thickly vegetated at its base and scrubby oaks growing out of cracks form excellent belays, yet the rock itself is remarkably clean. Where the path meets the left side of the cliff, *Gowbarrow Buttress* (hard S) offers a varied 130ft of climbing, with a groove, crack and chimney in succession. On the impressive wall rising above an expanse of lush undergrowth is the one-pitch strenuous crack climb called *Susan* (VS); this becomes extremely difficult at the point where it bends, especially when wet, and a jamming technique is needed to gain a comforting flake above. At the lowest point of the buttress starts the four-pitch *Birkett's View* (hard VD), its lower pitches taking a line up a wall whose upper part is shattered, where the rock must be treated with especial care. Higher up, follow a crack and a final corner ending with a strenuous pull over a jammed flake to a rocky belvedere with a commanding view. A girdle traverse has been made from right to left, giving 250ft of climbing with sufficiently exacting problems to merit deservedly a hard VS grading.

During the post-war period when the search began not only for 'new' crags but also for hitherto neglected valleys, Swindale was the first in which some low-level routes were worked out. This secluded valley lies to the east of Mardale, separated from it by a long ridge from Rosgill to the grassy hump of Selside Pike with steep broken rocks dominating its head. This area has the distinction of being the most easterly climbing ground of Lakeland and is well away from the main currents of tourism, even though it is easily reached from Bampton, Rosgill or Shap and is near both the A6 and M6 roads. The main attraction is Gouther Crag (38) about three miles up the valley on its south side opposite Truss Gap farm. It consists of five buttresses, though the one on the extreme right has only a few unnamed scrambling lines; while they face north-west, their low sheltered position makes them attractive in winter and the rock is sound and clean. On the extreme left (east), the North-East Buttress has several recently developed climbs, while the adjoining *Truss Buttress* gives a nice VD route up a clean-cut prominent ridge. Farther right is Fang Buttress, so called after the *Fang*, one of the first climbs to be worked out in the area, a hard S which has maintained its original grading. The start is made on the right, followed by an obvious traverse line left to a ledge, where a piton is used to safeguard the leader for a very steep crack; above this are an attractive arête and a final twin-cracks pitch. *Sostenuto* (hard VS), some 40ft left of the Fang, gives

Page 125 The Napes Needle, Great Gable

Page 126 (above left) The Abbey Buttress, the Napes, Great Gable; (above right) Witch, Buckbarrow, Wasdale; (below) Great Gable from Down in the Dale, Wasdale

a more difficult and quite exposed climb with four varied pitches, finishing up the last pitch of the *Fang*. On this area of slabby rock (following the canine nomenclature initiated by the *Fang*), the *Foreleg* and the *Kennel Wall* (both VD) form worthy routes. At the top of this wall is *Hindleg Crack* (mild S), on which a rather broken chimney contains some loose blocks which need care, ending in a strenuous pull out left above the overhang. The *Nymph* (hard VS), situated on the fourth buttress, gives 150ft of steep unrelenting climbing and is quite the best route in the valley.

Buckbarrow Crag (13) forms a conspicuous outcrop on the southwestern slopes of Tarn Crag, a lonely grassy summit overlooking the upper reaches of Long Sleddale. About twenty climbs of varying difficulty are available; despite its lonely situation, several were made during an early phase of exploration around 1929–31, though most of the harder ones were worked out in the 1960s. As one approaches the crag it looks most impressive, though on closer acquaintance it is seen to have much vegetation and the rock is more broken than seemed at first sight.

Down to the left Low Crag comprises a series of broken ribs and grooves providing some quite hard climbs; on its right edge the easier *Waterfall Buttress* (D) follows an arête which however degenerates into rather broken rocks. The higher crag is divided by the sloping and deeply cut Cleft Gill into two sections, The Dandle and High Crag. The former offers *Dandle Buttress* (hard D), which takes the obvious left-hand ridge starting below a big cave in Cleft Gill. Farther to the right *Dandle Slabs* (S) is a long climb of nearly 350ft taking a leftish line up The Dandle, with several good slabs and chimneys; these two climbs were in fact the first to be made on Buckbarrow. On High Crag, dominated by a clearly defined sharp arête, are two good routes: the *Minotaur* (VS) up the arête itself, steep and exposed, and the much more amenable *Eagles' Nest* (hard VD), which follows a groove on the left-hand of the arête for 140ft, finishing up Cleft Gully.

H

7

LANGDALE

THE Great Langdale valley extends westward from near the head of Windermere into the heart of the high fells, though its floor almost up to the head lies at only about 300ft. It forms a line of transition between on the one hand the tourist frequented shores of Windermere and the gentle beauty of Rydal and Grasmere, and on the other the rugged mountains at the centre of the Lakeland massif. Eight miles of winding road lead from Ambleside to the Old Dungeon Ghyll Hotel (ODG) through the small picturesque villages of Skelwith Bridge, Elterwater and Chapel Stile, where most buildings are made of the locally quarried green slate. The valley is better supplied with hotels than most, several outdoor activities centres have been opened, and Youth Hostels are at Elterwater and on the Red Bank road to Grasmere.

At one time indiscriminate camping made the valley hideous during summer weekends, though it is now restricted to a few specified sites, notably a large and very popular one owned by the National Trust near the ODG. A successful development by the Lake District Planning Board at Neaum Crag near Elterwater takes advantage of a wooded hillside, with rocky outcrops, clumps of trees and rhododendrons, and expanses of turf providing naturally screened sites at different levels for chalets, caravans and tents.

Traffic problems are acute because of Langdale's ready accessibility from the south, involving at times both the choking of the access road from Ambleside and the saturation of the limited parking space; suggestions have been put forward by the authorities for some form of control. Though Great Langdale is not a cul-de-sac, there is a distinct tidal flow of traffic up and down the narrow valley during summer weekends, complicated by the essential service buses. From beyond the ODG a road climbs out of the valley southward over a col and past Blea Tarn, then down a rocky valley floored with rough grazing and bracken and studded with clusters of dark juniper, so into Little Langdale, the valley of the River Brathay, attractively secluded and peaceful for much of the year.

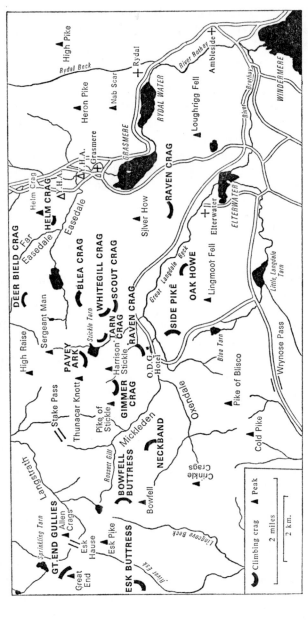

FIG 6. The Langdale district

The motorist can then continue either eastward back to Ambleside or westward over Wrynose Pass into Dunnerdale; these roads are steep, winding and narrow, lined with stone walls from which projecting boulders await an incautious motorist's wing and during summer weekends they are best avoided.

The steep northern wall of Great Langdale rises to a broken grassy plateau-ridge extending in a north-westerly direction from Loughrigg Fell above Grasmere over Silver How, Yew Crag and Tarn Crag towards the Langdale Pikes. Here the high ground is continuous with the north—south ridge between Borrowdale and Thirlmere, culminating in the undistinguished grassy summit of High Raise. The valley sides are craggy, scree slopes alternating with thick bracken, scattered holly and juniper, and rough grazing.

Few mountains so dominate a Lakeland view as the twin Langdale Pikes when viewed either distantly from the main road along the eastern shores of Windermere and from the terrace of the National Park Centre at Brockhole, or more nearly in Great Langdale itself (plate p 90). It is difficult to believe that the higher of the two Pikes, Harrison Stickle, rises barely 2,000ft above the valley floor, for it is the concentrated nature of this rise that gives it emphasis and impact. Unlike many Lakeland mountains the Pikes present their boldest profiles where most people can see them, that is, from their cars on a nearby road. The nature of the Borrowdale Volcanic rocks has dramatic effects upon the relief; tough beds form prominent buttresses, terraces and steps on the valley flanks, emphasised by the gentler slopes of less resistant rocks and by deeply incised gullies. But though hard the rocks are strongly jointed and prone to frost shattering, so that scree streams away below the crags; a narrow tongue of pale scree where recent falls of rock have obviously occurred descends from the gap to the east of Pike of Stickle almost to the valley bottom. On the southern side of the Pike an outcrop of rock was the source of raw material for a flourishing Neolithic and early Bronze Age industry: the making of axes for export to many parts of Britain.

Rounding the last sweeping curve of Great Langdale, the aspect of the Pikes changes into a series of rocky turrets on its northern wall, ceasing to dominate the valley head, which is now seen to be split by a long ridge known as the Band projecting boldly eastward from the summit of Bowfell. To its north lies Mickleden; its floor, flat, turf carpeted and neatly patterned with stone-walled fields, then becomes hummocky before rising to the surrounding rim of broken crags and scree. To the south of the Band is the more remote Oxendale, at first flat-floored and swampy, its upper recesses craggy and boulder strewn, gathering its headstreams (Browney and Crinkle Gills and Buscoe Sike) from the serrated ridge of the Crinkle Crags through deeply cut ravines. Now it becomes evident that the dominating peak of Langdale is Bowfell, though it is of course shared with Eskdale and Langstrath; despite its mild-sounding name this is one of Lakeland's eminent mountains.

FELL WALKS IN THE LANGDALE DISTRICT

From the head of Great Langdale well trodden ways lead across the mountains to the western valleys. A track runs up Mickleden to where Rossett and Stake Gills converge near a sheepfold to form the Great Langdale Beck, where diverge two clearly marked tracks. One zigzags steeply to the left of Stake Gill, then rises more gently through the marshy floor of Langdale Cove to the Stake Pass at 1,576ft, descending into Langstrath and hence to Stonethwaite and Borrowdale (p 91). The other path, eroded by the boots of generations, bears wearily beside the steep gash of Rossett Gill to a pass which just tops the 2,000ft contour before dropping to the darkly brooding Angle Tarn, rising again to the shelter below Esk Hause (p 177) and so by way of Sprinkling Tarn to Sty Head and Wasdale. This is possibly the most popular walker's route in Lakeland, since it crosses the heart of the central dome and from it several valleys and summits can easily be reached. The most direct line between Langdale and Eskdale goes by way of either the Band or Oxendale to the watershed ridge at Three Tarns, where three tiny pools lie in hollows on the col between Bowfell and the Crinkle Crags at a height of about 2,300ft. This col is extensive and rather featureless except for the tarns, and in bad weather conditions it is all too easy, unless working strictly by compass, to lose one's sense of direction and land down in the remote recesses of upper Eskdale in mistake for Langdale.

Profusely cairned, heavily scarred paths make their ways to the various summits, all popular and frequently ascended. Alternative lines lead up Harrison Stickle from behind the New Dungeon Ghyll

Hotel (NDG), half a mile down the valley from the ODG; the most interesting follows the deeply incised course of Dungeon Gill, with its fine cascades, deep pools and ravines, the upper parts of which are less visited and much more attractive than the lower reaches. At the top of the highest ravine, eroded in the crumbling reddish rocks, a scrambling line to the right leads to the summit rocks of Harrison Stickle. Alternatively, a path up Mill Gill valley goes from behind the NDG into the combe containing Stickle Tarn, enclosed by a man-made dam at its south-eastern corner and backed by the deeply gullied crag of Pavey Ark. A winding path leads from the tarn to the summit of Harrison Stickle, or a direct, quite steep scramble may be made up its rocky north-eastern ridge. Pike of Stickle, about a half-mile west of its twin, is reached across a marshy depression, followed by easy scrambling to its summit, variously described as a thumb, a thimble, a sugar loaf or a beehive according to the angle from which it is viewed. It is surprising that there is so much rock on the two Pikes yet so little real climbing, though a few possibilities have been recorded. Ascents of Pike of Stickle can be made directly from Mickleden alongside Troughton Beck or more easily from the top of the Stake Pass. After a day on Gimmer, the climber can continue to the summit of Loft Crag, not even named on the 1″ OS map, of which Gimmer is its southern buttress, thence easily to either Pike; the three tops are located at the apexes of a triangle and strictly therefore the Langdale Pikes are triplets rather than twins.

Several ridge walks are possible from the Pikes, though in contrast to their steep and rocky Langdale flanks the northern side of the group consists of a series of not very interesting grassy eminences which swell gently from a broad ridge trending away northward. From the hump of Thunacar Knott the walker can continue to High Raise, sometimes called the true central summit of all Lakeland, a splendid viewpoint if a disappointing top, then to Greenup Edge and Ullscarf (p 92). The walker bound for Grasmere can cross Sergeant Man and drop down either into the rocky recesses of Easedale by way of Codale and Easedale Tarns, or into Far Easedale, the next valley to the north, chiefly notable because the fine buttress of Deer Bield projects from its southern wall.

Bowfell can be climbed by several alternative routes from Langdale, the most obvious taking the Band from Stool End Farm, a clearly defined and gradual trod over grass, stones and occasional slabs, keeping mainly to the Oxendale flank of the ridge until it levels off into a grassy, rather marshy plateau. The shapely summit cone, triangular in profile from almost any angle, can then be reached either directly ahead up scree and easy rock or by a path swinging leftward to the Three Tarns col, thence by a tediously stony plod up the south ridge. The main charm of the ascent through Oxendale is the rock scenery and waterfalls in the beds of the gills, notably the spectacular Whorneyside Force and the steep trench of Hell Gill containing Buscoe Sike, the most northerly headstream, and so to Three Tarns. The walker from Borrowdale has a long tramp up Langstrath (p 91) before arriving at Angle Tarn, beyond which he can either detour to the col at about 2,600ft between Bowfell and Esk Pike known as Ore Gap, presumably because of the reddish iron-stained rocks, or scramble directly up a stony gully to the summit ridge.

On the north-eastern side of Bowfell several prominent crags are separated by scree slopes, reached from the Band by a high-level traverse across the face at a height of about 2,600ft, the start of which is not altogether easy to find in mist; under snowy conditions this path appears quite exposed. The face can also be reached, somewhat laboriously, direct from Mickleden over steep slopes of grass and boulders, or by ascending Rossett Pass and traversing southward across the shoulder of the mountain. Under the summit is Cambridge Crag, easily recognisable because, except after prolonged drought, a powerful gush of cold spring water issues from a joint plane near its base. To the right is the steep North Buttress, and lower down across a scree fan looms the prominent prow of Bowfell Buttress. Also of interest, situated to the left (south) of these crags and visible from the summit of the mountain, is an enormous low-angled slab, the upper exposure of Flat Crags, a great pile of strongly bedded volcanic rocks. Several scrambling routes, interesting under winter conditions, can be made directly to the summit from the traverse, notably up the sloping rake below and to the left of Cambridge Crag and between the latter and the Buttress. The Eskdale face of Bowfell is likewise craggy, with a series of broken buttresses separated by gullies, the whole known as Bowfell Links (plate p 107); they consist of rotten rock and are best avoided except when everything is hard frozen.

The Crinkle Crags form another section of the watershed ridge between Langdale and Eskdale, with five distinct knobs or 'crinkles' falling on each side to broken crags and boulder slopes. A well scratched track twists in and out, up and down, along the ridge, though the scrambler can choose his own line, preferably keeping to the exact crest. The traverse even includes a miniature 'bad step', a tiny gully with a chockstone, when descending the fourth crinkle (in order from north to south). Between the second crinkle (at 2,816ft the highest) and the third is the easily recognisable Mickle Door, a broad gap with scree on either side, a useful reference point in mist, and if the ridge is continued northward towards Three Tarns, two more knobs on Shelter Crag are crossed. While the traverse of the Crinkles in summer is an easy scramble, under real winter conditions it can provide a stimulating even exacting expedition.

A recommended day's outing is the round of Oxendale, or better still of the whole head of Langdale, starting from Pike of Blisco in the south-east, distinguished by its tall shapely cairn visible from virtually every direction. It can be reached either from the top of Wrynose Pass which gives a start of 1,270ft of height but requires the collaboration of a car driver, or from Wall End in Langdale and up the valley of Redacre Gill, leaving the prominent Kettle Crag on the right and scrambling up a series of terraces to the summit. From Blisco a short descent leads to Red Tarn, thence up to Cold Pike with its three rocky summits, after which a marshy plateau is crossed for almost a mile before the first rocks of the Crinkles are gained; these are traversed to Shelter Crags and down to Three Tarns, then up again to Bowfell. The walk can be continued down Bowfell's north-eastern ridge to Rossett Pass and along the ridge above the head of Mickleden to the Stake Pass, finally back to the NDG by way of the Langdale Pikes. This provides a fine high-level route of about eleven miles with varied terrain and superb views; an average time is about eight hours. One is not committed to the entire length, for several earlier lines of descent by way of the Band or Rossett Gill can be taken if desired.

ROCK CLIMBING IN THE LANGDALE DISTRICT

The numerous crags of varied character in the Langdale district have provided scope for climbers of successive generations. In the 'chimney and gully' phase (p 31) the great cliff of Pavey Ark offered obvious lines. In the 'slab and wall' epoch the silver-grey outcrop of Gimmer rising enticingly above the valley offered ample opportunities for those who could venture on to smooth rock with small holds and a degree of exposure; some of these climbs, such as the earliest of the 'alphabet' routes, were climbed during the early years of this century, and there was a tremendous acceleration after World War I, mainly under the influence of G. S. Bower. After World War II the ready accessibility of Langdale encouraged a great expansion of activity and the total number of ascents each year is far greater than in any other district. The major crags have been combed by leaders with the necessary technique and outlook; this was especially true of Pavey Ark, once visited only for its gullies and chimneys, now festooned with over fifty routes up its slabs, culminating in the XS *Astra* and the *Hobbit*. Gimmer too was the scene of 'fill-in' activity of a high order, including such landmarks as R. J. Birkett's *F* route in 1941, the last so far of the lettered series on the western face, and Arthur Dolphin's *Kipling Groove* (hard VS), which takes a superb line up the angle between the west and north-west faces (plate p 90); this was only one of his many climbs (perhaps his greatest was Deer Bield Buttress), before he lost his life in 1953 on the Aiguille du Géant in the Mont Blanc massif. The north-eastern face of Bowfell has also yielded some very hard routes, including the *Sword of Damocles*, an XS on the North Crag climbed as early as 1952, so called because of a large and insecure flake pointing ominously downwards. The sheer pressure on the climbing resources of the valley inevitably led to the combing of so-called minor crags: White Gill, Raven Crag, Deer Bield and others. The 1967 edition of the F&RCC Guidebook to Great Langdale by J. A. Austin, who has figured so prominently in the list of recent first ascents, is the bulkiest in the series. It includes 250 climbs on more than twenty crags; nearly a third are of mild Severe or easier grade while sixty are hard VS or XS, so that the district caters for everyone from beginners to experts. Low-lying

crags provide for short days or in winter, escaping much of the
low mist which so often carries a threat of rain and can be damaging
to harder climbs by causing a greasy film on the rocks, while the
higher crags offer splendid long routes as part of a mountaineering
day.

GIMMER CRAG (36)

This buttress leans against the northern wall of Great Langdale
to the south-east of the summit of Loft Crag. It is a singularly
compact mass of hard rock, structurally separated from the mountain by the shatter belt of a massive, steeply inclined fault which
manifests itself in the two bounding clefts: the short South-East
Gully facing down the valley and on the opposite side Junipall Gully
(plate p 90) falling steeply into the scree-filled North-West
Gully. Each forms a convenient line of descent from the top of
the buttress, though care is needed in PA's on loose scree and in
places damp vegetation. From the ODG a path traverses scree across
the face of the mountain; Gimmer comes welcomingly into sight
after crossing a little col, where a good impression is obtained of
its profile. The broken lower rocks rise in tiers for about 300ft,
when the angle abruptly steepens and the face sweeps up smoothly
to its gently rounded top.

Gimmer has three major faces. The narrow south-east face is
split by the distinct parallel cracks of Gimmer Chimney, while the
west face rises above the terraces at the foot of the steep section.
This abuts round the corner on to the north-west face, of very
different character, for here can be seen the effects of closely parallel
faults at a high angle, producing a series of steeply inclined grooves,
cracks and slabs. In addition to the main crag, the flanking rocks
on either side offer further routes: on the right (east) of South-
East Gully is Main Wall, on the left of Junipall Gully is Pallid
Buttress. Thus Gimmer provides a variety of routes on superlative
rock, which, since the crag has been popular since the beginning of
this century, is clean and well scratched, so much so that some
moves have become more difficult because of the wearing and
polishing of the holds. The climbs meet all moods, whether one is
inclined to tiptoe precisely in PA's up splendidly continuous slabs,
revelling in the fine sense of exposure, or to cope with something
more strenuous 'round the corner'.

On the south-east face *Gimmer Chimney* (VD) provides an old-time route with short pitches and good belays; it consists of closely parallel twin cracks, using the left one as far as the fifth pitch, where it is necessary to walk a few yards along a terrace to the foot of the much easier right-hand chimney and continue up that. The much more strenuous upper section of the left chimney is included in the excellent route known as *Bracket and Slab* (mild S), which gives a varied climb of nearly 300ft from near the base of the crag. It includes some delightful pitches, notably a traverse followed by a groove (the Bracket) and a delicate little move up a diagonal ledge and a thin crack called the Neat Bit.

The west face is reached by an easy scramble up the Bilberry Chute, hence over stepped rocks to Ash-tree Ledge where the climbs start. Here the alphabet climbs from *A* to *F* pursue their elegant lines, with their named and well loved pitches. *A*, an excellent hard VD climb, though given an S rating in the earlier Guidebooks, goes off left up Thomson's Ledge (he was a Gimmer pioneer), then via the Forty Foot Corner to the greenish Lichen Chimney. *B* (mild S) moves right to a slanting crack on a little overhanging wall; this is Amen Corner, supposedly called from the pious murmurings of the second man in response to his leader's imprecations, though it is easily climbed by a layback with hands and feet close together, three quickly transferred pounces reaching the top of the corner. Above is the Green Chimney, at the top of which a traverse right leads to a neat ledge known as the Crow's Nest, and then a sweep of easy slabs to the top. *C* (S) takes a straight line between *A* and *B*, steep but with superb holds wherever needed. The lower part of *E* (hard S) was originally made as an alternative start to *A* but later an independent finish was worked out via the bottom of Lichen Chimney and a rising traverse to the steep wall parallel to *C*. *D* (S) is short but steep, including the Forked Lightning Crack, while *F* (VS) takes a strenuous line to the left of *D* up an overhanging crack.

The north-west face is divided into two parts, a lower section on which some short climbs finish at Ash-tree Ledge, and the main upper section. Among the several hard routes of character on the former (notably *Asterisk* (hard S) and *Joas* (VS)) are two milder climbs well worth doing, *Herdwick Buttress* and *Ash-tree Slabs*

(both hard VD). If the latter is followed by *D*, just across Ash-tree
Ledge to the right, a fine route of over 250ft can be enjoyed.

The upper section of the north-west face has half a dozen good
routes, of which the *Crack* (mild VS) is outstanding, since it
follows a natural and continuous line to the top of the crag (plate
p 90). Though only 240ft overall, it is split into nine concise pitches,
well supplied with stances, thread belays and opportunities for fixing
runners before each crucial move. Though the Crack itself is followed closely, on the third pitch a neat traverse on small flakes on
to the left-hand wall avoids a particularly strenuous continuation;
this bypassed section has now been climbed and forms part of the
XS *Gimmer String*, at present the hardest route on the crag, taking
the very steep arête between the Crack and Kipling Groove. The
Crack is rejoined higher up at a vertical slot (Sentry Box), where
a hard move leads to a ledge (Bower), above which the crack is
followed to its final problem, an appreciable overhang. To the left
of the Crack *Hiatus* (VS) takes a line up the slabs to a series of
overhangs, beneath which an exposed leftward traverse provides
the main feature of this excellent climb.

Away to the left of this face on the wall of Junipall Gully is
Juniper Buttress (mild S), involving a long horizontal traverse to
the right into an obvious groove, succeeded higher by a traverse
back along ledges on which the junipers still grow despite the
passage of boots. The central section between the two traverses
forms part of the long continuous *Godiva Groove* (mild VS), whose
top pitch is very steep and exposed; this was climbed right through
twenty-eight years after the first ascent of the Buttress which had
borrowed its mid-section.

Finally, the stretch of pale grey rock to the left of Junipall Gully
yields several climbs, of which *Pallid Slabs* (S) is the most attractive. It is steep and in parts quite delicate, though its line is somewhat wandering; holds are sometimes rather infrequent but always
adequate.

PAVEY ARK (76)

Pavey is an enormous bow-shaped crag overlooking Stickle Tarn
to the north-west of Harrison Stickle, visible from the road near
the NDG. From the eastern shore of the tarn it looks extremely
impressive, even intimidating, as it rises abruptly for over 400ft

from its base, narrowing and falling away to the scree-covered fell-side on either flank. Even from a distance it is obvious that the crag is much broken up, heavily vegetated and in places wet and black with moss, though there are also some fine sweeps of clean rock where the new very hard routes have been made. Over to the left are the black clefts of the Little and Great Gullies, then Stony Buttress with the white scars of recent rock falls and bounded on its right by a shallow, rather messy groove known as the Crescent.

The central part of the crag forms a blunted equilateral triangle, its apex cut by the diagonal Jack's Rake slanting up leftwards across the crag at an angle of about 30°, a remarkable structural line of a closely parallel pair of faults. It is normally an easy scramble with little sense of exposure, up rocky grooves interlinking grassy terraces, though we recall a winter ascent a few years ago, with snow on the ledges and ice in the grooves, which took several hours. At the top of the Rake, beyond the Great Gully, the rock changes from its rather slabby character to the roughest imaginable, a kind of volcanic agglomerate which has weathered to give a spiky surface. The Ark above Jack's Rake leans back in a series of buttresses separated by extensive vegetated ledges, with plenty of trees for belays. Over to the right is the finest piece of rock on Pavey, the East Buttress, which bends round to the right above Easy Gully to form the impending East Wall, where most of the recent hard VS and XS climbs have been made.

Obviously Pavey's gullies and chimneys offered routes beloved by the pioneers, and these were climbed before the end of last century. *Great Gully* (D) is quite entertaining, with its Cave Pitch and in the bed of the gully the Brant and Slape slab (Cumbrian for steep and slippery). The short *Gwynne's Chimney* (D), divided into two pitches by an oblong chockstone known as the Gun, and the much longer *Rake End Chimney* (D) over to the right, separated into two distinct sections by a walk up the open bed of the gully, are both pleasant if one likes chimneys.

One of the earliest routes to leave the immured security of these gullies was *Crescent Slabs* (S) to the right of the mossy parts of the central crag; this gives 200ft of good climbing, sections of slab being linked by small grooves and scoops. Above Jack's Rake a few routes pursue strenuous lines up steep sections, hard moves

being separated by vegetated ledges and scoops. The well named
Cook's Tour (VD) takes a wandering line for 300ft up these higher
parts, starting from a narrow chimney halfway along the Rake; it
is not altogether easy to follow, but in due course it reaches the
top of the crag.

Probably the best route on Pavey for average climbers is *Stoats'
Crack* (hard S), a long climb of nearly 400ft starting just right of
the toe of the East Buttress at the foot of Easy Gully. The crack
itself, formed by an immense flake leaning against the massive
wall, starts some 50ft up and is reached by a rather wet and
vegetated corner followed by a short traverse. Two-thirds of the
way up it is necessary to make a leftward traverse over several
interconnected ledges, unless one takes a much more severe alternative straight up the wall behind. The upper third of the climb
interlinks some slabs and short walls by grooves and ledges.

Nearly forty routes have been made on this crag, many of an
exacting character. One great disadvantage is that it is high-lying,
and with its extensive vegetation it takes a long time to dry out.
Nevertheless, it is a mountaineer's crag, well worthy of a visit,
especially as part of a long outing taking in several crags and tops.

BOWFELL

A small outcrop just under the summit of the Band on its Mickleden flank, called rather obviously the Neckband (73), provides a
number of short steep climbs. The original route on the right of
the crag, the *Neckband* itself (VD), was climbed as long ago as
1924 and its line is well marked. Apart from this, half a dozen
very hard climbs have been put up its mossy, rather dank walls,
including four of XS grade, a surprising distinction for what seems
after all a very minor crag.

A high-level traverse across the north-eastern face of the mountain (p 133) passes under several crags, of which the Cambridge
and Bowfell Buttresses (9) offer most prospects. Flat Crag has
only a couple of hard, rather contrived routes, while those on the
North Buttress, with its steep and formidable grooves, will extend
the expert. The Cambridge Crag consists of a bold mass 250ft in
height, split by a distinctive joint pattern into a series of ribs and
grooves. The *Cambridge* climb (D) starts from the base of the buttress below an obvious gangway slanting up to the right and then

works its way up by varied stages, including a chimney and a steep wall with excellent holds, though it fades out near the top and a loose gully leads to the summit ridge. This gives a mountaineering kind of route of about 250ft; though scratched, it has not been cleaned off very well and under damp conditions its difficulty increases considerably. Above and to the left is *Borstal Buttress* (S), so named as a debunking of the Cambridge climb, but it is an unsatisfactory route since most difficulties can be bypassed up rather messy grass on its flanks.

Bowfell Buttress is a massive prow connected with the mountain by a narrow little neck. The rock shows a well-defined parallel jointing at an angle aligned only slightly from the vertical, and as a result to the left of the prow are alternating grooves and ribs, while to the right the exposed joint-plane provides a sweep of smooth slabs. *Bowfell Buttress* is one of the very good routes of its grade, though technically of only hard D standard. Yet because it lies so high and is a nine-pitch climb of 350ft, it is quite an undertaking and under inclement conditions it can become serious. It was first climbed as long ago as 1902 and since it has maintained its popularity the line is well scratched. It starts from a small cairn to the left of the lowest part of the crag. The climbing is varied, including a traverse with an awkward leftward step on smooth, sloping holds, and has good stances and belays. An easier climb is the *Plaque* route (D), following a curving line on the left edge of the Buttress. If conditions are good, several harder routes include *Sinister Slabs* and the *Central* route (both hard S). *Rubicon Groove* (hard VS) takes a direct line up the most prominent sequence of sharp grooves rising steeply above the first pitch of the Buttress climb; the hardest climbing comes in the first part of the groove, after which the rocks lean back. Over on the right-hand wall of the Buttress several steep slab climbs have been worked out, including the rather contrived but very exacting *Eliminate* (hard VS).

RAVEN CRAG (83)

Climbers in the past bound for Gimmer were wont to take to the rocks and gain height by climbing *Middlefell Buttress* (D) as a change from the winding path. Another possibility was Raven Crag Buttress on the right by the *Original* route (mild S), starting at almost the lowest point of the crag, an agreeable climb, well scratched and easy to follow, steep in its middle section and with a rather exposed top pitch. As low crags became popular in their own right, their progressive opening up was inevitable and the name Raven is now applied collectively to the whole series, including Middlefell, Raven itself, East and Far East Raven Crags. The main crag, steep and crowned in the centre by overhangs, now has some twenty routes, together with a couple of 'artificials'. The *Holly Tree Direct* (VS) takes the natural line of a long groove crowned by a holly, difficult to enter because of its initial overhang which is in fact avoided by a delicate traverse. At the top of the third pitch this climb joins the *Holly Tree Traverse* (VD), which takes a rather wandering line but is well worth doing. Farther round the base of the crag, passing under the overhangs of *Pluto* (hard VS), the next climb of merit is *Bilberry Buttress* (VS) down to the right, which maintains its standard right up to its exposed top pitch, and *Savernake* (mild S) is its less direct companion. Up the scree on the right is *Revelation* (S), furnished with good holds, which are particularly necessary on a 50ft pitch comprising a wall with a strenuous crack start and crowned by a nose (plate p 107). Beyond Raven Crag a shallow grassy depression, the Amphitheatre, has several routes on its bounding walls, of which the most recommended is *Centipede* (mild S), which gives 300ft of varied climbing with a rib, several traverses and a steep wall.

On the first of the smaller East Raven faces are several routes of the 100ft, one- or two-pitch variety, the first group named with a Sherlock Holmes motif, the second with a Middle-eastern flavour. *Watson*, a single 100ft arête pitch (hard S), and *Schizen Groove* (mild VS) are typical. The real charm of this area lies about 300 yards farther on, where we would select *Babylon* (hard VS), which merits its ranking mainly because of the manner in which the last pitch, reached by relatively easy climbing, breaks through the summit overhangs by a very thin scoop. *Nineveh* (VS) gives a somewhat milder three-pitch line, which we found more pleasant than the Guidebook would suggest. *Samarkand* (hard VS) is an excellent climb on sound rock, the crux being a delicate leftward traverse from a piton in place in a groove, though the climb is compelled to finish up the last pitch of *Nineveh*. Perhaps the best climb of all on these crags is *Damascus* (VS); after scrambling to a tree, it consists of three strikingly different groove pitches, the

Page 143 The Flake Crack, *Central Buttress*, Scafell

Page 144 The *Gargoyle*, Overbeck Buttress, Yewbarrow

last one necessitating a stiff pull up at the start and some airy bridging to finish.

WHITE GILL CRAGS (108)

A short walk from the NDG diagonally across the grassy slopes into the boulder-strewn bed of White Gill, or by a path by way of the Scout Crags (p 147), leads up to the two fine crags on the eastern (true left) wall of the gully. The upper is the older climbing ground, where in 1930 *The Slabs Route 1* was led by our friend Geoffrey Barker of beloved memory, followed three years later by *Route 2* led by Sid Cross. These are the original classics of the crag, each of a genial mild S category, fine steep slab climbs on the left side of the buttress up rough rock with a plethora of holds; their scratched character is evidence of their popularity. The Chimney climb makes a brief excursus on to these slabs and the Girdle Traverse crosses at a third of their height.

The right-hand side of the slabs runs into the right-angled *White Gill Chimney* (S), formed by the overlapping overhang extending across the face; this was climbed seven years earlier than Route 1, though in fact the actual line does not really use the chimney much but makes brief digressions into it. It is a climb of impressive situations and one is conscious all the time of the overpowering rock on the right. Forty-three years after the original ascent of the Chimney an XS climb was made, laughingly called *Chimney Variant*, leaving the Chimney at the top of its second pitch and boldly striking up to the right through the enormous bulges. The ordinary climber is glad to continue up the Chimney, though here more of a groove, then leaving it for the wall on the left and later traversing back into its final section. One of the earliest of the harder climbs was *Gordian Knot* (mild VS), led after several attempts by J. W. Haggas. This takes a superb line, starting up a clean-cut slab of about 70ft until one is forced to work up leftwards on to its edge and so into a little cave under an overhang. A slightly descending traverse leads to the right over easy broken rocks to a ledge, succeeded by the crux, a thought-provoking corner move, though fortunately with good finishing holds (plate p 107). This is continued by a short but taxing corner-crack after which the final wall, though steep, seems pleasurably comfortable. Half a dozen other hard climbs have been made on this crag, including

I

the tremendously fierce lead by Joe Brown in 1957 up '. . . a particularly improbable line . . .', which produced an XS route punningly named *Eliminot* after all the other 'knot' and 'not' climbs of this area.

The Lower Crag, separated from its neighbour by a slanting grassy rake, is perhaps at first sight not as imposing or as frightening but on acquaintance it proves just as demanding for the climber. Except for one slashing diagonal fault, its structural lines are near vertical, a dozen or so sharply angled pinkish grooves, most ending in triangular overhangs from which it is necessary to escape by traversing to one side or the other. This wall leads to a broad heather-covered platform known as the Great Shelf, above which another tier of rock provides continuation pitches for some climbs. There is a considerable amount of vegetation on this crag, heather, grass, hollies and hyacinths, though apparently much less since a fire burnt everything off a few years ago.

The best route for the ordinary climber is *Hollin Groove* (S), a climb on the extreme left of the crag and including three excellent pitches; its initial groove is not easily entered, though hand-jamming helps. A higher groove of 80ft lands one on the Great Shelf, which rather interrupts the continuity, though the final pitches on the upper tier are well worth doing. Another route of character is *Inferno* (hard S) over to the right of the crag; the climb proper consists of a well defined groove of 120ft, reached by a couple of rather scrambling pitches. The lower part of the groove is complicated by the negotiation of an overhang by means of a bridging movement safeguarded by runners; care should be taken to avoid an apparently sound but actually loose block in the groove of the last pitch. The crag abounds in groove problems from its nature; just to the left of Inferno is *Laugh Not* (hard VS), another Joe Brown lead which as its name implies is an almost guaranteed smile remover.

Unlike its neighbour, this Lower Crag has some easier routes; in fact there are three of VD grade, but they are rather messy, taking lines through broken rock, steep grass and heather; they are probably climbed only when weather conditions make the harder routes out of the question and there are better routes of that grade elsewhere in the valley. *Why Not*, a few feet to the right of Hollin Groove, is the best of this bunch.

OTHER CRAGS IN LANGDALE

The valley has been combed assiduously for climbable rock with such success that there are now a dozen or so minor crags with routes. While these hardly merit a full day's visit, they may pleasurably fill an odd half-day or evening, or they may be visited briefly en route to something more important, such as Tarn Crag on the way to Pavey or Scout Crag as a preliminary to White Gill. The only danger is that they can sometimes take the edge off one's energy or enthusiasm, or prove so genial on a summer day that one never reaches the major crag at all.

Scout Crag (92) lies only a quarter of an hour from the NDG. Leaving the road at a barn, one first passes a huge boulder split vertically into three; its south-facing side has a crack that can sap one's energy for the day. The first outcrop is Lower Scout Crag, scored and polished by innumerable boots; possible lines run everywhere. Scout Crag itself, a few minutes away up the hillside, is a blocky sort of outcrop with some delightful upper slabs, with hollies and junipers growing everywhere. It provides a useful practice ground, especially valuable as training for beginners, and a dozen obvious scratched lines are of D and VD difficulty, with a girdle traverse called rather obviously *Scout's Belt* (VD). One much harder climb, *Salmon Leap* (VS), has been made over to the right under a big blunt overhang.

On the way to Pavey Ark by the Mill Gill path, the blunt cone of Tarn Crag (104) can be seen on the right, a broad buttress of grey rock separated from another narrow one by a grassy bay. The crag is split by parallel, near-vertical joints and the rock is rough; it faces south-west and so receives the afternoon sun. There are more than half a dozen routes, mostly D in standard; someone has obligingly scratched the initials of each climb near its start. *Orchid*, however, is of mild S standard, following a well defined crack and providing nearly 300ft of climbing.

Raven Crag, Walthwaite (85) stands out prominently, square-cut and flat-topped, on the hillside only 200ft above the road from Chapel Stile over Red Bank to Grasmere; the climbs, though short, are steep and quite demanding. On the left hand of the crag *Walthwaite Crack* (VS) requires some strenuous jamming movements; the Guidebook mentions this climb without comment or description, but it is exacting and in fact left us rather limp. The best climb of its grade is *Route 2* (S), starting at the lowest point of the crag near a small ash, while *Deuterus* (VS) nearby provides an exposed climb with a steep top pitch of 90ft requiring a good deal of thought. *Walthwaite Gully* (mild VS) lies in the rather green corner between the main crag and some slabs on its right; it does not look at all inviting but is worthwhile, if only for the layback movement needed to negotiate the 'fierce flake' on the second pitch.

In conjunction with a quiet visit to Blea Tarn, the not too energetic can spend an hour or two on Side Pike (99), a little subsidiary top of Lingmoor Fell. The summit cairn is actually on top of these rocks and though short the climbs are diverting, notably *Spider Crack* (mild S) and *Limpet Grooves* (mild VS). The former has an initial overhang usually avoided by traversing rightward into the crack above it; on our first visit, without the Guidebook, we unwittingly climbed it direct, finding it distinctly strenuous.

While in this neighbourhood a brief visit may be paid to Oak Howe Crag (74), a rocky buttress forming the end of Lingmoor Fell's northern ridge. The crag has been so shattered by weathering, yet is so steep, that no climbing is possible on it. By a quirk, however, a stumpy little pinnacle called *Oak Howe Needle* has survived, which provides climbing of sorts, easy on the short side, harder on the front using either of a pair of steep cracks.

CRAGS IN EASEDALE AND FAR EASEDALE

Far Easedale is reached by a pleasant path from Grasmere. Though the valley sides appear rocky, most is too shattered, vegetated and discontinuous from the point of view of the climber. However, soon after leaving Grasmere the small but steep Helm Crag (54) can be seen some 400ft up the slope on the right; it has five short routes, two of which (*Beacon Rib* and *Flarepath*) are of VS category, steep and delicate, while the all-weather *Holly Tree Crack*, with short pleasant pitches following a defined crack, is of VD standard. Less recommended is Gibson Knott, farther up the valley; it is steep but messily vegetated and only two rather poor climbs have been made there.

Soon after the path crosses the Far Easedale Gill, Deer Bield Crag (20) comes impressively into view, its base about 400ft above the valley floor on the left; the best approach is to strike off up the grass to the left and follow a faint path through a maze of angular boulders. The crag is split by a whole series of steeply inclined fault lines, one of which has completely detached the central mass from the main buttress behind; to the left rises a smooth wall of pale rock, to the right several grooves with over-hanging roofs. The major fault is responsible for two great fissures: on the right of the central buttress is the Chimney, on the left the Crack; when ascending either it is possible at one point to see into the other. Between the two is the formidable XS route *Deer Bield Buttress*, which takes a line through a sheaf of closely parallel, steeply angled and overhanging edges.

The **Crack* (VS) is very steep and formidable, a natural line of great character and unique situations. We found that the crux on the fifth pitch was best negotiated by keeping well out of the chimney, contrary to the Guidebook's recommendation to climb inside as long as possible, which results in an awkward traverse out beneath the overhang. The last pitch, a kind of tremendously exposed 'Amen Corner' (p 137), we climbed by the unusual method of bridging and facing out before a fine series of finishing holds could be attained.

The **Chimney* (S) provides an excellent route under most conditions; we recently climbed it in a February snowstorm. The fissure is choked at intervals with massive blocks, mostly circumvented on the right wall neatly or strenuously according to whether or not the rock is dry. On the whole the blocks seem stable, though changes do occur; a tree mentioned in the Guidebook on pitch five has disappeared and a recent rock fall has changed this former chimney into a through-route where the blocks should be handled with caution. The climb continues up the thin steep crack of the fault line, but a somewhat contrived finish leaves this after 20ft at a sloping platform, from which a huge triangular flake on the right is negotiated by a strenuous 15ft rising hand traverse with no rugosities for the feet; a considerate leader can hang a sling over the apex of the flake to assist the final violent clutch of his second man.

Several strenuous climbs have been made through the grooves to the right of the main buttress. On the pallid slabs to the left is a hard VS route of a somewhat artificial character, named the *Pendulum*; on its second pitch the leader has to flick a sling on to a rusty piton some feet away, put in position by the original leader who first abseiled to that point. An expert friend made twenty-nine attempts (the second man swears he counted!) before the sling stuck so that he could swing across and continue up on tiny finger holds; this is clearly a move on which one is committed and from which there is no retreat except by roping down.

Though plentiful scrambling can be found, the only outcrop of note in Easedale is Blea Crag (6), situated high above the tarn on the northern side of Blea Rigg, the ridge separating Easedale from Great Langdale. A few routes have been worked out on this rather vegetated buttress, including the *Blea Rigg* climb (VD), which involves one or two nice pitches amid a good deal of scrambling.

8

THE SOUTH-WESTERN FELLS

THE effective southern margins of the climber's Lakeland is indicated by the boundary of the Borrowdale Volcanic rocks (figure 1); this trends in a south-westerly direction from the head of Windermere, just skirting the northern end of Coniston Water. The eastern flanks of the Old Man of Coniston, a mountain scarred and pitted with quarries and mines, rise steeply above the woodlands and fields bordering the shores of Coniston Water. The village of Coniston, standing back a little from the lake, has numerous hotels and guest houses and two Youth Hostels, one situated about a mile north-west of the village centre in the Coppermines Valley, the main mining district in the past.

This south-western fell country comprises the compact mass of the Coniston Fells and several sprawling ridges separated by the long lakeless valleys of the Rivers Duddon, Esk and Mite. The Old Man is the highest of the seven distinct summits of the group; in fact he has the distinction of being the highest point in Lancashire, though triumphing by only a single foot over Swirl How about one and a half miles to the north, since the OS deprived him of 2ft on the 1970 edition of the 1″ map. Swirl How is really the geographical centre of the group, for from it radiate ridges on which stand the other tops, while the Old Man is merely the termination of the southern ridge. The eastern flanks of the Coniston Fells are deeply dissected by steep-sided craggy combes containing tarns: the tiny Blind Tarn enclosed by a rock bar and with no surface outflow; Goat's Water lying in the deep boulder-strewn hollow between the buttresses of Dow Crag and the western slopes of the Old Man; Low Water on a little rock shelf, with its outflowing stream spilling in steep cascades to join the Church Beck; Levers Water impounded by a dam to supply the nearby copper mines; and away to the north Greenburn Tarn which likewise served as a reservoir for the Tilber-thwaite mines, draining by Greenburn Beck into Little Langdale Tarn. These Coniston mountains present their most striking aspect to the east; by contrast their western sides drop away in grassy

slopes to the Duddon valley and Little Langdale. Beyond the
Walna Scar track, the walker's route between Coniston and Seathwaite in the Duddon valley, the upland slopes away to the south-
west as a moorland ridge, though when viewed from the west the
hill known as Caw, while only 1,735ft in height, has a surprisingly
prominent outline.

The Duddon rises near the crest of Wrynose Pass and flows for
about fifteen miles along the flat-floored, steep-sided Dunnerdale
before reaching its estuary, which is choked with vast stretches of
sand and mud. The upper valley, known as Wrynose Bottom as
far as the small cluster of farm buildings at Cockley Beck, is wild
and desolate, the river flowing among sheets of stones and boulders
swept down by the floods of a few years ago which closed the
Wrynose road for a considerable time. The valley now turns south-
west, dominated by the pyramid of Harter Fell, and becomes much
narrower, with such craggy knolls as Castle How rising above its
floor. The river is here enclosed in a rocky channel, chutes and
cascades alternating with deep pools; its gorge is particularly striking above the stone-arched Birks Bridge. The valley is so constricted
below this point that the outlet stream from Seathwaite Tarn, which
lies in a combe on the western side of the Coniston Fells, flows
almost parallel to the Duddon in its own valley for two miles,
though the two streams are less than half a mile apart, separated
by a rocky ridge; they finally converge below Seathwaite where the
valley again opens out.

The eastern slopes of Harter Fell have been planted by the
Forestry Commission, providing an example of quite successful
afforestation, helped by the stony slopes and protruding knobbly
crags which break the green continuity of the tree cover and by the
carefully casual use of deciduous trees along the road and the forest
margins. Just below Seathwaite rises Wallowbarrow Crag from
above the trees on the western side of the valley; in recent years
this has become a popular low-lying climbing ground. A few farms
stand among the fields on the valley floor and there are pleasant
inns at Seathwaite and Ulpha, the latter situated at the point where
a road zigzags surprisingly steeply on to the moorlands of Birker
Fell and over into Eskdale. These moorlands cover the broad ridge
between the Duddon and Esk valleys, splaying out to the south-
west for a dozen miles in great undulating tracts: Birker with the

lonely Devoke Water, Ulpha, Corney and other fells, the upland grazings of several lonely farms. Beyond the unfenced road over Corney Fell, wide enough only for a single car except at designated passing places, the Lakeland hills culminate in their final outpost, the humped mass of Black Combe, which just fails to attain the 2,000ft contour; its slopes fall away steeply to the narrow coastal lowland along the Irish Sea.

The River Esk, rising at a height of almost 2,500ft near Esk Hause in the heart of the Lake District, flows for twenty miles before entering the sand-choked and almost land-locked estuary which it shares with the Mite and the Irt. Upper Eskdale is a wild and remote area, with massive crags and boulder-strewn slopes overlooking the valley floor, and with torrents spilling down to the river as it wanders in some parts among sheets of bleached gravels laid down in flood, in others through steep-sided rocky trenches with deep pools. Though the mountains surrounding the head of Eskdale are shared with Langdale and Wasdale, they form perhaps the most impressive rim of any Lakeland valley, sweeping round from Harter Fell through Hard Knott, Crinkle Crags, Bowfell and Esk Pike to meet the Scafell range beyond Esk Hause. With the exception of Hard Knott Pass, this rim is crossed only by a few high-lying cols used by hill walkers.

Upper Eskdale is an awkward area in which to wander under bad weather conditions; several subsidiary ridges and knolls interrupt it, there are high-lying basins with steep steps leading downvalley and sometimes streams appear to be flowing in quite the wrong direction. Some sections are marshy, notably the extensive basin well named the Great Moss, lying at a height of about 1,200ft, the crossing of which is not recommended. After skirting this basin in an easterly direction, the Esk turns abruptly southward in a right-angle bend and descends about 600ft in a series of cascades to the confluence with its main headstream, the Lingcove Beck. The latter likewise is formed by several headstreams, one of which, the Yeastyrigg Gill, rises almost at Ore Gap before flowing down into another marshy hollow, the Green Hole, from which the Lingcove Beck falls through deeply cleft ravines with cascades and deep pools to its confluence with the Esk just above Lingcove Bridge, one of the old stone pack horse type. The ridge in the angle between the converging streams is known as Throstle Garth, called it would seem after the nearby walled enclosure or 'garth' where sheep are gathered from the surrounding fells.

Below Throstle Garth the river opens out into a valley with a more pronounced U-profile, with a flat grassy floor and boulder-strewn hillsides interrupted by projecting outcrops; Heron Crag, on the north-western side of the valley, has been developed as a climbing ground of exceptional quality. It vies, in fact, with Esk Buttress (named on the 1" map as Dow Crag, which can lead to confusion with the crag of the same name near Coniston) as the premier climbing venue in Eskdale. It is interesting to note that the eighteenth century writer William Hutchinson in *An Excursion to the Lakes in 1773 and 1774* made specific mention of '. . . Doe Cragg and Earn Cragg, remarkable precipices, whose fronts are polished as marble, the one 160 perpendicular yards in height, the other 120 yards . . .' These figures are pretty accurate and such an evocative statement would be a stimulating challenge to a modern climber; in fact 'Doe Cragg', ie Esk Buttress, was not climbed until 1920 and 'Earn Cragg' (Heron Crag) until 1955. The opposite side of the valley to Heron is lined with more shattered outcrops on the flanks of Hard Knott Fell; from some angles the prominent stumpy obelisk of the Eskdale Needle, marked on the 1" map as the Steeple, can be seen in profile.

The Esk is joined below the little hamlet of Boot by another tributary, the Whillan Beck, which rises as Hardrigg Gill on the western slopes of Slight Side, the grassy ridge running south from Scafell, and then flows into Burnmoor Tarn on the marshy col between Eskdale and Wasdale; oddly the stream leaves again only a few yards from its point of entry. A charming walk from Eskdale crosses the Burnmoor col to Wasdale Head, either from the Burnmoor Inn at Boot up the Whillan valley or by a stony path, well marked by white crosses on the rocks, up the hillside behind the Woolpack Inn.

The upper part of the Esk valley has been eroded across the Borrowdale Volcanic rocks, but in its middle section the river crosses on to a large mass of granite (p 15 and figure 1). This coarse-crystalled rock is exposed in several tor-like bluffs and also in quarries where it has been worked for many years; most buildings in Eskdale are constructed of its square-hewn blocks. The middle and lower valley, otherwise rugged, is clothed with remarkably luxuriant vegetation, including groves of ornamental trees and prolific rhododendrons and bamboos, and the Forestry Commission's plantations. Outcrops of crenellated rock appear among and above the trees, an appearance emphasised by the sharp profile of Harter Fell in the distance and by the serrated ridges of Crook and Green Crags rising above the moorlands of Birker Fell.

The narrow ridge of Muncaster Fell, also of granite, projects almost to the sea between the valleys of the lower Esk and the smaller Mite, which flow in almost parallel courses barely a mile apart towards their common estuary at Ravenglass. The head-streams of the Mite rise vaguely on the marshy moorland to the south of Burnmoor Tarn, though separated from it by a low in-determinate watershed. Upper Miterdale is lonely and secluded, bounded on the north-west by the long ridge of Whin Rigg and Illgill Head. It is reached from Eskdale Green by a narrow road which at Low Place Farm degenerates into a track continuing to Miterdale Head, a group of former farm buildings now leased by Wyndham School in Egremont and used as an activity centre. The valley is broad and open, though rising to some bold granite crags at Great Bank on its northern flank. Its upper reaches form ex-tensive fell grazing, though lower down the slopes are covered with the conifers of Miterdale Forest.

The little village of Eskdale Green straggles along the road from Eskdale to Santon Bridge and Nether Wasdale. This road passes through a low gap between the Mite and Esk valleys; so too does the narrow-gauge Ravenglass and Eskdale Railway ('laal Ratty', as it is affectionately called), which follows the Mite along the northern flanks of Muncaster Fell before swinging into Eskdale to its terminus at Dalegarth near Boot. Eskdale is well provided with accommodation, including several inns of character, guest houses and a large purpose-built Youth Hostel, and in Eskdale Green are the spacious buildings and wooded grounds of the Outward Bound Mountain School (OBMS) grouped around an ornamental lake.

While upper Eskdale is a cul-de-sac for motor traffic, the road up the valley breaks out to the east by way of Hard Knott Pass, a narrow road climbing to its summit at 1,291ft by zigzags which in one place attain a gradient of one in three. About a third of the way up the pass on a shelf overlooking the Esk valley is the site of a fort, strategically placed by the Romans to command the route from their harbour at Ravenglass (*Glannaventa*) across the mountains to Ambleside (*Galava*). The road descends the far side of the pass to the Duddon valley at Cockley Beck, and the eastward line is continued over Wrynose Pass into Little Langdale and so to Ambleside. This is a fine trans-Lakeland route, at one time of great notoriety and used by RAC and other rallies, but now it is metalled and there are frequent passing places.

WALKS IN THE SOUTH-WESTERN FELLS

The compact group of the Coniston Fells, with their smooth grassy ridges, are well suited to high-level walking (plate p 108). Inevitably the most popular summit is that of the Old Man, and it must be one of the most frequented Lakeland tops because it rises boldly and obviously above Coniston, a challenging objective for the ambitious visitor. Several signposted tracks, many of them once serving the mines and quarries and marked by continuous lines of cairns, wind up its eastern face to the summit with its massive slate platform and OS column. This forms a fine viewpoint, not only for the Lakeland mountains but also for the softer hill country and the Morecambe Bay estuaries to the south. A more interesting ascent is by way of the crest of the Walna Scar pass at just under 2,000ft, then around the ridge surrounding Goat's Water, over Brown Pike, Buck Pike and Dow Crag to Goat's Hause and so to the top of the Old Man. After climbing on Dow, one can finish the day along some section of the ridge. If the car has been left near Seathwaite we continue northward over Brim Fell, Swirl How, Great Carrs with its eastern crags overlooking the Greenburn valley, and finally Grey Friar, thus rounding the hollow in which lies Seathwaite Tarn. If, less usually, we are based on Coniston, we swing north-east from Swirl How towards the long whaleback of Wetherlam, returning down either the curve of the Lad Stones ridge or the Red Gill valley, so to the copper mines district and by the track along the Church Beck to the village. With the co-operation of a car driver, an unexacting walk starts from the top of Wrynose, ascends the northeastern ridge (Wet Side Edge) of Little and Great Carrs by an easy path over the grassy slopes, and continues southward over Swirl How and the Old Man to Coniston, a distance of only about six miles.

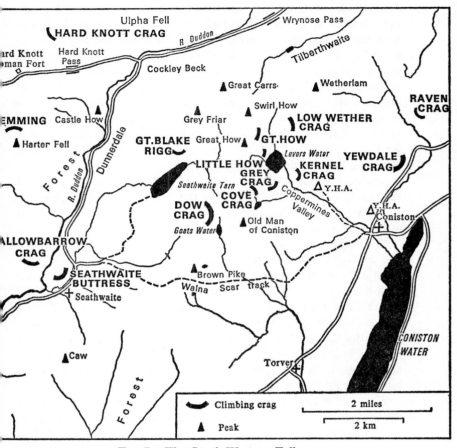

FIG 7. The South-Western Fells

Harter Fell stands on the ridge between Dunnerdale and Eskdale, best climbed either from the latter valley or by a wandering line among marshy hollows and rocky outcrops from the top of Hard Knott Pass, since the Duddon flanks have been closely planted with trees. Few mountains have such a profusion of crags and rough slabs, and several quite continuous scrambling lines can be worked out to its triple turreted summit. On its northern slopes Demming Crag has recently been opened up.

Several routes make for the ridge-line around the head of Eskdale, all easy to follow in clear weather, though some are difficult, even confusing under bad conditions. From Brotherilkeld Farm, near the foot of Hard Knott, Bowfell dominates the skyline on a clear day. Tracks up either side of the valley lead to Throstle Garth, where routes diverge. One winds up the slopes to the right (east) of Lingcove Beck into Green Hole and strikes up near Swinsty Gill into a shallow grassy embayment, known delightfully as Adam-a-Cove, hence to a col at the southern end of the Crinkles ridge (p 34). Other paths from Green Hole head directly up the Lingcove Beck to Three Tarns and to Ore Gap between Bowfell and Esk Pike, the latter a summit which the OS omitted to name until the appearance of the 1970 edition of the 1″ tourist map. A fast and interesting return to Eskdale from the top of Esk Pike follows its knobbly southern ridge, known as Yeastyrigg, so to the east of Gait and Long Crags to Throstle Garth.

The upper Esk valley can be reached either by a path up the left side of Throstle Garth and along the edge of Great Moss, or more directly from Taw House lower down the valley by a zigzag path beside Cowcove Beck and over a little col to the west of High Scarth Crag, then dropping down to Great Moss. A poorly defined trod beside the upper Esk, its last section along the bed of a ravine cut in the shattered red rocks, leads ultimately to Esk Hause. This is quite a dramatic walk, enclosed on the left by the crags, gullies and screes falling steeply from the Scafells, on the right by the long south ridge of Esk Pike.

The walker heading for either of the Scafells branches off from the previous route near some enormous boulders, known as Sampson's Stones, below the massive but broken Cam Spout Buttress, and follows a somewhat tiring stony ascent past the Cam Spout Falls. Higher up he passes under the tremendous overhangs of Scafell East Buttress, one of England's premier climbing cliffs, to Mickledore. If bound for Scafell, the climber either strikes off left below the East Buttress and ascends a rocky gully to Foxes Tarn, hence up an easy scree slope to the cairn, or he negotiates the square blocks of Broad Stand from just below Mickledore. Broad Stand is moderately easy but quite exposed and several fatal accidents have occurred there; if conditions are wet or icy a rope is essential. Scafell Pike, however, is only an easy walk up a rough blazened path from Mickledore.

An attractive alternative way to the Pike continues up the valley just beyond Esk Buttress and turns into Little Narrowcove. This is a remarkably secluded place; for years we had missed it until one snowy winter's day we scrambled beside the stream in its rocky course into a high-lying basin, far more extensive than we had anticipated, surrounded by the shattered buttresses of the Pike itself, Broad Crag and Ill Crag. We proceeded up a tongue of hard snow to reach the col between Broad Crag and the Pike, then leftward up a curving slope of snow to England's highest point.

The rounding of upper Eskdale by its mountain rim provides one of Lakeland's finest expeditions. Starting from Hard Knott Pass (a lift by car to the top will give an unearned though welcome bonus of nearly a thousand feet of height), the route heads for Hard Knott Fell, then swings north-eastward on to the Crinkles ridge and Bowfell to Esk Hause, Great End and the several tops of Scafell Pike to Mickledore. From here Scafell is reached by either Broad Stand or the more circuitous Lord's Rake route (p 179), and finally down the long southern ridge of Slight Side to Eskdale. The distance is about fourteen miles, involving a total ascent (assuming no initial lift up Hard Knott) of about 7,000ft, a truly fine day of about ten hours of steady going.

We once made a cross country trip from Wasdale Head to Coniston, with heavy rucsacs for good measure, taking as straight a line as possible: up to Mickledore, down the Cam Spout track, across the Lingcove Beck and down Moasdale (a curious variant of the widely used Mosedale) to Cockley Beck; then we took a diagonal line to the summit of Grey Friar (heavy going this), along the ridge to Swirl How and so over the Old Man to our destination; in all, about fifteen miles of mountain country.

ROCK CLIMBING IN THE SOUTH-WESTERN FELLS

DOW CRAG (24)

This splendid crag can be reached easily either from Coniston by way of the first two miles of the Walna Scar track, followed by a path forking right into the Goat's Water combe, or from Dunnerdale by the Walna Scar pass and the south ridge. From the latter a steep gully just before the main outcrop leads down to the base of the crags, where the blue first aid equipment box stands out clearly.

Dow consists of five distinct buttresses (figure 8), denoted by letters A to E. The tallest and most continuous is A on the left (south), especially well defined where it overlooks the deeply cut Great Gully. The upper parts of B, C and D lean back above a distinct shelf known as Easy Terrace, which can be reached from the left up an easy, well scratched slanting rake from near the foot of Great Gully, or from the right by a gentle scoop which leads out of Easter Gully. Practically all the climbing on these buttresses, with the exception of a few routes on the left of B, finishes at Easy Terrace, since the upper section consists of broken crags. E Buttress is a broad rather indeterminate mass, with few attractive routes.

Dow has had a long and honourable history, for it was opened up at an early stage more completely than most crags. This popularity was largely the result of its accessibility, since it was the only Lakeland climbing ground near a railway, little more than an hour's walk from Coniston or Torver stations. It therefore had its regular visitors from the south, perhaps breaking their journeys en route to Wasdale, as well as its faithful band of devotees from Barrow and other parts of the Furness district. As a result, before 1914 more than twenty good routes of remarkable character and identity had been worked out; over half a century later these retain their traditional popularity, charm and standard. After World War I another surge of activity added nearly as many climbs again; conspicuous among these were the *Eliminate* routes on A, B and C (all VS), so called because they deliberately chose lines which excluded any easy rock and avoided existing climbs, and the *tour-de-force* of *Great Central* (VS) in Easter Gully, which though climbed as early as 1919 is still regarded as an arduous effort. Not a lot was left to be done, other than a few very hard lines by exceptional climbers; R. J. Birkett, as ever, appeared on the scene, making *North Wall* (mild VS) on A and *Leopard's Crawl* (hard VS) on B. Then in the sixties three great climbs on A Buttress were led by Les Brown: the XS *Side Walk* on the tremendously steep right-hand edge and the hard VS *Isengard* and the *Balrog* in the centre.

One of the great charms of Dow is the wide variety both in the character and grading of its climbs, for it offers satisfying lines with a sense of achievement for climbers of all standards. *C Ordinary*

(D), for example, is an excellent route for beginners, as evidenced by the highly scratched nature of every hold, a logical nine-pitch climb with good stances and belays. But it is possible to mention here only a few of the very attractive possibilities.

On the left of A Buttress the *Trident* route (mild S) is so called from the three distinctive sections of slabby rock (plate p 108) well

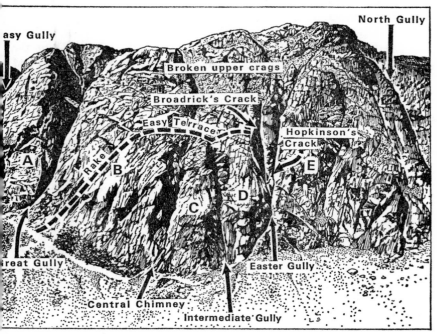

FIG 8. Dow Crag

furnished with neat positive holds. Two closely associated climbs are *Gordon and Craig's* (VD) and the **Arête, Chimney and Crack* (mild S); their middle four pitches are identical, including a big chimney and a superbly exposed traverse right across the face of the buttress. The introductory pitch of G&C is an easy diagonal scoop followed by some stepped ledges, while ACC takes a much harder arête, quite steep and thin near the top. Higher up G&C continues to be the end of the traverse to a slab, while its companion takes a steep but remarkably safe and easy crack. **Eliminate*

K

A comes into the category of the great routes, steep and exposed, but well protected and with good stances and belays. It works its way up the wall overlooking Great Gully before moving left on to the face of the buttress; the famous *rochers perchés*, two detached flakes mentioned in the Guidebook, have now disappeared, making the leftward move at that point somewhat harder. Near the top it crosses the G&C traverse and finishes up a corner to the left of the latter's crack pitch.

B Buttress has a host of good things: *Broadrick's* route (hard S) on the edge of Great Gully; the slanting *Giant's Crawl* (D) up the slabs to Easy Terrace, with some moderate climbing beyond; and the three well known eponymous routes, *Murray's* (S), *Abraham's* (S) and **Woodhouse's* (hard VD); the last, described in early editions of the Guidebook as '. . . the most popular climb on the crag . . .' and then graded only D, sometimes takes quite good climbers by surprise because of its oddly awkward character and has now been upgraded. **Murray's* is a delightful route, though wandering a bit about the crag, with a fine traverse across a big slab near its foot. *Abraham's*, another piece of excellent route-finding by the redoubtable Keswick brothers in 1903, is much harder than one expects, up a groove into a cave, a steep wall and some rightward slabs known as Pilgrim's Progress. One of us, unwisely attempting this route with a novice in the gathering gloom of a cold January day, got to the top of these slabs and, then unaware that the correct continuation is a descending traverse to the left, climbed with some desperation the wall ahead. This later turned out to be Giant Grim, a pitch on *Eliminate B* (VS); the novice had a hard time before he finally made it.

The **Central Chimney* (mild S) between B and C is really a corner-crack, with a stretch of slabs on the right up which this fine route mainly goes. C Buttress provides some delightful slab climbing, including the very popular **Ordinary* route (D), *Southern Slabs* (mild S) on pockmarked quartzy rock, the rather easier *Lazarus* (VD) round the corner, and the fine *Hawk* route (S). *Eliminate C* (VS) is quite short and lacks the variety and situations of *Eliminate A*, though the third pitch (including a delicate move to a spike on the arête) is technically very interesting.

Between C and D Buttresses the famous **Intermediate Gully* (hard S) consists of a string of steep cracks and chockstones, climbed way back in 1895; its standard varies enormously according to conditions and it involves moves which are at the same time strenuous and neat. However, it is a very safe climb and is much easier to descend than ascend. It is useful to know that a spring which rarely fails issues near the foot of the gully.

Beyond D Buttress, with its nice little *Raven* (mild S) and *North-East* (VD) routes, is Easter Gully, its base filled with an enormous boulder generally turned on the left by a steep polished slab and a traverse back into a vast stony amphitheatre, from which over a dozen routes begin. The two long cracks to left and right are *Broadrick's* and *Hopkinson's* (hard S), most entertaining and well provided with chocks so that runners on thread belays can be placed *ad lib*. Between them the steep pillar of *Great Central* (VS) affords a most strenuous climb, including the fierce South America Crack and the wall above the Bandstand. The Guidebook states that the latter was originally climbed using combined tactics; we found we could not get up otherwise. *Jones's route* (O. G. Jones was here in 1898), though only of hard VD standard, is interesting, involving the lower part of Broadrick's Crack, then an awkward crack to the Bandstand, a traverse across Hopkinson's Crack and a finish up an annoying little scoop. Several runners should be placed to safeguard the traverse; some time ago a grievous accident occurred when all three climbers were pulled off as a result of a fall from the traverse by one of them.

Finally, for those who like girdle traverses, that of Dow is exceptionally fine. It starts up the first pitch of Trident on A Buttress and finishes some hours and a thousand feet of climbing later by one of the right-hand exits from Easter Gully. All in all, Dow is one of our favourite places.

CRAGS IN THE COPPERMINES VALLEY
Tracks from Coniston lead north-westward on either side of the Church Cove Beck into what is generally known as the Coppermines Valley. Here copper and slate have been worked for centuries and the unlovely evidence of this activity abounds: expanses of sterile washings and spoil dumps, black dripping shafts and adits which should be cautiously avoided and numerous ruined buildings, some of which have been repaired to serve as a Youth Hostel and as climbing huts.

Apart from the man-made desolation, this is an exceptionally rugged district, with outcrops of rock, scree, cascading streams and boulders; the course of Low Water Beck is usually referred to as Boulder Valley. These boulders can give strenuous exercise on a wet day; one in particular called the Pudding Stone has several hard routes on it, including a vertical groove on its eastern side which is both hard to enter and to continue.

Several minor crags are well worth a visit. In the angle between Low Water and Levers Water Becks is Grey Crag (50), an elongated line of steep mossy slabs, with some black cracks and in the centre piles of squared blocks leaning against the face. Some hard climbs include *Viking Crack* (hard S), a deep right-angled fissure on its left wing. Cove Crag (18), overlooking Boulder Valley to the right of the cascades where Low Water Beck spills out of the combe, is an outcrop of unwelcoming aspect, usually rather wet, but providing a few routes, including the prominent *Cove Crack* (VS).

Below Levers Water is a prominent hump, Kernel Crag (61), which offers two interesting little climbs on rough sound rock with enormous sharp holds; these are *Pinnacle* route and the *Gangway* (both allegedly hard D, though much overrated), forming safe bad-weather climbs.

The party making a day's tour of the Coppermines Valley can then proceed to the Little and Great How Crags (44) on the slopes to the west of Levers Water. These look more impressive from a distance than they prove to be, but several climbs have been made, notably the *Original* route (hard VD) on Great How, which follows a prominent ridge in the centre of the outcrop and provides a pleasant climb up slabs, cracks and grooves. Finally, Low Wether Crag (67) projects from the western side of the Red Dell valley on the slopes of Black Sails ridge. Though rather messy and vegetatious, especially in its upper section, a few climbs have been made lower down. *North Buttress* (D) gives an easy 250ft climb up the right-hand edge, which can be continued up broken rocks to the ridge and so to the summit of Wetherlam.

OTHER CRAGS NEAR CONISTON

The small hill known as Ivy Crag, about two miles from Coniston, has several rocky spurs, one of which closely approaches the road along Yewdale. Its south-eastern face forms a steep crag slanting diagonally up the fellside, in places with overhanging walls and with breaks cutting across it in the form of gangways and rather mossy grooves. This has the somewhat unoriginal name of Raven Crag (81), one of half a dozen in Lakeland. From below the fore-shortening effect rather minimises the extent and character of climbable rock, and the half-dozen routes actually prove to be much harder and more exposed than a casual visual assessment would suggest. The quality of the rock is likewise better than one might expect, at times yielding surprisingly good incut holds. The low-lying crag gave us some very satisfying climbing on a recent cold dank February day. *Chrysalis* (hard S) at its left-hand end proved an excellent route, with some exposed moves on spiky holds, start-ing up a right-slanting gangway which proved to be surprisingly easy. The third pitch involves an airy move from the tip of a large apparently safe flake, which has to be used as a foothold, then round a nose on the right, rather like the famous Nose on Pillar (p 64) but in the opposite direction. The climb of 190ft can be ex-tended by taking a cracked wall to the right of the top belay, fol-lowed by a corner and some slabby rocks with quartzy holds. Farther right is *Josies Jog*, given a VS rating from its second long pitch on which the holds are not too good; higher up it shares the nose pitch of Chrysalis. Next come the exposed *Tarantula* (VS) and *Cobra* (VS) and higher up is *Laverock* (mild S). We finished the day on *Marabou* (S); starting with some reluctance because of the Guidebook's comment of 'mossy with vegetation' but encouraged by the remark 'more climbing than is apparent', we found it quite enjoyable and since our visit it has considerably less moss, the removal of which exposed some good holds, rather essential under the wet conditions. A memorable move near the top involved a rightward traverse, with an awkward step into an undercut groove above a grassy recess, the groove then being followed to the top.

Other crags which provide a few routes, rarely meriting a specific visit but worth taking in during the course of a mountaineering day, include Hen Crag on the eastern side of Wetherlam above the swampy hollow in which rise the headstreams of Tilberthwaite Beck, Blind Tarn Crag on the eastern side of the ridge running south from Dow, and Yewdale Crag (110) near the road a mile north of Coniston.

CRAGS IN DUNNERDALE

It is truly surprising that Wallowbarrow Crag (106) should have been neglected until the early 1950s, when the first routes were made by instructors from the Eskdale OBMS. Possibly the thick woodland below the crag helped to camouflage its real quality, or perhaps Dunnerdale was simply off the beaten track for climbers. Yet it faces south, it is sheltered, its base is at little over 750ft so that climbing can be pleasant here when the high crags are out of condition, and it can be reached quickly by the road to Wallowbarrow Farm. The rock is rough and has been so assiduously gardened by the heavy traffic of OBMS and other parties that much vegetation and suspect rock has been removed.

The main features are indicated on figure 9, on which are marked the eight climbs we like best out of the twenty or so available. The steep clean West Buttress is separated from the longer but more broken East Buttress by the obvious Red Gully, while a long rake to the right forms an easy line of descent. Far East Buttress provides a few easy scrambling routes, and the tree-shrouded Lower Crag has one climb of quality.

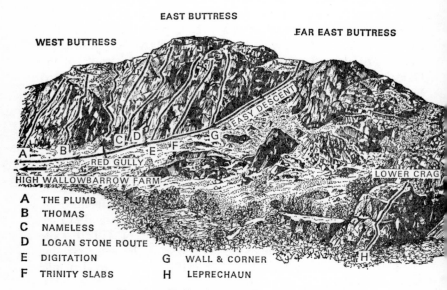

FIG 9. Wallowbarrow Crag, Dunnerdale

Away to the left the *Plumb* (VS) is a fine exposed route (plate p 108), its lower pitch up a rib, the other a very steep groove succeeded by a narrow chimney. *Thomas* (S), in some ways the most attractive climb on the crag, involves a groove surmounted by a wall; one of us had a hold come away on the upper section, though fortunately when well placed. Beyond Red Gully is the popular *Nameless* (VD), whose main feature is a traverse leftwards from a groove, followed by a couple of steep pitches on delightfully adequate holds. The *Logan Stone* route (S) is a climb of splendid situations; after a groove leading to the top pitch of Nameless, a remarkable structural line forming a gangway is continued to the right to a tiny exposed ledge where once stood the block which gave the route its name; here a runner can be fixed before negotiating a steep and awkward little groove. Above this a rib involves a delicate mantelshelf move at about halfway. *Digitation* (mild VS) takes a diagonal line rightwards up Oak Tree Slabs, so called from an oak growing on a ledge two-thirds of the way up. The right-hand edge of these slabs gives two pleasantly easy routes, with clean pitches well supplied with belays, *Trinity Slabs* and *Wall and Corner* (both D). Despite its messy approach over grassy ledges and broken slimy rocks, *Leprechaun* (hard S) is both strenuous and delicate, with four varied pitches of steep walls and cracks and a neat traverse near the top.

Near the road up the valley just beyond Seathwaite, the small Seathwaite Buttress (95) rises among the trees, reached by crossing Tarn Beck near the little church. We spent a day of pouring rain on the three short routes of about 100ft, named with great originality *Snap* (D), a safe crack on the left, *Crackle* (mild S), a steep little arête in the centre, and *Pop* (mild S), a crack on the right ending with a wall.

Great Blake Rigg (41) overlooks Seathwaite Tarn on the southern flanks of Grey Friar, which we once visited in the warm evening sunshine after a leisurely day on Dow and a ramble around the tops. We were surprised at the amount of rock, though very broken. A few climbs have been made and recorded, including a mild VS, and we think we followed one of them, the *Gangway* (hard S), though this is a crag on which to take the rock as one finds it and work out some kind of upward line.

HERON CRAG (55)

During the walk up Eskdale from Brotherilkeld, Heron Crag on
the north-western side of the valley first appears as a mere ex-
crescence but gradually reveals itself as one of the most impressive
masses in Lakeland; as an article in the *F&RCC Journal* puts it,
'. . . its steepness is fearsome'. Three buttresses fall to rounded
bases above the boulder-studded grassy slopes. That on the left is
broken and discontinuous, that on the right is dark, mossy and
usually dripping, though hard, determined men have put up
some routes, including the frightful looking XS named the
Flanker.

The central buttress forms a tremendous sweep of clean grey
rock, so devoid of vegetation that it dries rapidly. It was first opened
up in the mid-1950s by instructors from the Eskdale OBMS, logically enough following the natural breaks. The only climb of less
than hard S grade is *Heron Corner* (VD), the first to be climbed,
following the left-hand edge, which has now been well cleaned and
gardened. *Kama Sutra* (VS) is a nearby short climb, which likewise has been much improved by usage. It works its way up a
prominent corner, then by a step right to a sloping ledge; an overhang is surmounted by a strenuous pull, followed by some fine
flakes leading to a belay below a groove which is hard to enter.
The climb finishes up a steep wall and an arête to broken ground
above the big gully. Farther to the right a chimney groove has such
a profusion of trees and heather growing out of its depths that
presumably its name *Babylon* (hard S) was derived from these
hanging gardens; though still somewhat messy and usually rather
damp, it provides a good continuous line.

The best climb on Heron Crag is undoubtedly *Gormenghast*
(hard VS); some would claim this to be the best in Lakeland. It
begins at the foot of the central pillar and goes steeply to a neat
niche with a piton belay in place. Then follows a really magnificent
pitch, 90ft of continuously hard rock involving difficult moves
which have to be worked out in very exposed positions. From the
belay a wall is climbed on flat holds, then an ascending move to
the right is followed by a steep crack. A groove leads to a holly
growing from a ledge, and a long pitch includes a traverse followed
by a short descent to a crack, thus circumventing a nose of rock.
A pinnacle is climbed direct to a large ledge, on which are the

remnants of a huge nest, and a final groove leads triumphantly to the top, in all 300ft of sustained climbing. Although allegedly easier than the last, a climb up the left side of the central pillar, known as the *Yellow Edge* (VS), is in some ways more exacting; after beginning up Babylon, it works out right to a grassy ledge and then moves back on to the edge, first up a thin groove with little beetling overhangs and a final steep arête; after the miniscule holds in the groove the last pitch, though airy, goes comfortably.

A prominent groove defining the right-hand side of the central pillar yields a hard VS route named *Bellerophon*. Despite its rather wet and mossy character, it is a climb of great character, involving several hard though well safeguarded cracks and grooves. The most exacting pitch is an overhanging crack near the top, with strenuous finishing moves, though this is sometimes avoided by taking the last pitch of Gormenghast nearby on the left, which brings the overall grade down to VS.

ESK BUTTRESS (29)

This great buttress on the eastern flanks of Scafell Pike overlooking the valley of the upper Esk is a superb piece of rock which at first sight cannot fail to impress, even overpower, with its vertical lines and steep grey walls 400 to 500ft high alternating with dark cracks and gullies. As one approaches the crag something of this impressive quality is lost because of the broken and vegetated section below the central mass, which also rather masks the location of the individual climbs, but when the actual base of the steep rock is reached the buttress reasserts itself intimidatingly. Its dominating feature is the Central Pillar, defined by deeply cut chimneys. The crag is clearly a place for those who like steep rock and long arduous routes, for there is nothing here under hard S standard and there are two XS's. Yet it is comparatively low-lying and dries off quickly, partly because of its south-easterly aspect, partly because of its relative freedom from vegetated ledges.

For long, Esk Buttress had only two climbs, both deservedly named after their pioneer leaders: *Bower's* and *Bridge's* routes, each over 400ft, steep and exposed and with varied pitches. Yet these are only of hard S standard, a tribute to their route-finding qualities; the first was climbed as early as 1920, the second twelve years later. *Bower's* route on the right-hand side of the Buttress begins with a 100ft sweep of slabs, then a diagonal leftward traverse followed by a groove to the foot of a steep crack. This is climbed on good holds, and the next very steep pitch includes a little bulge and a traverse to a niche known as the Waiting Room; a strenuous chimney follows, then a more open V-chimney and easier slabs to the top. A great charm of this route is the excellent stances and belays, and runners are comparatively easy to fix. *Bridge's* route lies to the left of the Central Pillar; starting up fairly easy rock the difficulties increase progressively as height is gained: a steep crack, several awkward grooves, two exposed and delicate traverses, the higher leading away from the impending upper section of the pillar into a rather mossy groove.

Esk Buttress remained a two-climb crag until 1944 when R. J. Birkett added the first of his ten high quality routes. These included *Great Central* (VS) of over 500ft, the longest on the crag, taking the lower part of the central pillar but moving out to the right under its upper rocks by a traverse and a short abseil down a groove, higher up joining Bower's route at the Waiting Room. Another line of a quite different character is *Square Chimney* (VS) up the left-hand wall of the Central Pillar. The actual chimney, reached by 150ft of fairly easy climbing, is an infuriating place, requiring some strenuous backing-up followed by a distinctly awkward exit to the left at the top. A little higher, where the chimney opens out into a groove, Bridge's route traverses across its line. Two more climbs of VS standard, *Medusa Wall* and *Gargoyle Groove*, were made on the same day in 1947 by Arthur Dolphin.

There things again rested after this surge of activity until a memorable Sunday in June 1962, when two parties with designs on the completion of the upper section of the Central Pillar arrived at its base. But Peter Crew and M. Owen were first on the scene and achieved their design, an XS route of almost 500ft which took the first four pitches of Bridge's route and then moved right to climb directly the final steep tower. This great climb is not only a triumph of modern climbing technique, using an inserted chockstone and pitons for protection, but at the same time a tribute to A. W. Bridge whose original line, made thirty years previously up more than half of its total height, was still found to be the most logical. The second party arrived too late for the main prize, but achieved two other remarkable *tours-de-force, Black Sunday* (hard VS) and the *Red Edge* (XS), closely parallel direct lines on the steep rib to the left of Square Chimney.

MINOR CRAGS IN ESKDALE

This is a very craggy valley; probably many routes have been made of which no record exists. Thus, for example, behind the Youth Hostel are several slabby outcrops on which people scramble on summer evenings, there are numerous crags on Hard Knott Fell, and one can find climbable rock all over Harter Fell.

About a mile from Eskdale Green along the road to Birker Fell a minor road branches off to Bootle; a short distance along this, a small tor-like crag rises on the left above the River Esk, only a few minutes up the hillside. This is Brantrake Crag (11), which has been opened up by the Eskdale OBMS as a training ground; some bolts have been considerably fixed into the rock at the top to serve as belay points. The crag is unique in Lakeland in that it consists of granite, split by vertical cracks along the joint-lines, with edges rounded by the characteristic weathering of this rock. There are several tiers of crags; large white numbers painted at the base of the top tier indicate routes 1, 2 and 3, of D or VD standard. Several other quite hard lines, including an obvious VS crack, are also possible.

Higher up the valley, on its south side near Birker Force, is Gate Crag (33), where half a dozen routes have been made, including some short but intense VS climbs. Demming Crag (21) is on the north-western side of Harter Fell, reached by a wandering line from Hard Knott Pass. The crag has a considerable expanse of slabs, up which several routes have been made, including the VS *Barbarian*; some of our knowledgeable friends believe this to be a coming crag. Not far from the pass on its northern side, Hard Knott Crag (51) is another outcrop with great possibilities, since it is steep and in places overhanging, so much so that there are several hard VS routes.

When walking up the valley beyond Brotherilkeld, the Eskdale Needle stands out on the right skyline, the surviving portion of a shattered outcrop with enormous vertical joints, among a chaos of angular boulders. On the long side of the Needle, huge blocks leaning against it form a slightly overhanging crack, leading to a platform from which a short face climb attains its flat top, bedecked with a patch of bilberries. The short side gives an easy but exposed climb with big holds.

Mention may be made of High Scarth Crag (58) near the Cowcove track from Taw House to upper Eskdale; here the rock is broken but provides half a dozen routes, and Throstlehow Crag in the angle between the converging Esk and Lingcove Beck. Finally, Cam Spout Crag (15) in upper Eskdale to the south-west of Cam Spout waterfall is hardly a minor crag; in fact it is a very considerable mass, though much interrupted by broken rock and vegetation. It has very striking structural lines, slashed across by prominent parallel faults sloping down to the left. Over on the left is Peregrine Gully, an unpleasant place to visit in summer, though it may give a good climb under winter conditions. To its left four long climbs of VS standard have been made up the grooved buttress.

9

WASDALE

From the wide stretches of sand along the shores of the Irish Sea between Seascale and Drigg, the fells present a purple profile, a bold backcloth to the east. It is only as one drives inland along winding roads that it becomes evident that Wasdale penetrates far into the heart of the Lakeland dome. Near the foot of the valley Nether Wasdale is an area of rocky knolls and tree-covered morainic humps, part of the natural dam of clay and boulders which encloses Wastwater, out of which wanders the River Irt on its ten-mile course to the Ravenglass estuary. Small green fields, clumps of woodland, whitewashed farms and a few large houses, their grounds ablaze in late spring with massy rhododendrons, are interlinked by narrow stone-walled roads. The village of Strands, its houses and farms strung loosely along a wide-verged road set in trees and with the cliffs of the Screes rising behind, is possibly one of the best kept, least spoilt and most attractive villages in the Lake District.

Wastwater, three miles in length though less than half a mile across, lies in a straight-sided, rock-floored trough, its south-eastern shores rising steeply and uninterruptedly to the vast, continuous curtain of the Screes, ribbed with crumbling buttresses and gashed by deep black gullies; here if anywhere is the proper name merited for this characteristic mountain feature. The wear and tear of the rotten crags continues through weathering; occasionally a rock fall leaves a pale scar and a fan of fresh debris on the slope below. The dominant mood of Wasdale is sombre, yet on a spring day Wastwater can assume a sparkling quality.

From the coast road the approach is through Gosforth, a little town which has grown rapidly in recent years, and the left-hand side of the valley is first dominated by the craggy face of Buckbarrow, then by the rocky tiers of Middle Fell and Long Crag. To the north lie the undulating hills of Copeland Forest, culminating in the summit of Seatallan which always seems strangely aloof, perhaps because it requires a special outing to reach its top, though it attains only 2,270ft; the Caw Fell—Haycock—Scoat Fell ridge

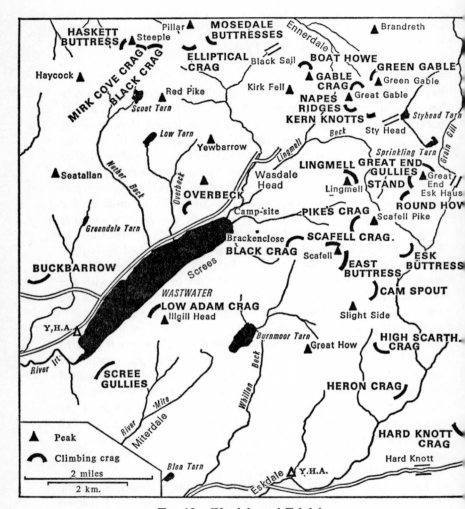

FIG 10. Wasdale and Eskdale

beyond forms the watershed with Ennerdale. The road now drops to the lake shore, meeting another from Santon Bridge, and the view unfolds dramatically towards Wasdale Head. Seen from a prominent rocky peninsula the head of the valley is framed by three peaks: on the left the ribbed ridge of Yewbarrow, in the centre the pyramid outline of Great Gable (appearing so different from the massive dome overlooking Ennerdale), on the right Lingmell, the supporting buttress of the Scafell massif; this striking three-fold mountain profile was adopted as the emblem of the Lake District National Park. The summit of Scafell Pike lies back out of sight, though Scafell farther to the right is visible, separated from Lingmell by the deeply cut valley of Lingmell Gill, its headstreams rising in the amphitheatre of Hollow Stones under Scafell and Pike's Crag.

The road to Wasdale Head keeps close to the shore until it reaches the head of the lake, fringed by a curving shingly beach except where the inflowing Lingmell Beck is building out a marshy delta. The flat valley floor extends for about one and a half miles above the lake, its lower part covered with stones and boulders swept down by past floods (p 24), among which grow scrubby oaks and silver birch, holly and gorse, with patches of smooth turf. Here a large camp site, with a warden during the summer months, was established a few years ago by the National Trust when indiscriminate camping along the lake edge was prohibited. Across the valley, reached by a side road, near the foot of Lingmell Gill and hidden in a little oak-wood, is Brackenclose, a 'hut' owned by the Fell and Rock Climbing Club. Unlike most such buildings which are usually converted barns or cottages, this was constructed in 1937 of local stone and slate; it is, of course, restricted to members of the Club and their guests.

The road then crosses a hump-backed stone bridge and continues to the tiny hamlet of Wasdale Head. Apart from a few scattered farms, there are only two or three buildings, notably the slate-roofed church sheltered by a group of dark yews and claimed to be the smallest in England, and the whitewashed Wastwater Hotel, for over a century the traditional haunt of climbers whose exploits were duly recorded in a log-book as a guide to others. The first three lines of *British Mountain Climbs* by George Abraham are today something of an over-statement: '. . . In mountaineering circles Zermatt and Chamonix, the two greatest Alpine centres, are scarcely more famous than Wasdale Head . . .' But about the turn of the century the comparison was justifiable, for all the pioneer British climbers foregathered there at one time or another. If Wasdale Head did not see the actual birth of British rock climbing (the Pillar Rock in Ennerdale retains this distinction), certainly its early stages were nurtured and developed there. The Hotel remains an immensely popular centre for visitors.

The valley floor is divided by stone walls into a mosaic of tiny fields, the precious valley-pasture to which the Herdwick ewes are brought down from the mountains for the May lambing. In early October 'the Shepherds' Meet' is held in a field behind the Hotel; this began as a gathering of fell farmers to return animals which had strayed into neighbouring valleys, a sorting out of the flocks before the winter, and has developed into an annual show attended by large numbers of visitors as well as locals.

At Wasdale Head the profile of the valley rim again changes. Away to the left (north) is Mosedale, a secondary dale-head surrounded by the craggy slopes of Yewbarrow, Red Pike, Pillar and Kirk Fell, the last a bulky mountain separated from Great Gable by the high Beckhead col and with a grassy south-western ridge descending from its summit directly towards the Hotel. Beyond the little village green, a stony road leads up the main valley to the long low buildings of Burnthwaite, a farm which has royally entertained visitors for many years. Now the valley head closes in, dominated even more by the pyramid of Great Gable (plate p 126), with its sweeping scree-covered flanks, the prominent buttresses of the Napes and the broken Westmorland Crags fringing the summit plateau. Away to the right Lingmell now falls into place as an outlier of the Scafells, though its summit is well worth visiting if only for the view, situated as it is in the heart of Wasdale. While its tall cairn can easily be reached up a gentle rise of less than 300ft from Lingmell col, a bonus before or after the ascent of Scafell Pike, its north-eastern face is steep and rugged, split by gullies which may provide some hard climbs in winter. The rocky Wasdale aspect of the Scafell Pike ridge is revealed right up to Great End in the north-east, its flanks deeply gashed by ravines: Skew Gill, Grains Gill, Greta Gill and the deeply incised bends of Piers Gill; the immense scale of the last can only be appreciated by a closer visit.

FELL WALKS IN THE WASDALE DISTRICT

Since the head of Wasdale extends into the heart of the mountains, several much frequented walker's routes link it with neighbouring valleys. From Burnthwaite a track follows the valley floor beside the stony bed of Lingmell Beck for half a mile before ascending diagonally across the scree-covered breast of Gable to Sty Head at a height of 1,600ft. An alternative, slightly longer but much more pleasant, is the Old Sty Head track, which keeps to the boulder-strewn valley floor until just beyond the confluence of Piers Gill with a small right-bank tributary, Spouthead Gill, where it zig-zags up a grassy ridge before bearing left to the pass, marked by a great cairn; a short distance away to the north-east lies Styhead Tarn. This pass is one of the focal points of the western fells for crossings between Wasdale Head and Borrowdale and (via Sprink-ling Tarn and the shelter below Esk Hause) between Wasdale and Langdale. Also from the pass, routes radiate to the summits of Great and Green Gable, Scafell Pike and Great End.

Another walker's route out of Wasdale goes up Mosedale, swinging away from its flat marshy floor in a north-easterly direction to the crest of Black Sail Pass and hence descending to the Black Sail Youth Hostel in Ennerdale (p 49). Upper Eskdale may be reached by a long grind over Mickledore which lies at about 2,700ft, and lower Eskdale by a delightful walk from the head of the lake over gentle moorlands, brilliant with heather in the autumn, past Burnmoor Tarn and so down either to the Burnmoor Inn at Boot or to the Woolpack Inn farther up the valley. While in this neigh-bourhood, mention should be made of the attractive walk along the ridge of Illgill Head and Whin Rigg, with occasional careful views beyond the crumbling edge on the right down the face of the Screes. The return to Wasdale Head can be made along the lake shore at the foot of the Screes, at either end of which is a sur-prisingly good path, though the intervening section provides a quarter-mile of really strenuous boulder clambering.

As in other popular valleys, the mountains around Wasdale Head may be ascended by numerous well marked trails. The boulder-strewn summit of Great Gable, now so dotted with cairns that under misty conditions they defeat their original purpose of indicating various routes, can be reached by half a dozen lines not

L

only from Wasdale, but also from Ennerdale, Borrowdale and Buttermere. An expedition of considerable interest is a clockwise traverse of the flanks of the mountain at about two-thirds height, following a cairned track from Sty Head under the foot of the prominent buttress of Kern Knotts, past a rocky corner from which issues a little fault-spring, and then ascending diagonally over the reddish scree slopes to the Napes ridges; here the non-climber can scramble along a rocky path and obtain a fine view of the Needle, the Eagle's Nest and Arrowhead ridges. The trod then contours the scree-clad western slopes of the mountain under Gable Crag (p 68) to Windy Gap and so reaches the summit up the short north-eastern ridge.

By virtue of being the highest point in England, the summit of Scafell Pike is attained by an enormous number of people every year, a kind of pious pilgrimage, as the white-scarred trails over the boulder-covered plateau ridge testify. The 'tourist route' winds interminably from Sty Head past Sprinkling Tarn to Esk Hause, then in a south-westerly direction across Calf Cove on to the ridge, crossing Ill Crag and Broad Crag cols in turn before the final 300ft to the huge summit cairn. A much more attractive ascent from Sty Head is the Corridor Route, which traverses a distinct shelf across the face of the mountain, crossing the foot of the deeply gashed Skew Gill and the heads of Greta and Piers Gill in turn. Another impressive way from the valley floor follows the Lingmell Beck to its junction with Spouthead Gill, climbs up to the right over steep grass, crosses the foot of Greta Gill and skirts the upper edge of the long diagonal ravine of Piers Gill, with dramatic views into its shattered depths, until reaching its final right-angle, where it strikes up to join the previous route. At this point one can either take the shallow gully leading to Broad Crag col or walk more gently to Lingmell col, from each of which an ascent over rough scree and boulders leads to the summit. All these lines are easy and straight-forward in good summer weather, but the mountain can be a diffi-cult, even hazardous proposition in winter or in bad weather when the risk of exposure may add to the danger of an accident.

Scafell Pike is separated from its lower neighbour Scafell by the gap known as Mickledore, which can be reached by an easy scramble down a well scratched path; a mountain rescue box is located on the Eskdale side of the col. A short divergence to the left before Mickledore leads to a small rock-pool known as Broad-crag Tarn, which lying at 2,746ft has the distinction of being the highest named tarn in Lakeland, just exceeding Foxes Tarn on the Eskdale side of Scafell. Mickledore is reached from Wasdale by a steep ascent up Brown Tongue, a long grassy rib between the head-streams of Lingmell Gill, into Hollow Stones, the amphitheatre between the facing buttresses of Pike's Crag and Scafell Crag. While much of its floor is stony as its name would indicate, patches of soft turf provide good camp sites and several boulders offer a degree of shelter for a bivouac. On the right between Scafell Crag and Scafell Shamrock a loose rocky cleft known as Lord's Rake leads to a tiny col, beyond which an up and down traverse is made to the open fellside and then easily to the summit of Scafell. Alter-natively the West Wall Traverse breaks out of Lord's Rake before the first col and follows a distinct shelf into the upper part of Deep Gill between the impressive walls of Scafell Pinnacle and Deep Gill Buttress; a steep, rather crumbling slope of red shale leads to the summit plateau, from which a walk of 200 yards in a direction just west of south across a saddle brings one to the cairn. The direct ascent of Scafell from Mickledore via Broad Stand, or its circumvention by Foxes Tarn, has been mentioned (p 158). Scafell is a mountain of remarkable contrasts, fringed on the north and east by tremendous crags but falling away gently to the south-west in sweeping slopes of grass and heather. Even more than Scafell Pike, it can be a dangerous mountain in winter for the inexperienced, for hard slopes of snow persist long in the gullies and Lord's Rake and the West Wall Traverse may then provide a difficult descent. The tragedy of a few years ago, when four were killed in a fall down an icy Deep Gill, emphasises the dangers inherent under such conditions.

As in the case of other Lakeland valleys, the circuit of the sur-rounding tops is an outstanding expedition. Starting from Bracken-close, the walker takes the Brown Tongue route and traverses Scafell to Mickledore, then up the stony track to the Pike and along the ridge to Esk Hause. The conscientious purist can turn aside to visit the fine rocky dome of Great End; its chief virtue, however, is its north-eastern face seamed with three prominent gullies, which under good conditions provide some of the best winter climbing in the district (p 46). Instead of the detour by way of Esk Hause, time

will be saved in clear weather by a direct descent from Great End
to the left (west) of these crags down a grassy, boulder-strewn
slope known as the Band, to the right of Skew Gill and so to Sty
Head. The walker then crosses Great Gable to Beck Head, traverses
the twin summits of Kirk Fell, and strikes down the south-western
ridge of the mountain to the Wastwater Hotel. If sufficiently fresh
he can include the round of Mosedale along a section of the Ennerdale horseshoe (p 55) to Black Sail, Pillar and Wind Gap, then
traversing scree slopes to the summit rocks of Mosedale Red Pike;
the prefix is necessary to distinguish this mountain from the other
of the same name only three miles away on the Ennerdale—Buttermere ridge. Mosedale Red Pike is a fine mountain, with broken
crags falling abruptly on the east, and its south ridge is followed to
Dore Head, a scree-shoot descending almost to the floor of Mosedale. If the walker is still anxious to press on and complete the
whole round, a scramble up the broken rocks of Stirrup Crag
gains the long summit ridge of Yewbarrow, which is traversed and
its southern ridge descended to the lake shore. Yewbarrow, though
not much above 2,000ft, is a fine mountain in its own right, with
a crest nearly one and a half miles long. The rocky outcrop of
Bell Rib on its south ridge can be climbed direct by an easy
scramble, and at the top of this buttress one arrives suddenly at a
prominent cleft, visible in profile from across the valley, known as
the Great Door. On the south-western side of this ridge Overbeck
Buttress provides a number of good climbs.

The Wasdale Head Round, beginning and ending at the Wastwater Hotel, totals about seventeen miles with a total ascent of
about 8,000ft; while this makes a strenuous day, it is a splendid
and worthwhile expedition. A still more exacting trip, the complete
round of Wasdale itself, was mentioned on p 29.

ROCK CLIMBING IN WASDALE

SCAFELL

The climber toiling up the spur of Brown Tongue from near the
head of Wastwater into Hollow Stones finds his view of Scafell
masked by the dark bulk of the Shamrock until he reaches a huge
boulder at the foot of steep scree slopes, where the full glory of the
great sweep of Scafell Crag, from Mickledore round to the Sham-

rock, is revealed, a series of massive buttresses and pinnacles
separated by deeply cut gullies (figure 11). A steep scramble up a
scree cone leads to the foot of Lord's Rake in the sombre angle
between Scafell Crag and the Shamrock. Nearby on the rock face
a carved cross commemorates four climbers who were killed in
1903, striving to emulate O. G. Jones's route up Scafell Pinnacle,
the narrow, well defined line of slabs between Steep and Deep Gills.
From Lord's Rake a walker's path to Mickledore skirts the foot of
a broken plinth of steep, rather loose rock, though most climbs
actually start from a higher terrace known as the Rake's Progress,
which is in places quite exposed.

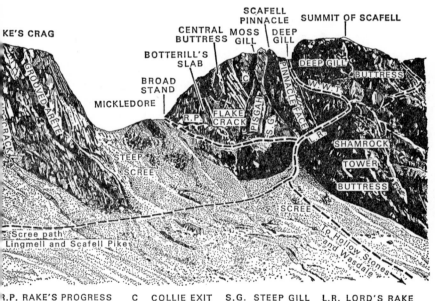

R.P. RAKE'S PROGRESS   C   COLLIE EXIT   S.G. STEEP GILL   L.R. LORD'S RAKE

FIG 11.   Scafell and Pike's Crag

Perhaps only Dow can emulate Scafell in the contribution made
to climbing history by the pioneers, who have left a legacy of much
loved eponymous routes, pitches and individual moves: Woodhead's Slab, Herford's Finish, Collier's Chimney, the Collie Step,
Jones's Arête, Sansom's Traverse, Slingsby's Chimney and many
more. Here the climber is treading ground rich with associations.

Scafell Crag is high-lying, facing almost due north, and so is mostly in the shade and slow drying. Often when Pike's Crag opposite is bathed in sunshine, Scafell has a chilly feel, its rocks cold and greasy. But on a late summer evening, when the sun at last comes round on to the crag, its rocks can be welcoming and rewarding.

Several short routes are found on the Mickledore (left) wing of the crag, including *Collier's* climb, of D standard except for a difficult first pitch (hard S) up a shallow, rather mossy scoop. Next to the right is the **Keswick Brothers'* climb, although only of VD standard, a surprisingly exposed and quite strenuous route which works its way rightwards over some projecting blocks to a prominent pinnacle known as the Pulpit, then up a steep little crack to a large ledge which is actually the top of **Botterill's Slab* slanting up from the right. This remarkably clean-cut, pale coloured slab of a consistently high angle provides a precisely delicate VS climb. Its main 90ft pitch can be climbed direct, though no protection is possible unless the leader moves into the chimney-corner on its right edge to affix a runner before resuming his ascent.

Botterill's marks the left-hand edge of the rock face known as the **Central Buttress* (hard VS), mentioned on p 38 as one of the great climbs with immense tradition. It starts from the Rake's Progress up a long slab with the dominant leftward structural slant of the crag, then up some easy walls to a grassy shelf known as the Oval. Above is the Flake Crack (plate p 143), in the past climbed by elaborate combined tactics though now always led direct, safeguarded by a runner round a fortunately placed chockstone, either by a strenuous layback or by hand-jamming; few moments in life can compare with the ecstasy of grasping the sharp horizontal crest of the Flake after the struggle below. The rest of the climb involves several traverses, one of extreme delicacy, then up to join the top pitch of Moss Gill Grooves. Several variations have been made, including more direct starts and finishes. For long, this was the only climb up the Buttress and in fact no other line was considered possible until 1966 when Les Brown led the *Nazgul* (XS), which takes the left-hand side of the Flake, using several pitons and slings for aid; higher up it twice crosses the ordinary CB route.

The right-hand edge of the Central Buttress is sharply defined by **Moss Gill*, a splendid classic gully of hard VD standard under reasonable conditions, but when wet or icy becoming much more formidable. With a total length of over 400ft, it has eleven pitches, including such features as the steep little Tennis Court Wall and the traverse left out of the back of a huge cave, known as the Collie Step after the leader who on the first ascent chipped a tiny foothold in the rock with his axe. But who are we to censure such an action? On one winter ascent, when we found the Step sheeted with ice, we used three pitons to make the move. After traversing back into the Gill a large stony amphitheatre is reached, with several possible exits. The two most usual take either the long sweep of broken slabs on the left (the Collie Exit), or the steep green chimney on the right (Collier's Chimney); the latter, well endowed with chockstones, gives 130ft of climbing, including a through-route up a hole behind a jammed boulder where it is all too easy to stick. Under real winter conditions, Moss Gill may afford a superlative climb with the issue in doubt to the end.

Several climbs leave Moss Gill and slant leftwards up the edge of the Central Buttress. The finest is *Moss Gill Grooves* (hard S), a delightfully delicate climb up a series of slabs; it includes the so-called 'irreversible move' on one steep slab, achieved by crossing the right leg inside the left on minute holds. Dr G. Graham Macphee not only proved it reversible by making the first descent, but had the satisfaction of using his initials to summarise the climb as 'M.G.G.; G.G.M.'

To the right of Moss Gill is Pisgah Buttress, named by the Biblically minded pioneers with the same association of ideas as was evident on the Pillar Rock (p 61). This provides several long continuous climbs, including the *Direct* route (mild S) of 450ft which takes a very good line up the centre. Steep Gill to the right of Pisgah is a gully to avoid except under winter conditions, when it may provide a really formidable and indeed rarely successful climb. Many climbers, however, enter its lower recesses to strike out right on to the flanks of Scafell Pinnacle to a huge rock crevasse. Above this the rather awkward and undercut *Slingsby's Chimney* (hard D) leads to the top of Low Man, the lower summit of the Pinnacle and then up a much scratched Knife-edge Arête to High Man. This gives a varied expedition of over 300ft, providing an excellent first acquaintance with the Pinnacle; its summit stands quite isolated, with a short descent on sloping polished holds leading into Jordan Gap.

The Pinnacle Face is a fine sweep of clean rock leading to a prominent ledge with a cairn, originally built by the Hopkinson brothers in the 1880's who had descended to it on a rope. Half a dozen climbs have been made up the face, starting with O. G. Jones's original route *Direct from Lord's Rake* (S) in 1898 and culminating in the *Right Hand Edge* (hard VS) in 1961. Under dry conditions in PA's these climbs, with their traditional eponymous pitches and situations, go very comfortably despite the slabby and sloping nature of the rock; notorious for the absence of belays, the use of slings with nuts has eased this problem. A justifiable piton has been placed as a belay on Moss Ledge, just below the steep Herford's Slab leading to Hopkinson's Cairn; this can be reached by the very fine *Moss Ledge Direct* climb (mild VS), with a top pitch runout of 120ft.

The Deep Gill wall of the Pinnacle, rising boldly from the reddish scree and boulders at its base, has quite a maze of routes. One of the best is *Jones's Route from Deep Gill* (mild S), following a long curving crack and then a square-cut arête to the top of Low Man. On the right-hand corner of the Pinnacle *Woodhead's* climb (mild S) starts with a perplexing slab on which one teeters ridiculously before stepping up towards a prominent pinnacle and so by *Herford's Finish* up a bulging wall.

The *Girdle Traverse* of Scafell, starting from the *Professor's Chimney* (D) in the right-hand angle of the Pinnacle, makes a splendid expedition of about 1,100ft of climbing, with one or two alternative sections. Its general standard is hard S, unless the logical finish up Botterill's Slab is included which involves a VS pitch. Two of us leading through took about two and a half hours on one occasion, though conditions were then superb, and at other times we have taken twice as long.

There are a few good climbs on Deep Gill Buttress to the right of Deep Gill and on the Shamrock. For modest climbers the *West Wall* (D) to the right of the deeply incised Great Chimney is attractive, while its left-hand wall is followed by the *Upper West Wall* climb (S), with a hard introductory groove succeeded by easier rocks. One of the longest climbs in Lakeland is the *Tower Buttress* (hard S) of almost 700ft, starting right down at the base of the crags; it has fourteen varied pitches and the main difficulty is adhering to the route.

On the way up to Scafell from Wasdale a large diamond-shaped mass of rock standing darkly out on the fellside is known as Black Crag (4); rarely is a climber enticed on to it if his ultimate objective is Scafell, since its dark vegetated nature is not alluring. On closer inspection it indeed proves to be mossy and greasy, crossed by numerous grassy ledges; obviously it requires a good spell of fine weather before climbing is at all pleasant and then one would presumably prefer Scafell. However, three routes have been made and on one occasion we forced ourselves to climb the 400ft *Sinister Ridge*, only of hard VD standard but sufficiently extending to require socks over rubbers to negotiate its eleven pitches of grooves, walls and corners separated by grassy ledges.

One of the remarkable features of Scafell is that while its familiar and much loved main crag has many fine routes of all grades, it also has a hidden treasure for the expert in its East Buttress (91), reached from Mickledore by a short descent on the Eskdale side down the scree past Broad Stand. This is a most striking wall, vertical even palpably overhanging at its base, with enormous grooves and corners, though the upper section eases back into the mountain and does not at first give a true impression of its height and of the length of the climbs, of the order of 200 to 300ft. The buttress is high-lying and carries much natural drainage, so that it has a dark wet appearance except after a period of drought. There have been some bad summers during the last decade when it was literally impossible to climb there; a few big routes, made under dry conditions, were unrepeated for several years not merely because of their technical difficulty (though this is usually considerable) or the shortage of able leaders, but because of the unremittingly wet or greasy conditions. On the other hand, a good summer such as 1966 and 1968 makes the East Buttress irresistible to the experts, and experts they must be, since except for one or two flanking chimneys, the routes are all of VS or XS grade. Their number is steadily increasing, about twenty-five when the Guidebook was published in 1967, but since then at least half a dozen more have been made and the Buttress now has five XS's.

We can mention only a few of the more amenable routes within our capacity, starting with the *Great Eastern* (mild VS), one of the early classics climbed in 1932 by Maurice Linnell, later killed on Ben Nevis, and Sid Cross. One of us has vivid memories of being last man on the first ascent in nailed boots, led by R. J. Birkett in 1938. After the first 15ft pitch, the steepness of the rock asserts itself in the form of an overhanging crack, and after crossing a slab a series of cracks leads to a stance below a prominent roof. Here the Guidebook's direction is '. . . ascend on good holds', whereas the move is easier by descending slightly and continuing an upward traverse to the right to a small crevasse. The climbing now relaxes and finishes up a corner near the top of the prominent White Slab. This is a route well within the competence of an adequate climber, with none of the desperation of the harder lines yet affording an excellent example of the 'feel' of the Buttress. For those who are in form for sterner stuff, the *Yellow Slab Variation taking off at pitch three gives 175ft of hard VS climbing, strenuous in its lower section, exposed and delicate in the upper.

Another of the older classics is *Mickledore Grooves (VS); in fact the Guidebook goes so far as to call it the classic of the district. It is a delicate climb up slabs, walls and grooves away to the right of the crag near Mickledore Chimney; its third pitch requires an overall runout of 140ft before a satisfactory belay is reached, though several runners may be fixed. Another climb of quite reasonable character is *Morning Wall (mild VS), taking the prominent overhanging wall on the south-eastern flank facing Bowfell. It shares its start with three other climbs, and the real work does not begin until the second pitch, a thin, almost holdless crack on which a leader need not be too proud to accept his second man's shoulder in order to gain height. Reassuringly this is the hardest section of the climb, and the continuation of the long leftward traverse, followed by a chimney and some slabs, is comparatively easy.

Two other recommended climbs on the right-hand flank of the Buttress are the closely associated Mayday (hard VS) and *Overhanging Wall (VS). The former starts about 30ft left of Mickledore Chimney, the latter a further 20ft on. Both are strenuous, particularly memorable being a thin and rather fierce scoop on Mayday, and each has pitons in place, though on our last visit the one on Overhanging Wall was rusty and looked and felt unsafe; perhaps it has recently been replaced. The more attractive finish to Overhanging Wall is the so-called White Slab Variation, rather than the upward continuation of the original line. The White Slab is a fine-looking mass broken into two pitches of 50ft each by a very convenient block which affords an excellent belay; this whole section is delightful after the strenuous character of the wall below.

CRAGS ON THE SCAFELL PIKE RANGE

On occasions when we have been heavily engaged in the shadows of Scafell Crag we have looked across Hollow Stones with some longing towards Pike's Crag (77), which is in sunshine most of the day. This is a flanking buttress of Scafell Pike, whose summit lies a third of a mile to the east. It rises from a broken plinth of little walls and grassy ledges, and culminates towards its centre in the prominent Pulpit Rock, which can be reached by an easy scramble from the plateau behind and affords a magnificent view of Scafell. As a climbing ground, of course, Pike's Crag does not compare with Scafell, for it is much more broken, but closer inspection reveals several continuous ribs of good rock.

For many years attention was paid only to the black-looking gullies to the left, lettered A to D, but though B contains a quite difficult chimney pitch, they are hardly worth visiting in summer. Under winter conditions, however, they may provide some good climbing.

The rib which sweeps up to the Pulpit Rock gives several good routes; the *Wall and Crack* and the **Juniper Buttress* are among the best of the VD category, long, varied and on sound rock. The former is a good safe climb in winter, with short pitches, big holds and very good belays, while the top 50ft pitch of the latter is remarkably steep and exposed for its grading, with excellent holds up a thin crack. It is of interest that these two were first climbed on successive days in April 1924 by H. M. Kelly, who is so prominently associated with Pillar, and on the next day his party in the same surge of activity added two more, *Grooved Arête* (VD) and *Southern Corner* (S) farther to the right on the more broken crags overlooking the screes below Mickledore. While Southern Corner is technically harder, it is interrupted by easy rock and grassy ledges, and the Grooved Arête is a much more satisfactory climb, including a good pitch which takes a steep crack and then traverses off left on to a clean-cut rib.

Several harder climbs have been made up the right-hand wall of the Pulpit buttress, including the *Sentinel* and the *Citadel* (both VS) and the unattractive *Urchin's Groove* (hard S), from which we retreated on a damp day because of its greasy mossy nature. On the whole, if one wishes to climb VS routes there are abundant good ones across the way on Scafell, and we suspect that some of these harder lines were evolved on Pike's Crag when it just happened to be in better condition than its big neighbour.

The western face of the range between Lingmell and Great End abounds in outcrops, many of which provide scrambling of good quality, as is evidenced by the well-scratched lines on rocks near the Corridor Route. Stand Crag (100), just below this popular trod to the left (true right) of the big fall in Greta Gill, has half a dozen routes of varied quality on sound rock with excellent holds; the best is *Deerstalker* (S), though this is so deficient in belays that a piton is advisable. Higher up the Corridor Route, just before crossing the upper section of Greta Gill, Round How (88), a small outcrop with well-marked glacial striations, has several routes, including the mild *Wyvern Groove*, an obvious deeply cut line on the right.

Lingmell (64) has an impressive north-western buttress, but this is so shattered and interrupted that worthwhile climbing routes are unlikely. However, its north-eastern slopes are deeply gashed by Piers Gill and its confluents; the ascent of the Gill is well worth doing for the dramatic quality of its narrowly enclosed gorges, pinnacles, cascades and pools, though this is practicable only after a spell of reasonably dry weather and may be utterly impossible after heavy rain. This expedition involves much scrambling among boulders on the stream bed, wading through pools (it is preferable to abandon at an early stage any thought of keeping dry), and several steep waterfall pitches where the rock is distinctly unsound. One of us was negotiating a vertical corner while trying to keep out of the main waterfall when a hold came away and he executed what must have been the finest sitting high dive ever seen in Wasdale into the pool which fortunately awaited him. Actually the two main waterfall pitches can be avoided by taking to the walls, traversing back above each fall into the bed of the Gill. Above the higher fall a massive boulder forms the easily recognisable Bridge Rock, beyond which the rocky bed of the upper gill can easily be followed to the Corridor Route about 200ft below Lingmell Col. If morale is still good and the party is not too wet or cold, it is preferable to leave the Gill just beyond the Bridge Rock and scramble up its tributary Straight Gill to the right. Followed by a long broken scoop and a rather shattered arête, this will lead ultimately to the summit of Lingmell. The entire expedition from the lower reaches of Piers Gill, allegedly providing 2,000ft of climbing and scrambling (though considerably more of the latter), has been christened *Pilgrim's Progress* (VD).

The northern and north-eastern faces of Great End (42) are extremely craggy and split by three well defined gullies, their base at about 2,500ft and almost reaching the summit plateau. Yet despite this abundance of rock, in summer the gullies offer very little climbing between long slopes of scree and boulders. In a good winter, however, the *South-East* and *Central Gullies* may provide really fine routes; we have climbed them during three of the last four winters and found quite different conditions on each occasion. The third and shortest gully is *Cust's* away to the right, readily recognisable from a jammed boulder bridging its upper cleft; this forms a good descent after climbing one of the others. From Wasdale Head the approach to these gullies can be made up the Old Sty Head track, turning right into the square-cut Skew Gill (the exit from which on one occasion up steep ice was quite difficult), and so to a prominent col, from which a traverse across the snow-slopes leads to the foot of the crag.

CRAGS OVERLOOKING WASTWATER

The great mass of rock falling from the summit of Whin Rigg towards the foot of Wastwater is split by several deep black clefts known as the Screes Gullies (93). Half a dozen of these, lettered A to F from east to west, are mentioned in the old Guidebooks, but only two, the *Great Gully* (S) and the **C Gully* (mild VS), are worth climbing. For long these had a dangerous reputation because of their rotten rock; during his second ascent of C Gully O. G. Jones had a fall when a great mass came away. However, more frequent usage seems to have cleaned them somewhat. Last year we climbed the Great Gully, raced along the summit ridge of Whin Rigg and down the path to the west of the crags to their base, and then continued nonstop up C Gully; this gave us 1,200ft of climbing and took us, leading through, about five hours. All the usual types of gully obstacle are present: chimneys, caves, cracks, chockstones and water slides, some climbed direct, others bypassed by traverses on the enclosing walls. The only point to remember in the

Great Gully is that after reaching a large amphitheatre it is essential to keep up the left branch for the right can lead into trouble, while in the C Gully the crux is the awkward wall and bulging corner of the top pitch. After much rain the gullies should be left alone, since they rapidly become tremendous cascades.

Low Adam Crag (66) is an outcrop on the slope of the screes about 750ft above the lake and below the summit of Illgill Head. While the Guidebook description of the climbs as being '. . . steep, loose and coated with lichen' is not very alluring, the crag is not entirely deserving of rejection. One of us has respect for *Dexedrin* (VS), having participated in its first ascent in 1964. The piton runner on the groove of the first pitch proved to be a welcome rest-point, where one could hang on and take some of the strain off the feet which had been overworked on the meagre wrinkles below. This pitch ends with a thin move leftward around a small overhang, followed by a steep rib, and it shares the last pitch with *Pituitrin* (also VS). All the other climbs are of VS category and almost all are named with drug associations; one could sum up the crag by describing it not in the words of the Guidebook '. . . strictly for the connoisseur', but rather for the addict.

On the north-western side of the lake above the road near Green-dale the rocky outcrop of Buckbarrow (13) stands out prominently as one approaches from Gosforth. It is surprising that for so long very little attention was paid to these bluffs; presumably climbers were too intent on getting to Wasdale Head. The outcrops comprise two separate sections, the more easterly having the early climbs of *Rowan Tree* (mild S) and *Forked Gullies* (S) and the pleasant little *Central Face* climb (hard S) which takes an obvious line up its centre.

The popular Buckbarrow routes have been made on the larger steeper crag to the west, where a large pillar leans against the main mass. *Gargarin* is an excellent climb of VD standard on the left of the pillar, with five varied pitches; the second is a wall with a somewhat problematical start and a neat exit on to a slab. At the top of this an exposed ridge directly above the central pillar is gained by way of a steep crack with good holds. *Witch* (VS) works its way up the chimney-crack on the right side of the pillar (plate p 126), involving bridging, then a thought-provoking move to a little niche on the right and a short steep wall, above which the crack is regained and followed to the top of the pillar, in all a fine 90ft pitch. Finally an exposed open groove is shared with its neighbour *Harmony* (VS). Above this buttress a terrace is topped by a line of broken crags which provides some scrambling routes to the top of the hill. At the right-hand of this upper tier the prominent *Buckbarrow Needle* (VS) forms a two-pitch problem with an over-hanging crack start (avoidable by a traverse in from the left or by another crack around the corner) and a very steep wall-pitch climbed on minute holds.

Overbeck (75), a small compact outcrop on the south-western flanks of Yewbarrow overlooking Bowderdale, is barely a half-hour from the lakeshore road and ideal for short climbs on a summer evening. It offers an assortment of chimney, crack and slab climbs, including two good routes of VS standard; their shortness is the only disadvantage. *Overbeck Buttress* (mild S) follows the clean-cut right-hand edge of the crag; its third pitch forms the crux, a slight bulge on the steep section of the arête where a delicate step is made to the right and the wall above climbed on good holds. To the left of the last climb is the *Bowderdale* climb (S), which has a neat little 'sentry box' at about mid-height, from which a leftward traverse over rather mossy slabs leads to a stance with an old yew serving as a belay; the finish is up a steep wall on small but adequate holds. A prominent feature of Overbeck is a protruding bracket on the right-hand edge of a small overhanging wall, after which the *Gargoyle* (VS) is named. The third pitch is the crux, where a vertical and very strenuous crack is negotiated to reach the Gargoyle itself (plate p 144); this involves a bold lead, though mitigated by the fixing of runners before pulling over on top of the Gargoyle. Though somewhat discontinuous, the *Central* route (S) has some good individual pitches, particularly a slanting chimney in the middle of the climb.

Towards the centre of the crag three prominent chimneys, *B* (D), *Central* and *Ash Tree*, start from a narrow ledge known as the Catwalk. The two last are of VD standard and are worth a visit in any weather conditions; Ash Tree can be lengthened by pre-facing a groove which lies directly below the usual start. *Curving Crack* (S) is a better route than might initially appear, for the broken nature of the lower rocks improves with height; at about 30ft it is necessary to make an awkward little move to the right, and the top pitch is a short chimney-crack with rather sparse holds.

GREAT GABLE

Though the great crag on the northern face of Great Gable belongs
indubitably to Ennerdale (p 68), two outcrops on its southern flanks
are clearly included in Wasdale: Kern Knotts and the Napes.

Kern Knotts (62) is a small compact buttress of superb rock
situated about a quarter-mile west of the summit of Sty Head. It
can be reached from Wasdale Head by leaving the Sty Head track
at a grassy bluff and scrambling directly up towards the outcrop.
A small secluded cave among the boulders, where we have on
occasions sheltered snugly, is passed, though it is difficult to find
unless one knows its exact entrance. Just above the cave the small
outcrop of Lower Kern Knotts is split by a difficult 30ft crack with
an awkward little overhang halfway up, while on the right the
Slab climb (S) takes a neat line on tiny but sufficient holds. Lower
Kern Knotts West, another little outcrop a hundred yards to the
west, has a couple of interesting if short climbs, one a quite severe
buttress route. We have spent several wet days here, based in the
cave and forcing ourselves out periodically on to one or other of
these small outcrops.

A faint path winds up the scree to the main Kern Knotts which
rises prominently from a chaos of huge angular boulders at its
foot. It consists of a massive nose structurally detached from the
main mass by a fault, thus forming the *Chimney* (D) on the west,
the *Crack* (mild VS) splitting the near-vertical wall on the east.
Beyond the Chimney a steep grey wall extends westward, interrupted only by the prominent right-angle of the West Chimney,
until it fades out into the broken rocks and scree of the mountainside. On the right (east) the East Buttress has a single S route up a
wall with good holds.

The whole mass is only about 100ft high, the wall containing the
Crack a mere 70ft, so that Kern Knotts has been rather contemptu-
ously dismissed as an 'overgrown boulder problem' and a great
place for close-up spectator participation; we once saw someone
climb the Crack blindfolded, which, though admittedly done for a
film, savours of stunting. Yet the rock is steep, clean and massive
and a dozen memorable climbs, most of VS category, have been
made, all of them before 1934 with the exception of the *Cenotaph*
(VS). This was made in 1955 up the right-angle between the East
Buttress and the main wall, involving near the top a very strenuous

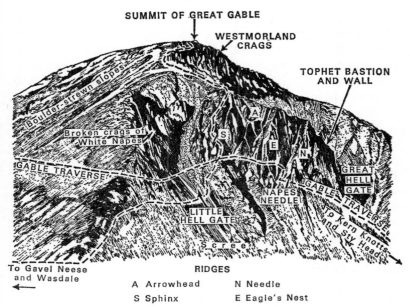

SUMMIT OF GREAT GABLE

WESTMORLAND CRAGS

TOPHET BASTION AND WALL

Boulder-strewn slopes

Broken crags of White Napes

GABLE TRAVERSE

A

S

E

N

GREAT HELL GATE

NAPES NEEDLE

GABLE TRAVERSE

LITTLE HELL GATE

To Kern Knotts and Sty Head

S c r e e

To Gavel Neese and Wasdale

RIDGES

A Arrowhead   N Needle
S Sphinx   E Eagle's Nest

FIG 12.   The Napes, Great Gable

move out of an overhanging crack and up over a triangular roof into a steep finishing groove. Kern Knotts is a splendid place for climbing on the tips of the fingers and the edges of PA's on clean rock with minute holds. The routes include the steep layback crack and sensational hand traverse of *Sepulchre* (VS); the very thin *Innominate Crack* (VS) which was such a strain on the fingers for the 60ft pitch until the use of nuts and runners gave reassurance; *Kern Knotts Crack* itself, which used to be S but in the recent edition of the Guidebook has been promoted to mild VS, presumably because it has been so polished during its seventy years' career since the first ascent by O. G. Jones, especially the slab on the right of the Sentry Box; the beautiful three-pitch *Buttonhook* (hard VS), so called originally because a piece of wire was carried to poke a piece of line through a hole to make a thread belay at the top of the first pitch; and the *Buttress* (hard VS), which includes a most awkward step to the right from the big platform on the Chimney on to a faintly sloping foothold, particularly if one doesn't know about a high little incut for the right fingers to steady

M

the move across. Five more climbs lie west of the Chimney, including two steep routes of mild VS category, the *Central* climb and the *West Buttress*, both on sound rock with small though adequate holds. The end route on the left is the *Flake* climb (mild VS), which follows a long slanting flake known as the Cat Walk to a chimney near the top of the buttress.

Three of us once spent most of a broiling day doing the **Kern Knotts Chain* (hard VS), a mini-girdle of the whole buttress, which we took from right to left, the reverse of the Guidebook's suggestion, starting up the Sepulchre and finishing along the Flake. Probably the hardest moves involved crossing the sections of vertical almost holdless wall between the Innominate and Kern Knotts Cracks and between the latter and the Buttress. It was in all an exacting exercise.

From Burnthwaite the Napes ridges (72) stand out boldly at a height of about 2,000ft on the southern flanks of Great Gable (plate p 126), bounded on either side by extensive scree slopes falling steeply to the valley floor. They can be reached either from Sty Head by the South Gable Traverse or from Burnthwaite by the long plod up Gavel Neese to a little obelisk known as Moses' Finger, then by a rough rightward ascent to join the South Gable Traverse just west of the Napes. They consist of a series of prominent arêtes and buttresses, separated by shattered gullies (figure 12) which should be strictly avoided because of stone fall; not only are these dangerously loose, but they funnel stones dislodged from the intervening ridges.

Steep and remarkably sound in their lower sections, the several arêtes lean back and merge into a narrow horizontal crest which runs into the mountainside. With their sound rock and sunny southerly aspect, the Napes have long been popular, as indicated by the scratched and highly polished holds. Four distinct ridges may be distinguished, while on the east a series of more broken tiers end in the clean-cut Tophet Wall overlooking the red screes of Great Hell Gate. At the foot of the Needle Ridge near the east of the crags is the unmistakable obelisk of the Napes Needle (plate p 125). Within this limited area of rock are concentrated nearly fifty climbs, ranging in time from the Needle Ridge climbed in 1884 and the Needle two years later to such 'fill-in' climbs as the *Pod* (VS) and the *Merry Monk* (mild VS) made as late as 1968 on the west-

ern flanks of the Eagle's Nest Ridge, and the tremendously strenuous crack on Tophet Wall, long regarded as a major outstanding
problem and finally solved in 1969 to give an XS climb, the *Viking*.

Starting from the west the first mass of rock is known as the
Sphinx Ridge after the curiously shaped rock at its base which
from some aspects looks indeed like the profile of the Sphinx,
though from others like a sitting cat with a projecting tail; the
move from its tail to its head gives a little 15ft problem. *Sphinx
Ridge* (hard D) takes a natural line from the gap, while *Rainbow
Ridge* (hard S) lies on another ridge higher and to the right; it
starts with a steep delicate slab and traverses to a delightfully rough
arête. Across the gully the sharply defined *Arrowhead Ridge* is
so called because it leads to a clean-cut diamond-shaped rock, the
Arrowhead itself. A fine series of slabs, quite exposed though only
of VD standard because of the superb holds, leads directly to the
tip of the Arrowhead; the gap is crossed to the easier upper ridge,
followed for another 120ft to the top, crossing en route another
steep little gap known as the Strid. An 'easy way', also useful as a
quick descent, leads from Eagle's Nest Gully to the gap behind
the Arrowhead.

Across the Eagle's Nest Gully rises the finest of the Napes ridges,
the Eagle's Nest itself, split by the West and Ling Chimneys into
several steep ribs. On the left is the very good *Abbey Buttress*
(plate p 126) (VD) starting from a large crevasse formed by a pinnacle at the base of the buttress. The first section ascends for about
100ft, followed by an awkward little traverse to the right under an
overhang, though with good holds and plenty of possible runners,
finishing straight up to the top of the buttress, where it joins the
Eagle's Nest route. A much harder climb, *Long John* (mild VS),
takes the wall between Ling and West Chimneys, involving one or
two very hard moves on minute holds. The *Eagle's Nest Ridge
Direct*, first climbed in 1892, starts from a prominent terrace known
as the Dress Circle because of its excellent view of the Needle
opposite. Over the years the naturally small and sloping holds have
become so polished that the climb has been elevated from its former
S grading to mild VS; it is almost impossible to arrange any form
of protection for the 70ft runout of the main pitch, though on dry
rock in PA's all that is needed is a series of steady balanced rises.

One of our favourite climbs is *Tricouni Rib* (mild VS), originally so called because its holds were admirably suited to tricouni nailing, negotiating the steep wall to the right of the Eagle's Nest Direct. After the initial easy pitch from the Dress Circle, a grass ledge with a large block is reached beneath a steep wall. A difficult step up is made by a finger or nut jammed in a thin crack to reach a horizontal traverse line of holds to the edge of the buttress. Continuing up this edge a small, often wet, chimney is reached, which can either be climbed direct or by a couple of moves up its outside wall, regaining it just below a chockstone. A final easy slanting chimney with small footholds but good hand-jams leads to the main Eagle's Nest Ridge.

These various routes merge to follow the long easy upper part of the ridge for about 200ft. The deeply cut *West Chimney* (D) is a mildly pleasant way of joining the Eagle's Nest Ridge above the two hard pitches on the Direct route, while *Ling Chimney* (hard VD) to the right is a steep and narrow chimney-crack with good holds.

The **Napes Needle* (plate p 125) rises from a plinth at the base of the Needle Ridge and provides a spectacular little climb of about 60ft (hard VD). Several routes by way of either the Wasdale or Lingmell Cracks or the neater arête on its western angle lead to the upper platform known as the Shoulder. The top block is so polished that its ascent is now more difficult than in the past, but since the leader is merely a few feet away from his second it is only a slight balancing trick to step up on to a mantelshelf at its right end (the left end is possible but much harder), traverse delicately left and pull up on to the top block. The belay here is unique, since a loop is lowered beneath the overhanging block by means of a kind of skipping-rope swing and a handy little knob hooks it in position as the free rope is taken in and thus the leader ties himself on to the block. Though on the first visit it may not seem so, the descent is actually much easier than the ascent. The *Obverse* route (S) swings boldly across the face of the Needle from the Shoulder above the gap opposite the Needle Ridge and climbs the corner of the top block by a 'monkey up a stick' movement on rounded holds. There is even a *Direct Obverse* (hard VS) straight up from the gap, but this requires a very tall leader with exceptional reach and it is usually necessary for his foot to be held on the initial tiny sloping holds. Finally, a girdle of the Needle which though quite easy looks most spectacular from the Dress Circle can be made at the level of the Shoulder on excellent holds. The *Needle Ridge* (VD) is an extremely popular climb of well over 300ft; from the gap it starts up a smooth slab with some neat little thumb-holes and continues up a series of walls, ribs and grooves to the top of the Napes. This and the other ridges lend themselves to continuous climbing, up one and down another, stringing them together in various combinations as the mood suggests.

To the east of the Needle the rock becomes much more broken and indeed in some places suspect, but several short routes have been made, including the *Chantry Buttress* (hard VD). Its second pitch involves an awkward traverse to the left, followed by a difficult little corner, but runners can be fixed before these slightly exposed moves.

The eastern section of the Napes is bounded by the massive Tophet Buttress, which on the south side forms a long, though rather broken arête known as **Tophet Bastion* (hard VD). This gives a good climb, suitable for wet conditions, with large holds and belays, up a series of walls, corners and grooves; the climb can be extended up a prominent sharp-angled pillar to the left, the *Shark's Fin*, providing two quite difficult pitches on small holds. To the east of this arête the steep expanse of Tophet Wall provides several very good climbs, of which the **Tophet Wall* route itself (S) can be highly recommended. It works its way across the wall from left to right, including an exposed traverse high up on superb flake holds before finishing up a rib.

All the Napes ridges merge at their apex to a narrow grassy col, behind which rise the broken Westmorland crags, on which several scrambling routes or a more continuous climb, the *Westmorland Ridge* (VD), can be taken to the top of the crag at the southern edge of the summit plateau. Here a massive cairn was built in 1876 by the brothers Westmorland to indicate what they regarded as Lakeland's finest view, with Wastwater to the south-west and the Scafell Pike range across the great gulf of upper Wasdale to the south-east. A short walk over the boulder-strewn plateau leads to the summit of Great Gable, with the bronze War Memorial plaque of the Fell and Rock Climbing Club set in the solid rock.

Thus Wordsworth's 'wheel' has indeed come full circle, as we look from Gable down Ennerdale where we started our itinerary. This is our mountain heritage.

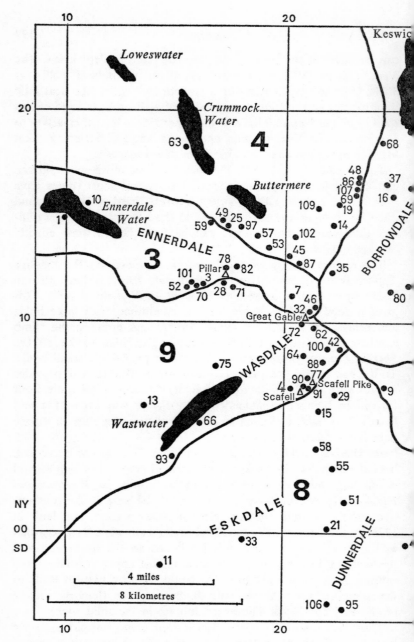

FIG 13. Location map of the climbing crags. The large number[s]
indicate the seven topographical chapters; the small numbers indica[te]
each climbing crag, listed in the table on p 200. National Grid lines a[re]
inserted at 10km intervals

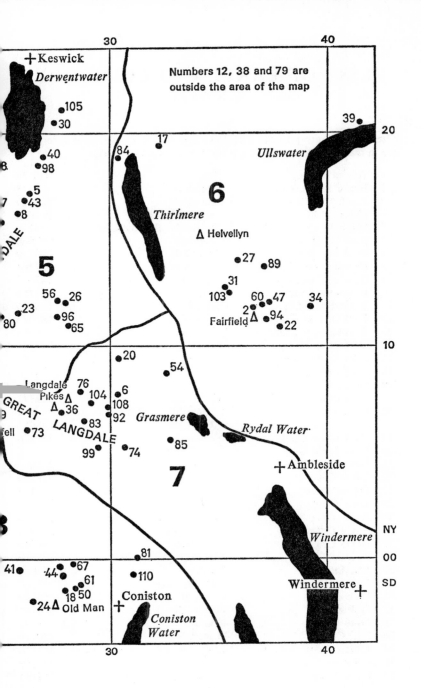

+Keswick
Derwentwater

Numbers 12, 38 and 79 are
outside the area of the map

●105
●30

●40
●98

Ullswater

39●

●5
●43
●8

Thirlmere

6

Δ Helvellyn

5

●27
●89

56● ●26

●31
103●

60● ●47

●23

●80

●96
●65

Fairfield Δ ●94
2● ●22

34●

●20

●54

Langdale
Pikes Δ ●76
●104
●6

GREAT Δ●36
●108
●92

Grasmere

Rydal Water·

●83

fell ●73

LANGDALE

99●
●74

●85

7

+Ambleside

Windermere

●81

41● ·44●
●67
●61

●110

Windermere

18●50
●24 Δ Old Man

Coniston

*Coniston
Water*

LIST OF LAKELAND CLIMBING CRAGS

The number refers to the location map, figure 13. All grid references are in the NY 100km square except where stated otherwise.

1	Angler's Crag	Ennerdale	098150
2	Black Buttress	Deepdale	362118
3	Black Crag	Ennerdale	166117
4	Black Crag	Scafell, Wasdale	201068
5	Black Crag	Troutdale, Borrowdale	264172
6	Blea Crag	Langdale	302080
7	Boat Howe	Ennerdale	200110
8	Bowderstone Crags	Borrowdale	257164
9	Bowfell Buttresses	Langdale	245070
10	Bowness Knott	Ennerdale	111155
11	Brantrake Crag	Eskdale	SD 146986
12	Buckbarrow Crag	Long Sleddale	483073
13	Buckbarrow Crag	Wasdale	136058
14	Buckstone How	Buttermere	224145
15	Cam Spout Crag	Eskdale	214056
16	Castle Crag	Borrowdale	250160
17	Castle Rock of Triermain	Thirlmere	322197
18	Cove Crag	Coppermines Valley, Coniston	SD 278985
19	Dale Head Crag	Newlands	227156
20	Deer Bield Crag	Far Easedale	303096
21	Demming Crag	Eskdale	223003
22	Dove Crag	Dovedale	376109
23	Doves' Nest	Comb Gill, Borrowdale	256117
24	Dow Crag	Coniston	SD 263980
25	Eagle Crag	Birkness, Buttermere	173146
26	Eagle Crag	Borrowdale	277121
27	Eagle Crag	Grisedale	356140
28	Elliptical Crag	Mosedale, Wasdale	172117
29	Esk Buttress	Eskdale	222064
30	Falcon Crags	Derwentwater	272205
31	Falcon Crag	Grisedale	350127
32	Gable Crag	Ennerdale	212105
33	Gate Crag	Eskdale	SD 186999
34	Gill Crag	Dovedale	390119
35	Gillercombe Buttress	Borrowdale	217116
36	Gimmer Crag	Langdale	276069
37	Goat Crag	Borrowdale	245165

38	Gouther Crag	Swindale		516128
39	Gowbarrow Crag	Ullswater		414205
40	Gowder Crag	Borrowdale		266187
41	Great Blake Rigg	Seathwaite, Dunnerdale	SD	257997
42	Great End	Scafell range		227085
43	Greatend Crag	Troutdale, Borrowdale		259170
44	Great and Little How	Coppermines Valley,	SD	274999
	Crags	Coniston	SD	271997
45	Green Crag	Buttermere		203131
46	Green Gable Crag	Ennerdale		216107
47	Greenhow End	Deepdale		369120
48	Grey Buttress	Newlands		233166
49	Grey Crag	Birkness, Buttermere		171148
50	Grey Crag	Coppermines Valley,		
		Coniston	SD	282987
51	Hard Knott Crag	Eskdale		227017
52	Haskett Buttress	Ennerdale		155114
53	Haystacks Crag	Buttermere		196132
54	Helm Crag	Far Easedale		326089
55	Heron Crag	Eskdale		222028
56	Heron Crag	Langstrath, Borrowdale		275118
57	High Crag	Buttermere		183144
58	High Scarth Crag	Eskdale		215040
59	High Stile Crags	Ennerdale		167147
60	Hutaple Crag	Deepdale		365118
61	Kernel Crag	Coppermines Valley,		
		Coniston	SD	284991
62	Kern Knotts	Great Gable, Wasdale		216095
63	Ling Crag	Mellbreak, Crummock		
		Water		154183
64	Lingmell	Wasdale		208084
65	Lining Crag	Borrowdale		283112
66	Low Adam Crag	Wasdale		158048
67	Low Wether Crag	Coppermines Valley,		
		Coniston	SD	284002
68	Maiden Moor Crag	Derwentwater		244184
69	Miners' Crag	Newlands		232158
70	Mirk Cove Buttress	Ennerdale		159116
71	Mosedale Buttresses	Mosedale, Wasdale		176116
72	The Napes	Great Gable, Wasdale		210100
73	Neckband	Langdale		262061
74	Oak Howe	Langdale		305055
75	Overbeck Buttress	Wasdale		169079
76	Pavey Ark	Langdale		285080
77	Pike's Crag	Wasdale		210072
78	Pillar Rock	Ennerdale		172125

N

79	Rainsborrow Crag	Kentmere		444067
80	Raven Crag	Comb Gill, Borrowdale		247115
81	Raven Crag	Coniston		312003
82	Raven Crag	Ennerdale		175128
83	Raven Crag	Great Langdale		285064
84	Raven Crag	Thirlmere		304189
85	Raven Crag	Walthwaite, Langdale		325057
86	Red Crag	Newlands		234166
87	Round How	Buttermere		206128
88	Round How	Wasdale		218082
89	St Sunday Crag	Grisedale		367135
90	Scafell Crag	Wasdale		208069
91	Scafell East Buttress	Eskdale		210067
92	Scout Crag	Langdale		298070
93	Screes Gullies	Wasdale		150035
94	Scrubby Crag	Deepdale		367116
95	Seathwaite Buttress	Dunnerdale	SD	229964
96	Sergeant Crag	Langstrath, Borrowdale		273114
97	Sheepbone Buttress	Birkness, Buttermere		179144
98	Shepherd's Crag	Borrowdale		263185
99	Side Pike	Langdale		294054
100	Stand Crag	Wasdale		219088
101	Steeple Buttress	Ennerdale		158117
102	Striddle Crag	Buttermere		205140
103	Tarn Crag	Grisedale		352126
104	Tarn Crag	Langdale		290073
105	Walla Crag	Derwentwater		274210
106	Wallowbarrow Crag	Dunnerdale	SD	222968
107	Waterfall Buttress	Newlands		233160
108	White Gill Crags	Langdale		298073
109	Yew Crag	Buttermere		214153
110	Yewdale Crag	Coniston	SD	309992

ONE HUNDRED GOOD CLIMBS

A DIFFICULT/VERY DIFFICULT

A route, Gimmer, Great Langdale
Abbey Buttress, The Napes, Great Gable, Wasdale
Arrowhead Ridge Direct, The Napes, Great Gable, Wasdale
Birkness Gully, Birkness Combe, Buttermere
Bowderstone Pinnacle, Borrowdale
Bowfell Buttress, Bowfell, Great Langdale
C route, Dow Crag, Coniston
Corvus, Raven Crag, Borrowdale
Curving Gully, Hutaple Crag, Deepdale
Gimmer Chimney, Gimmer, Great Langdale
Harrow Buttress, Grey Crag, Birkness Combe, Buttermere
Jones's route *from Easter Gully*, Dow Crag, Coniston
Juniper Buttress, Pike's Crag, Wasdale
Keswick Brothers' climb, Scafell, Wasdale
Little Chamonix, Shepherd's Crag, Borrowdale
Mitre Direct, Grey Crag, Birkness Combe, Buttermere
Moss Gill, Scafell, Wasdale
The *Needle*, The Napes, Great Gable, Wasdale
New West climb, Pillar Rock, Ennerdale
North-East climb, Pillar Rock, Ennerdale
High Man via Steep Gill and Slingsby's Chimney, Scafell, Wasdale
Tophet Bastion, The Napes, Great Gable, Wasdale
Westmorland's route, Dove Crag, Dovedale
West Wall climb, Pillar Rock, Ennerdale
Woodhouse's route, Dow Crag, Coniston

B MILD SEVERE/MILD VERY SEVERE

Arête, Chimney and Crack, A Buttress, Dow Crag, Coniston
B route, Gimmer, Great Langdale
Bracket and Slab, Gimmer, Great Langdale
Bridge's route, Esk Buttress, Eskdale
Brown Crag Wall, Shepherd's Crag, Borrowdale
Centipede, Raven Crag, Great Langdale
Central Chimney, Dow Crag, Coniston
C Gully, The Screes, Wasdale
Chrysalis, Raven Crag, Coniston
Deer Bield Chimney, Deer Bield, Far Easedale
Digitation, Wallowbarrow Crag, Dunnerdale
Doctor's Grooves, Eagle Crag, Grisedale
Eagle's Nest Ridge Direct, The Napes, Great Gable, Wasdale

Eve, Shepherd's Crag, Borrowdale
Fortiter, Grey Crag, Birkness Combe, Buttermere
Gillercombe Buttress, Gillercombe, Borrowdale
Gimmer Crack, Gimmer, Great Langdale
Girdle Traverse, Scafell Crag, Wasdale
The *Gordian Knot*, White Gill, Great Langdale
Green Gash, Bowness Knott, Ennerdale
Hailstorm, Bowness Knott, Ennerdale
Hedera Grooves, Falcon Crags, Derwentwater
Hollin Groove, White Gill, Great Langdale
Honister Wall, Buckstone How, Buttermere
Intermediate Gully, Dow Crag, Coniston
Jones's route *Direct from Lord's Rake*, Scafell Pinnacle, Wasdale
Kestrel Wall, Eagle Crag, Grisedale
Logan Stone route, Wallowbarrow Crag, Dunnerdale
Morning Wall, Scafell East Buttress, Eskdale
Moss Gill Grooves, Scafell Crag, Wasdale
Moss Ledge Direct, Scafell Pinnacle, Wasdale
Murray's route, B Buttress, Dow Crag, Coniston
Newlands Buttress, Miners' Crag, Newlands
North-West climb, Pillar Rock, Ennerdale
Pedagogue's Chimney, Striddle Crag, Buttermere
Revelation, Raven Crag, Great Langdale
Rib and Slab climb, Pillar Rock, Ennerdale
Scorpion, Shepherd's Crag, Borrowdale
Sergeant Crag Gully, Langstrath, Borrowdale
Shepherd's Chimney, Shepherd's Crag, Borrowdale
South-West climb, Pillar Rock, Ennerdale
Stoat's Crack, Pavey Ark, Great Langdale
Suaviter, Grey Crag, Birkness Combe, Buttermere
Summit route, Raven Crag, Combe Gill, Borrowdale
Thomas, Wallowbarrow Crag, Dunnerdale
Tophet Wall, The Napes, Great Gable, Wasdale
Tricouni Rib, The Napes, Great Gable, Wasdale
Troutdale Pinnacle, Black Crag, Troutdale, Borrowdale
Valedictory, Raven Crag, Thirlmere
Walker's Gully, Pillar Rock, Ennerdale

C   VERY SEVERE/HARD VERY SEVERE

Botterill's Slab, Scafell Crag, Wasdale
Central Buttress, Scafell Crag, Wasdale
Communist Convert, Raven Crag, Thirlmere
Damascus, Raven Crag, Great Langdale
Deer Bield Crack, Deer Bield, Far Easedale
Eagle Front, Eagle Crag, Birkness Combe, Buttermere

Eliminate A, Dow Crag, Coniston
Fool's Paradise, Gowder Crag, Borrowdale
The Gargoyle, Overbeck, Yewbarrow, Wasdale
Gomorrah, Pillar Rock, Ennerdale
Gormenghast, Heron Crag, Eskdale
Great Central route, Dow Crag, Coniston
Great Eastern (Yellow Slab Variation), Scafell East Buttress, Eskdale
Grooved Wall, Pillar Rock, Ennerdale
Hiatus, Gimmer Crag, Great Langdale
Illusion, Falcon Crags, Derwentwater
Kern Knotts Chain, Kern Knotts, Great Gable, Wasdale
Mickledore Grooves, Scafell East Buttress, Eskdale
Obituary Grooves, Black Crag, Troutdale, Borrowdale
Overhanging Bastion, Castle Rock of Triermain, Thirlmere
Overhanging Wall, Scafell East Buttress, Eskdale
Rogue's Gallery, Shepherd's Crag, Borrowdale
Smuggler's Chimney, Gable Crag, Great Gable, Ennerdale
Sodom, Pillar Rock, Ennerdale
Zigzag, Castle Rock of Triermain, Thirlmere

LIST OF PEAKS EXCEEDING
2,000ft (610m)

		(ft)	(metres)	(National Grid reference NY except where stated)
1	Scafell Pike	3,206	977	215072
2	Scafell	3,162	964	207065
3	Helvellyn	3,113	949	342152
4	Skiddaw	3,054	931	260291
5	Great End	2,984	910	226084
6	Bowfell	2,960	902	245065
7	Great Gable	2,949	899	211104
8	Pillar	2,928	892	171121
9	Nethermost Pike	2,920	890	346143
10	Catstycam (Catchedicam)	2,917	889	348158
11	Esk Pike	2,903	885	237075
12	Raise (Helvellyn)	2,889	881	343175
13	Fairfield	2,863	873	358118
14	Blencathra (Saddleback)	2,847	868	324278
15	Crinkle Crags	2,816	858	248049
16	Dollywaggon Pike	2,810	856	346130
17	Great Dod	2,807	855	342204
18	Grasmoor	2,791	851	175204
19	Scoat Fell	2,760	841	159114
20	St Sunday Crag	2,756	840	369134
21	Stybarrow Dod	2,756	840	340187
22	Eel Crag	2,753	839	193203
23	High Street	2,719	829	441110
24	Red Pike (Mosedale)	2,707	825	165105
25	Hart Crag	2,698	822	369112
26	Steeple	2,687	819	158117
27	Lingmell	2,649	807	209081
28	High Stile	2,644	806	170148
29	High Raise (High Street)	2,634	803	448135
30	Coniston Old Man	2,631	802	SD 273979
31	Kirkfell	2,630	802	195104
32	Swirl How	2,630	802	273006
33	Haycock	2,618	798	145107
34	Brim Fell	2,611	796	SD 270986
35	Green Gable	2,603	793	215107
36	Dove Crag	2,603	793	374104
37	Grisedale Pike	2,593	790	197225
38	Rampsgill (Ramsgill) Head	2,581	787	444128

		(ft)	*(metres)*	(National Grid reference NY except where stated)
39	Great Carrs	2,575	785	270009
40	Allen Crags	2,572	784	236087
41	Thornthwaite Crag	2,569	783	432100
42	Glaramara	2,560	780	248106
43	Kidsty Pike	2,560	780	448127
44	Dow Crag	2,555	779	SD 262978
45	Red Screes	2,547	776	396087
46	Harter Fell (Mardale)	2,539	774	461094
47	Grey Friar	2,536	773	260005
48	Wandope (Wanlope)	2,533	772	187198
49	Sail	2,530	771	199204
50	Hobcarton Pike (Hopegill Head)	2,525	770	187223
51	Great Rigg	2,513	766	355104
52	Wetherlam	2,502	763	288011
53	High Raise	2,500	762	281096
54	Slight Side	2,499	762	209050
55	Mardale Ill Bell	2,496	761	447102
56	Hart Side	2,481	756	359198
57	Red Pike (Buttermere)	2,479	756	161154
58	Ill Bell	2,476	755	436077
59	Dale Head	2,473	754	222154
60	High Crag	2,443	745	181140
61	The Knott	2,423	739	438128
62	Robinson	2,417	737	202168
63	Seat Sandal	2,415	736	343115
64	Sergeant Man	2,414	736	287089
65	Harrison Stickle	2,403	732	281074
66	Kentmere Pike	2,397	731	465078
67	Hindscarth	2,385	727	216165
68	Clough Head	2,381	726	334225
69	Ullscarf	2,370	722	291121
70	Froswick	2,359	719	435085
71	Thunacar Knott	2,351	717	279080
72	Lonscale Fell	2,344	714	285271
73	Brandreth	2,344	714	215119
74	Knott	2,329	710	297330
75	Pike of Stickle	2,323	708	273074
76	Whiteside	2,317	706	171219
77	Yoke	2,309	704	438068
78	Bowscale Fell	2,306	703	333305
79	Pike of Blisco	2,304	702	270042
80	Pavey Ark	2,288	697	284079

		(ft)	(metres)	(National Grid reference NY except where stated)
81	Caw Fell	2,288	697	132110
82	Grey Knotts	2,287	697	219127
83	Rest Dod	2,278	694	433137
84	Seatallan	2,270	692	140084
85	Loft Crag	2,270	692	278071
86	Great Calva	2,265	690	291312
87	Cold Pike	2,259	689	264035
88	Brown Pike	2,237	682	SD 261966
89	Sheffield Pike	2,232	680	370182
90	Ullock Pike	2,230	680	244289
91	Scar Crags	2,205	672	210206
92	Loadpot Hill	2,202	671	457181
93	Tarn Crag	2,176	663	488079
94	Wether Hill	2,174	663	457169
95	Carrock Fell	2,174	663	341337
96	Whiteless Pike	2,159	658	180190
97	High Pike	2,159	658	319350
98	Place Fell	2,155	657	405169
99	High Spy	2,143	653	233162
100	Great Sca Fell	2,131	650	291339
101	Harter Fell (Eskdale)	2,129	649	SD 218997
102	Fleetwith Pike	2,126	648	207142
103	Base Brown	2,120	646	225115
104	Rossett Pike	2,106	642	250075
105	Middle Dod	2,106	642	398097
106	Little Hart Crag	2,091	637	388100
107	Starling Dodd	2,085	636	142158
108	Yewbarrow	2,058	627	173085
109	Causey Pike	2,035	620	219210
110	Great Borne	2,020	616	124165
111	Hartsop Dod	2,018	615	411119
112	Heron Pike	2,003	611	356082

BIBLIOGRAPHY

It is inevitable that the English Lake District should have evoked an enormous and still growing literature, which it is hardly necessary to summarise here; the various aspects are fully covered by Millward, R., and Robinson, A., *The Lake District* (London, 1970), chapter 11, 'The Lake District and the arts', with a very full bibliography. They discuss the contributions by guidebook writers catering for the ever-growing surge of tourists, the poets, the regional novelists, the geologists and topographers, and the archaeologists.

From the strict viewpoint of the climber, two immensely detailed and complementary series of Guidebooks must be cited.

(i)   Wainwright, A., *A Pictorial Guide to the Lakeland Fells* (Kendal).

Book One: *The Eastern Fells* (1955)
Book Two: *The Far Eastern Fells* (1957)
Book Three: *The Central Fells* (1958)
Book Four: *The Southern Fells* (1960)
Book Five: *The Northern Fells* (1962)
Book Six: *The North Western Fells* (1964)
Book Seven: *The Western Fells* (1966)

In these seven volumes, totalling some 2,000 pages, he describes in meticulous detail the topography of 214 separate peaks, the routes up, down and between them, and the views from each; all the material, maps, drawings and letterings, is beautifully executed in his own hand.

(ii)   The Fell and Rock Climbing Club of the English Lake District, founded in 1906, has been responsible for the publication of a series of detailed rock climbing Guidebooks. The first editions appeared soon after World War I, and they have been several times revised and enlarged to keep pace with the development of climbing. The current volumes were edited by J. Wilkinson and printed by the Cloister Press Ltd, Heaton Mersey, Stockport. Immensely detailed and indispensable to the climber, they include historical and topographical introductions, followed by climb by climb, pitch by pitch descriptions of every recorded route, with its length and grading, and illustrated by beautifully clear line-drawings of the crags by the eminent Lake District artist, W. Heaton Cooper. The volumes are as follows:

Nunn, P. J. and Woolcock, O., *Borrowdale* (1968)

Soper, N. J. and Allinson, N., *Buttermere and Newlands Area* (1970)

Miller, D., *Dow Crag Area* (1968)

Drasdo, H. and Soper, N. J., *Eastern Crags* (1969)

Fearnehough, P. L., *Great Gable, Wasdale and Eskdale* (1969)

Austin, J. A., *Great Langdale* (1967)

Cram, A. G., *Pillar Group* (1968)

Oliver, G. and Griffin, L. J., *Scafell Group* (1967)

Climbs made subsequent to the publication of these Guidebooks are recorded in *The Fell and Rock Journal*, edited by G. Dyke, in a section entitled 'New Climbs and Notes'.

Mention should be made of a book which truly deserves the term 'classic': Jones, O. G., *Rock-climbing in the English Lake District* (Keswick, first edition, 1897). A contemporary writer who probably more than anyone evokes sheer joy in the mountains of Lakeland is A. H. Griffin; his five books, published between 1963 and 1970, are *In Mountain Lakeland*; *Inside the Real Lakeland*; *Pageant of Lakeland*; *The Roof of England*; and *Still the Real Lakeland*.

GENERAL INDEX

Plates are indicated by italic numerals
(*B* = Buttress; *C* = Crag; *L* = Lake; *R* = River)

211